To Dorothy—
May you always find
joy in being
awakened to God
Shalom,
Fran

Awakening to God

The Sunday Readings in Our Lives

YEAR B

Awakening to God

Fran Salone-Pelletier

The Sunday Readings in Our Lives

TWENTY
THIRD *23rd*
PUBLICATIONS

Twenty-Third Publications
A Division of Bayard
One Montauk Avenue, Suite 200
New London, CT 06320
(860) 437-3013 or (800) 321-0411
www.twentythirdpublications.com

ISBN:1-58595-533-7
Library of Congress Catalog Card Number: 2005929696
Printed in the U.S.A.

Dedication

To my family and friends
who have been the bread of life for me.

To my college professor Margaret Mooney
whose question, "Why don't you write?"
was seed firmly planted in my subconscious
for late harvest.

Special gratitude goes to my husband Jean,
my constant companion,
challenging and consoling me
as I look into the darkened mirror and see Light.

Acknowledgments

I am extremely appreciative of the warmth and cooperation that Bayard/Twenty-Third Publications has extended to me, and I am especially grateful to Gwen Costello, who saw possibilities to awaken a wider audience to God's presence. I am also in awe of the superb and meticulous editing done by Mary Carol Kendzia, who always managed to safeguard the timbre and tone of the reflections' content while honing my words into sharpened quality.

Contents

Introduction

These reflections on the Sunday readings were born from my own deep-seated, personal need. Along with so many other Roman Catholics, the Second Vatican Council awakened me to the Scriptures. I noticed that the Bible was no longer being treated solely as an academic subject or a text used to prove a point. There was a deeper and fuller meaning to be gleaned from the biblical commentaries I read in preparation for teaching Scripture.

I soon discovered there were more questions than answers. How did the readings apply to my own daily life? What did they really mean to me? How did they affect me in my decisions and my choices, in my struggle in developing a relationship with the God of my belief, and in my relations with others? What was…what *is*…God…saying to me, to us?

What I have written is the result of my own prayerful reflection on the Word, as I hear the Lord speaking to me through my life experience—however joyful or difficult it might be. I began to notice how much the Scriptures were helping me. To my great surprise and delight, they also assisted those with whom I worked in ministry, community Bible groups, and the person in the pew.

The uniqueness of these writings lies in their flexibility. They can be used in Scripture study groups by utilizing the questions to facilitate discussion; as prayer starters for individual or communal retreat experiences; as homiletic tools; as spiritual reading, with or without the reflective questions; to assist those who participate as catechumens or sponsors in the Rite of Christian Initiation of Adults, as well as those in liturgy-based catechetical programs; to prepare for a more prayerful experience of Sunday liturgy, and more.

What I have written is the result of my own prayerful reflection on the Word, as I hear the Lord speaking to me through my life experience. Though personal, this word—as well as the suggested prayer at the end of each reflection—is also universal and meant for the People of God.

Awakening to God is a series of wake-up calls, challenges to plumb the depths of God's word. It commands a keen attentiveness to the God who is present to us always, if only we will allow ourselves to be alert to the divinity in our daily lives.

Deeply grateful for all that God has given me, I now give what I have received as gift to God's people.

Season of Advent

FIRST SUNDAY OF ADVENT

ISAIAH 63:16–17, 19, 64:2–7; 1 CORINTHIANS 1:3–9; MARK 13:33–37

Life is a waiting game

One of the most difficult tasks a human being can assume is the job of learning how to wait patiently and optimistically. The cartoon figure of a father-to-be pacing nervously up and down a hospital hall while awaiting the arrival of his firstborn always brings a knowing smile. It seems the anxiety and expectation can never be exaggerated. We wait for babies to smile, talk, crawl, walk. We watch and wait as they grow into toddlers, preschoolers, and onward through their adolescence into a companionable adulthood. In the process, our lives entwine and sometimes entangle!

We wait for day when the nights are long, and for night when the days are interminably painful. Spring is awaited after a cold, hard winter no less than fall is a welcome cooling on the heels of summer's hot aridity. T.G.I.F. is the weekly cry of working anticipators.

I guess it could be said that life is a waiting game.

During the recent past, my family has been engaged in that sort of endeavor. Over time, my elderly Mom had developed health problems that exploded into an emergency situation demanding surgery and subsequent convalescent care. Each day became a new episode of waiting. Emotions jumped from the terror that set telephone wires humming as the information was passed from family member to family member to the joy that caused us all to hop around the house in celebration. We moved from sipping coffee for a caffeine jolt to keep us alert to slugging a jigger or two to toast an apparently successful surgical procedure. Then the phone rang again. Dreaded words were heard. "There has been a complication."

With the utterance of that one short phrase, our "end times" were both faced and denied, anticipated and avoided. Our mother of four adult children, grandmother to eleven and great-grandmother of nine was seriously ill. In those days, after that suffering, our sun was darkened, our moon did not give its light, and our stars were falling from heaven. The central figure in our family solar system was in grave danger; the powers in our heavens were shaken.

At that moment, all we could do was wait—for the end to begin or the beginning to end.

Wait and pray. Pray and wait.

Vitality renewed, this was a time for us all to keep awake. We needed to be alert and aware—readied for listening to all the medical information we'd be given. We needed to be ever more attuned to minute changes in our mother's physical condition and in our own volatile emotional states. Life immediately attained critical attention. We were alive, perhaps more so than we had been for a long time.

Waiting moved from dire expectation to dynamic expectancy. Each of us responded personally and individually. All of us took keener notice of the reality that we are family. Family means that we must be "moving and being" as one unit while retaining our own uniqueness.

With the advent of illness comes the opportunity for change—the chance to permit our conversion, to allow and admit new vision instead of clinging to old shortsightedness. From the fig tree of dis-ease we can learn a lesson.

Life, indeed, is a waiting game, a lifelong contest of "wait and see!"

As I grow older, I realize how profoundly powerful that game can be. The more I wait, the more I see. The more I see, the more I know the potency to be found in waiting. Only within the folds of expectancy can we recognize the awesome deeds God is doing in our lives, works we did not expect that make mountains quake and quiver with delight in the reality of divine presence.

While my brother and sisters who lived in geographical proximity gathered around our mother, I waited from afar. Believing it was the better route to go (and with every ounce of strength it took), I entered into sacrificial waiting. I waited to hear word of progress or its lack. I waited for her to leave the hospital and enter interim convalescent care. I waited for my mother to gain enough strength for me to phone her and speak of my love. I waited to hear her voice and let her hear mine.

The sacrifice did what all true sacrifices do. It made me recognize what I had instead of regretting what I did not possess. Distance afforded me the gift of objectivity, time and space to ponder alternatives. It also bequeathed me the ability to return that gift to my siblings later, at a time when they needed a breather. I could travel at another time to tend to my mother's wants. Each of us might then be doorkeepers on the watch. Each uniquely awake to God's graceful presence. All in charge of our own work in our own way.

Our advent into this kind of guardianship has great potential. We can become family as we never have or had been previously. My siblings and I have been face-to-face with "what could have been." We have dodged a bullet and been given a distinct opportunity to forge relationships anew. What had been taken for granted can now be noted as grace. What had fallen from appreciation can now be embraced with wonder and awe.

Each of us is learning to wait and see. To see and wait. In the process, we are learning that our hearts can beat in unison, if we so choose. Our breathing can bear the words of Paul to his community in Corinth, if we so desire. Each of us is empowered to pray for the other and for our mother, "Grace to you and peace from God, our Father, and the Lord Jesus Christ. I give thanks to my God always for you because of the grace of God that has been given you in Christ Jesus, for in every way you have been enriched in him, in speech and knowledge of every kind, so that you are not lacking in any spiritual gift as you wait for the revealing of our Lord Jesus Christ. He will also strengthen you to the end, so that you may be blameless on the day of our Lord Jesus Christ" (1 Corinthians 1:3–8).

Life is a waiting game. Keep awake to play it well!

For Reflection and Discussion

- In what ways have you been asleep, unaware, not watchful to the advent of divinity? In what ways have you been alert to God's presence in your life? How have you responded to that presence?

Prayer

God of my clay time, God of my wandering ways,
I want to return to you and give you praise.
My hardened heart has gone far from your grace
As I find myself running in a terrible rat race.
In my sorrow, I seek only an awakening so grand
That I'll flee from the withering absence to hold your divine hand.
I beg that you cast your anger away
And call to me each passing day.
You are my potter; I am your clay.
Do with me what you will; I promise to stay
Awake and alert from morning to night
Searching only for your truth and your light.
Amen.

SECOND SUNDAY OF ADVENT

ISAIAH 40:1–5, 9–11; 2 PETER 3:8–14; MARK 1:1–8

Preparing while waiting: a seesaw of love

Everything we do in life demands a degree of preparation—even, perhaps especially, waiting. I recall the time when I was readying myself, my house, and my husband for a two-and-a-half-week absence while I attended to my mother's needs in Connecticut. Meals were made and frozen for future use. Schedules were rearranged to afford the least interruption of others' routines. Memos and lists were scattered throughout the house to ensure the smooth continuing of life until I returned. All the while, I was also trying to keep myself anchored in the present moment, honoring all that is as I lived in expectancy of what is yet to be.

It was, and still is, my seesaw of love.

In the meantime, my mother did her own waiting and preparing. Weak from surgery, she awaited the strength of her eldest child. Empty and longing for the return of normalcy and routine, she prepared for the worst while anticipating the best. She ate a little and hoped that would help. She waited eagerly for daily signs of healing and prepared to rejoice at each positive result. Wanting me to arrive immediately, she patiently counted the days until the future became the present.

Waiting while preparing, preparing while waiting. It was her seesaw of love.

On the one hand, I do not want to ignore the sense of timelessness that makes preparation significantly important. "With the Lord, one day is like a thousand years, and a thousand years are like one day." On the other, there is an urgency surging in my being. "The day of the Lord will come like a thief, and then the heavens will pass away with a loud noise, and the elements will be dissolved with fire, and the earth and everything that is done on it will be disclosed" (2 Peter 3:8, 10). What appears to be a dilemma is truly a challenge. How do I—how does each of us—live well today while remembering yesterday with expectancy for tomorrow? What does it mean for us to be preparing while waiting? How is this a seesaw of love?

It would seem that our primary response is that we all need to recognize and make real in our lives the fact that God is in control. God is in charge. Our very life is in God's hands, not ours. At the same time, we need to become increasingly aware that God's will is enacted through us. We are the messengers sent ahead to prepare God's way in the world. We are the voices crying out in the wilderness, "Make straight the paths of God" (paraphrase of Mark 1:3). The preparation is both challenging and comforting. It is hard work that is never fully accomplished and always being completed. It is loving and being loved; sitting as confidently on a grounded seat as on one soaring high in the sky.

To be preparing while waiting, one needs to speak tenderly of forgiveness—first of all to oneself. Each of us needs to accept God's desire to straighten our paths to divinity, to make a highway on which God might travel in our desert experiences. We need to know and rejoice in the fact that God's wish is for every valley to be lifted up and every mountain and hill to be made low. There is no area of our life that is uninteresting to God. No secret space or crowded cubbyhole that is unknown. God shall level the uneven ground of our commitment and make a plain out of the rough places of our sinfulness. Our task is simply to permit God to forgive us—and gracefully to accept that forgiveness.

In short, we must allow God to ride with us on our seesaw of love.

Only then will we be credible proclaimers of God's presence in the world. Only then will we be empowered with authenticity in our announcement of good tidings. Only then will others be able to believe that God will gather the lambs and gently lead the mother sheep to pastures beyond all reckoning.

When we deny God's forgiveness, we only enforce fear where faith could reign. When our voices are weak with apathy, we refute the power of God's strength. When we are slow to see that God lives in the here and now among us, we cloud humanity's vision of God and increase the inability of those who depend on our sight and light to decrease their myopia. As a result, there is no comfort for God's people, there is no dynamic, uplifting movement to the seesaw of love. There is only the static stagnation of people mired in discouragement.

Our call to be comforting challengers and challenging comforters remains. Our cry is to everyone to be preparing while waiting; waiting while preparing. Our mission is to discover and uncover the giftedness borne in the attitude of expectancy—to realize that "we wait for new heavens and a new earth, where righteousness is at home" (2 Peter 3:13).

There is but one way to ready ourselves to make righteousness at home. It is to be "comfortably present" in our lives. It is to practice righteousness, to hone at-one-ment, until its strangeness disappears into habit. It is to be as patient as is God with our lack of perfection, until we notice we are in the process of being perfected.

As for me, I awaited my journey to my mother's side, and she for my arrival. Each of us prepared and waited both for absence and presence by riding a seesaw of love. So, too, do all of us climb aboard a similar apparatus in God's earthly playground.

To ride the seesaw of love is to be preparing while waiting. It is to be ready and readied for our total presence to the God who is, was, and always will be waiting with us—the God who does not want any to perish but desires all to come to repentance.

For Reflection and Discussion

- In what ways do you live well today while remembering yesterday with expectancy for tomorrow? How are you preparing while waiting? In what way or ways do you perceive this as a seesaw of love? How have you been a person whose humility has led to bold action?

Prayer

God of my desert, lead me into a boldness I would never dare on my own. Give voice to my trembling. Let me cry out in the various wastelands in which I find myself. Help me always to remember that it is your path I am straightening, your way I am preparing, not my own. When I tire, help me to recall that, with you, one day is like a thousand years and a thousand years like one day. Help me to believe, always, that you will not delay with your promise and you will never cease to be patient with me. Amen.

THIRD SUNDAY OF ADVENT

ISAIAH 61:1–2, 10–11; 1 THESSALONIANS 5:16–24; JOHN 1:6–8, 19–28

Waiting to discover who I am

One of the most profound questions one can ask—or hear—is this, "Who are you?" There are days when I look into the mirror of life and am astounded at what I see. I stare curiously at an image I cannot believe is real and ask, "Who are you?"

Who is this person who has reacted with swift and sure anger at a remark innocently made or a question naively asked? Who is this woman who speaks confidently of nonjudgmental, unconditional love and then becomes perturbed when things do not go as planned? Who is she when she has difficulty with any and all who differ from her point of view? Who is this person who can see the beauty in those around her, but fixates on her own flaws, failings, and imperfections? Who is she?

As I ask the question, I live the answer: "Wait and see!" Wait on a Creator God who is continuing to fashion the marvel of divine image and likeness. Wait expectantly—always on the alert for calls to change, to be and become. Wait and rejoice always in God's labor of love. "Give thanks in all circumstances; for this is the will of God in Christ Jesus for you. Do not quench the Spirit, test everything; hold fast to what is good; abstain from every form of evil" (1 Thessalonians 5:18–21). Wait prayerfully, and see what happens.

Whenever I have given myself the experience of pregnant, patient expectancy, I am awestruck by the results. Whenever I refrain from quenching God's spirit and allow divinity time and space to work in me, I am amazed. The mirror image doesn't change; my perspective does. I see myself and all creation differently. All the "I am not's" disappear in the face of who I am. No longer is it important that I be the best and the brightest, the slimmest and the smartest. All that counts now is that I am permitting the Spirit of God to be upon me. I am letting God anoint me and send me to "bring good news to the oppressed, to bind up the brokenhearted, to proclaim liberty to the captives, and release to the prisoners" (Isaiah 61:1).

While I was waiting, I began to discover that I am who I am. My life is now a series of revelations, a continual unveiling of all I keep so carefully hidden, lest it be perceived as insufficient. Too often, I short-circuit the process. Rather than paining with the seemingly endless and ineffective passing of time, I push the panic button. Invariably, as my mother used to tell us, it is the last five minutes of waiting that cause us to act inappropriately and succumb to dire predictions of disaster. If only we'd waited out those moments, we'd have discovered that there was no fatal car accident, just an explainable, though tardy, arrival. All is well when we wait to see.

If I endure the many "five minute" intervals of trepidation and mistrust that crop up in life, I will find that I am a woman sent by God as a witness to testify to the light of God so that all might believe. So are we all. Male and female alike, we are God's chosen ones commissioned to witness to God's creating power, a light shining in the darkness of a world too preoccupied to wait and see.

We are not the light, but we are called to give testimony to it. If it means crying out in the wilderness, so be it. If it demands testing everything in order to discern what is good and hold fast to it, we'll do it. If it means cataloging all that we are not in order to discover who we really are, we'll take on the task. What remains of prime importance is that we continue to probe as we wait and wait as we probe the depths of God's image and likeness shining forth in each of us.

I find it both consoling and immensely challenging to wait for God. Consolation lies in the fact that I do not have to initiate anything. I am only asked to respond. Challenge lies in the same reality. I am a "take charge" person who tackles jobs with vim and vigor. At my best, I am a productive worker. At my worst, I am a major controller! My virtue in extreme is my vice supreme. Waiting does not come easily to people like me. I suspect it is no less problematic for those who are more "laid back." Their difficulty comes in the form of complacent procrastination. Both types need to come to terms with the power unleashed as we wait—to see and discover who we are.

Like John the Baptizer, we are called to do what God requires in the face of opposition and lack of credentials. "John confessed and did not deny it…I am not the Messiah. And they asked him, 'What then? Are you Elijah?' He said, 'I am not.' 'Are you the prophet?' He answered, 'No.'

"They asked him, 'Why then are you baptizing if you are neither the Messiah, nor Elijah, nor the prophet?' He answered them, 'I baptize with water. Among you stands one whom you do not know, the one who is coming after me; I am not worthy to untie the thong of his sandal'" (John 1:20–27).

John acknowledged who he wasn't and found who he was. He waited for that discovery. He waited to see. While waiting, he did what God called him to do, trusting that his life would not signal the end of an era but was to mark the beginning of one. With authenticity, he answered questions regarding who he was. Thus he ushered in a new age and gave birth to a new reality.

John did not simply wait to be. He waited to see, and sight was given him. He waited to discover, and his goodness was revealed to him. May we dare to live as John lived, truthfully responding to the most profound question one can ask, or hear, "Who are you?" May we know and believe that the one who asks the question is a faithful God of peace who sanctifies us entirely and keeps us sound and blameless for all time.

For Reflection and Discussion

- Thomas Merton's spirituality asks that we "seek the true self." How patient are you with God's Holy Spirit who slowly paints the portrait of your true self? In what ways might you increase the quality of your patience? What revelations about yourself have caused you to rejoice in God your Savior?

Prayer

I believe that the Spirit of the Lord God is upon me because the Lord has anointed me to bring glad tidings to the poor, to heal the brokenhearted, to proclaim liberty to captives and release to prisoners. I believe that God has clothed me with a robe of salvation and has wrapped me in a mantle of justice. I promise never to quench the Spirit of God in me. I will listen to the voice of the prophets in my midst. I will test everything and retain what is good. And I will rejoice always in the knowledge that the God of peace is making me perfectly holy as I await the coming of my Lord and Savior, Companion and Friend, Jesus the Christ. Amen.

Fourth Sunday of Advent

2 Samuel 7:1–5, 8–12, 14, 16; Romans 16:25–27; Luke 1:26–38

Creating a waiting place for God

There is a marvelous tool created by Myers-Briggs that is used for discerning preferences. Each of us wonderful human beings leans one way or another—the instrument states there are sixteen variations on the theme—as we make our choices in life. I am a classic ENFJ—extroverted, intuitive, feeling person who judges her actions. In short, that means I gain vitality and ideas from being with people rather than staying in solitude. I receive knowledge intuitively more than by noting sensory information, make my decisions with an emphasis on value judgments rather than being intensely analytical. Lastly, I am a scheduled list-keeper who is uncomfortable with open-ended and shifting possibilities. With all that being said, I guess I would be much like King David when it comes to creating a waiting place for God.

When God gives me rest from all those with whom I have difficulty, I sit in my own little prayer spot to relax in remembering. As the memories float to the surface of my consciousness, my own comfortableness invariably is shaken. Wanting to do for God what God has done for me, I look at all I've been given and seek to do something significant in return, such as find a place for God to dwell in comfort and ease. Instead of allowing God to determine the divine site, I am determined to provide one and thus control the God I profess to be founder of all freedom.

Thank God, I am also amused at the prospect. I am so like my predecessors in God's family who were likewise interested in creating a waiting place for God without understanding that God waits everywhere, always, and in all people. God's abode is dynamic. It is a movable feast, manifest to all who care to see and kept in creative motion by all who comprehend the crucial necessity of journeying into divinity. God is with us. All creation is God's waiting place. All humanity is blessed with divine presence.

The only house God wants is a place in our heart.

These are troubling words that challenge our status quo. Mary of Nazareth in Galilee found them disturbing; so should we. What she was told many years ago is a message for us today as well. "Do not be afraid, Mary, for you have found favor with God. And now, you will conceive in your womb and bear a son, and you will name him Jesus" (Luke 1:30–31).

Troubling words are marvelously creative. They are meant to shake us from complacency into charity, not to cause us terror. Do not fear. There is no reason to be afraid for we are already blessed, have already found favor with God. Our task, should we choose to accept it, is to conceive and bear the Christ child.

Obviously our birthing is not to be a biological reality as it was for Mary. God is being spiritually birthed in our being, as individuals who respond to God's call and as communities whose faith is expressed in a continuing *fiat*!

We are to give this child the name "Jesus." He is the one who saves us. The name is not our choice but God's. This Jesus is our named Messiah who lives in and with us. He and we are to be conspirators of deliverance, God's helpers in redeeming this world of ours. Together we bear and empower compassion in the place of morbid competition. Our "care-full-ness" is a crucial presence to suffering humanity. We are the house of God, a waiting place created and filled with the grace and power of divinity.

"How can this be?" we ask. We are still babes ourselves, untested by the rigors of harsh reality, innocent and unknowing in the face of those who would abort life unless it met their requirements or qualifications. How can we house a God who cannot be contained? What will people say? How can we explain this? What will happen to us in the process?

The answer is astonishingly simple. We are not in charge of the details. God is. We are not being asked to build a house for God, only to allow God to construct a dwelling within us. God's message is clear: "The Holy Spirit will come upon you, and the power of the Most High will overshadow you; therefore the child to be born will be holy; he will be called Son of God" (Luke 1:35).

What a relief! Neither you nor I need to worry about being powers-that-be any more than we need to be concerned that others might wield more potency than we. Our light, our power, will be overshadowed by the far greater, brighter, more intense light of God's powerful Spirit. Whatever is brought forth as a result of this creative collaboration will be holy. That is God's promise, for nothing is impossible with God. Nothing!

There is but one step left to take, and it is a leap into fidelity. Until and unless we are able to speak the words of Mary, all remains static, concretized into a concept, wonderful but wasted. It is an idea that awaits fruition; an ideal that seeks to be tried. Birth cannot happen without our consent. The world cries out for a Savior who promises to be God-with-them. Creation holds its breath in eager anticipation and anxious expectation. Will we open our hearts and minds and lips to say, "Here I am, the servant of the Lord; let it be with me according to your word" (Luke 1:38)?

Whisper it if need be. Shout it if possible. Pray it always. Let the *fiat* of faithfulness come forth from every crucible of doubt. Take a chance on God's ability to house divinity in our humanity. Do not be afraid. For we are highly favored ones. God is with us. We can let it be done according to God's word. Birth will occur. God's waiting place is already being created. We just have to be there to let it happen.

For Reflection and Discussion

- How do you see yourself as a conspirator of deliverance, God's helper in redemption? When did you ask "How can this be?" What resulted from that question? How can you house a God who cannot be contained?

Prayer

In the depths of my darkness, I wait, my God.
I watch and wonder which paths to trod;
I ask my questions and voice my doubts
Hoping that you will enter my fearful bouts
And let me know your presence is near.
In the midst of my pain, my terror clear,
I know in my heart that you are God-with-us,
A divinity whose promise I can trust.
I celebrate your coming, the Babe who saves all
From humanity's failure; humankind's fall.
For this gift I am filled with heartfelt thanksgiving
That is the beginning of my intensified living. Amen.

Season of Christmas

CHRISTMAS DAY

ISAIAH 9:1–6; TITUS 2:11–14; LUKE 2:1–14, 15–20

Unwrapping unexpected treasures

Christmas arrives in a flurry of anticipation and dashed expectations. Weeks of "hype," whispered hopes, and circled desires swiftly end in a heap of torn paper and crushed bows. Gifts hoped for are not received. Unexpected presents do not always match desires. Children, overwhelmed by the abundance of toys, cannot express their gratitude in the face of such bounty. Despite our best efforts to ignore the feeling, I think we all sense the death found in birth, the cross that shadows Christmas. Less than perfect, we walk in darkness, yet we are more than Scrooges who shout "Bah! Humbug!" wherever we go.

Somewhere deep inside a greater message surges upward and forward. In the midst of our darkness, we begin to see a great light. Our Advent waiting has come to an end. It is not simply a matter of enduring four weeks of hustle and bustle. It is an Advent attitude—given a lifetime and a lifeline to incorporate the apparent opposites of birth and death, cross and Christmas.

In the uneasy feelings that accompany Christmas presents, we begin to discover true Christian presence.

This was true for Mary and Joseph as they sought to comply with the law while laboring to give birth to love. There was no place for them in the crowds of Bethlehem, no one willing to make room for new life if it meant discomfort and displacement. To sacrifice their spot was a gift no one was willing to offer, a price too high to pay for a yet-to-be-unwrapped, unknown treasure.

Peace, banishment of oppression, and justice would seem to be universal desires. All humanity would prefer light over darkness. However, none of us yearns to unwrap those gifts. We do not want to tear at the paper that holds them captive, or break the ribbons that keep them bound. No one is eager to receive a gift that bears a price tag. We want bondage broken while we remain unscathed in the process. We look for light but not in a land of deep darkness. We seek multiplication of joy without any sorrow and endless serenity devoid of the pain found when we work for justice. We want the presence of Christ as an innocent child resting in a crib, even if it is a manger, not a challenging adult writhing on a cross. We want salvation without sanctification.

But Christmas is also about receiving gifts we had neither wanted nor sought and finding them to be unexpected treasures. Christmas is all about being shepherds living in fields, keeping watch over flocks by night when fright is found in shadows and terror tears at the heart. Christmas is being unafraid to stay in that darkness, finding good news in its clutches, seeing light in the nighttime blackness. Christmas is listening for good news of great joy in the midst of banality and commercialism, heartache and disaster. Christmas is unwrapping the unexpected treasure revealed when we allow the Savior to be born in our midst.

There are signs of Christmas presence all around us, deep within us, shared among us. We simply need to go with haste to our Bethlehems—our own houses of bread, places where we both give and receive nourishment. "Let us see this thing that has taken place, which the Lord has made known to us" (paraphrase of Luke 2:15).

We need to tell our own stories of birth and rebirth. We need to listen to those tales told by others, and treasure all the words, pondering them in our hearts until they pulsate with each breath we take. Ultimately, we need to unwrap the unexpected treasures we are—the gifts of presence we are meant to be—to a world that waits in darkness for great light to appear.

It is true that the Savior, the Christ, has come once and for all. His physical advent has already occurred and cannot be repeated in the same way, place, or time ever again. At the same time, the coming of God into human history is an ongoing phenomenon. It is a continuing and continual revelation of increased joy, divided plunder, broken yokes and bars of oppression, and endless peace. And we are the ones who are called to unwrap that unexpected treasure. We are the ones who are commanded to make room in the inns of humanity so that the zeal of the Lord God can create a marvelous birthing of divinity over and over again.

The magnificence of it all is that we just have to be there to let it happen.

Mary and Joseph were simply following the orders of their day, going to be registered in their towns of origin according to the prevalent Roman law. There was nothing singularly extraordinary about their journey. The unusual occurred in the midst of ordinary obedience. God's grace appeared, with its universal salvation, as Mary and Joseph labored and gave birth in a place where there was supposedly no room for such an experience. In places of comfortableness there is often exclusivity—no room for all to rest, to have shelter, to be comforted into wholeness. So, Mary birthed the Christ Child in a spot others loathed, a dwelling fit only for beasts. She placed him in a manger of uncomfortableness and gave him the solace of her undivided love.

Christmas presence, from its outset, was extraordinarily ordinary. God became human in a most surprising way. With human effort, divinity struggled to show us the way to image God. This continues to be true for us today and each day of our lives. With every dawn there is newness to the night of labor. With every hardship a gift is unveiled.

The truth is that "...the grace of God has appeared, bringing salvation to all, training us to renounce impiety and worldly passions, and in the present age to live lives that are self-controlled, upright, and godly, while we wait for the blessed hope and the manifestation of the glory of our great God and Savior, Jesus Christ" (Titus 2:11–13).

All that now awaits is our unwrapping of this unexpected treasure.

For Reflection and Discussion

- In what ways can you unwrap for others the gifts of peace, freedom, justice, and light that Christ came to give us? What do you think were the real feelings of the teenaged Mary at the birthing of Jesus? How do you experience the birthing of Christ within you and through you? What are your feelings about those occurrences?

Prayer

Dear God, you have chosen to join us in our infancy. You came into our world, just as we have, birthed from the womb of your mother. I give you thanks and praise for that precious gift of life begun infinitesimally and continued to its ultimate goal. Help me always to appreciate this Christmas presence and to share its beauty and grace with those who are most in need of a Savior who understands what it is to be a powerless babe. Let me share the wonder of Mary's Christmas, pregnant with possibilities that give birth to joy and peace. In gratitude, I pray. Amen.

Feast of the Holy Family

Sirach 3:2–6, 12–14; Colossians 3:12–21; Luke 2:22–26, 28–32, 36, 38–40

It's a matter of "relative-ity"

Each time the Feast of the Holy Family rolls around, I am struck by the same thoughts. Holy Family denotes Perfect Family. While I am perfectly aware that this concept is not found in earthly families, I also feel somewhat saddened that an unattainable ideal is fostered as a possibility to be attained. To have this placed squarely in front of us on the very first Sunday after being gifted with the Incarnation of Emmanuel dampens the spirit, if it doesn't stir it to meet the challenge. Is that the purpose of this celebration? Are we to be in competition with a family that knows no errors nor makes mistakes? Are we to strive for those goals? If not, what is this event all about?

I would offer another suggestion. Perhaps we can look at the Holy Family from the viewpoint that family wholeness ("holy family-ness") is a matter of "relative-ity." It is a matter of looking at relatedness (relationships) and unveiling their relative-ity to who we are, wherever we are, where we are going, and how we are getting there. How are the people with whom I interact on a daily basis relative to my very being? In what ways do they affect my wholeness? In a word, are we "family" together? As a result of being family, are we growing individually and communally into holiness? These questions cannot be answered easily or quickly. They demand a second look, perhaps many second looks, at ourselves and others.

My life experience is that sanctity is tested most severely in close encounters. I have always found it easier to put on a happy face or whistle a pleasant tune when I am with people who are casual acquaintances or business buddies. They touch my life, it is true, but on a sporadic or controlled basis. Family and deep friends, however, are forever. They walk with me even when I am unaware of their presence and affect me in ways mysterious. With those people, a strange phenomenon occurs. It is at once both more difficult to continue a pretense and more necessary! They see through my antics and postures to a deeper and truer me; so I become more transparent. As a result, I cringe or react negatively and put up a smoke screen to obscure their piercing view. What a dilemma! What a test of human holiness, of family wholeness!

I would suspect the same sort of push and pull plagued the unique "first family" of Nazareth. Their path of "relative-ity" cannot have been without its moments of dread and items of heated discussion. They were Mediterranean folks with high emotions, not plaster saints whose faces were fixed in a perennially placid composition. Theirs was not a pietistic view of life that admitted ecstasy without its accompanying agony. Theirs was a profoundly real beatific vision that knew pain and felt angst but remained obedient and committed to hearing and heeding the divine call each experienced individually and all lived as a family group. What happened to Joseph affected Mary's life and that of Jesus. What occurred to Mary did the same for her husband and son. In no less a fashion did Jesus' life experiences impact both Mary and Joseph. All three were ensconced in the holiness that is a matter of "relative-ity."

Jesus heard the words of God stating, "For the Lord honors a father above his children and confirms a mother's right over her children" (Sirach 3:2), and yet followed his heart, remaining in the temple to do God's work despite the anguish it caused. His was not an act of defiance but of definition. It was what he "had to do" even if his action was not completely understood or accepted. His holiness depended upon it. His family, once confronted, comprehended the fact that this, too, was a matter of "relative-ity." Their relatedness both veiled Jesus' presence and also revealed it. Together, they would become whole and holy. Separately, they would continue that growth in wisdom, age, and grace before all humankind.

Their path, as ours, is one clothed with compassion, kindness, humility, meekness, and patience. It is a life marked by forgiveness and the love that binds everything together in perfect harmony—a harmony that emerges from a descant that allows for difference without defiant dissonance! Obviously, this way of living does not fall upon us like the rain from heaven. It is a labor of love. It is a daily dying and rising, each to one's own foibles and failings and all to the inadequacies of the group.

My mother used to advise me that life is compromise, compromise, compromise. Obviously, she was right. Just as obviously, she was wrong. Yes, we need to "give a little to get a little." But, none of us can compromise to the point of losing our integrity. At the same time, all of us can compromise a lot—if we understand that word to indicate our need to promise together to be who we are called to be. Promising together demands and commands communication, cooperation, collaboration, discussion, and decision. It is the lifetime process that produces pearls from grains of sand and burnishes gold to shining splendor. It is a matter of "relative-ity."

This kind of sanctification means following the law when the law serves to encourage and enhance holiness. It means seeking, finding, and heeding those prophets, both male and female, whose sole purpose is to reveal messianic presence, surface salvation, unveil divine light, and give glory to God. It means traveling to extraordinary places of sanctification but always returning to the ordinary sites of daily living where holiness is both experienced and expressed in the tasks and relationships that we too often regard as mundane. It is an every day, every way, everywhere kind of relationship each of us must consciously live..

Like Joseph, Mary, and Jesus, we need to "finish everything required by the law of the Lord" (paraphrase of Luke 2:39) and then return to our Galilee, to our own hometown, where we can grow, become strong, be filled with wisdom, and know the favor of God. We need to go back to our roots where wholeness and holiness are best experienced in matters of "relative-ity."

For Reflection and Discussion

- How are the people with whom you interact on a daily basis or less frequently relative to your very being? In what ways do they affect your wholeness? In a word, are you family together? As a result of being family, how are you growing individually and communally into holiness?

Prayer

Beloved God, how wonderful it is to know that you live in a community of Father, Son, and Spirit. May our families be formed according to the model of your love, and may we receive from you the glory of your salvation. Reconcile all broken family relationships. Strengthen all families bearing heavy crosses. Heal all sickness and ills that cripple families. Restore peace to all families experiencing discord. May our family and all others find their true home in you. Amen.

SOLEMNITY OF MARY, MOTHER OF GOD

NUMBERS 6:22–27; GALATIANS 4:4–7; LUKE 2:16–21

A woman for all seasons

Many years ago I read an article in *Modern Liturgy* entitled "A Woman for all Seasons." It stated that "New Year's Day in America is often a 'let-down' day when people stay home, watch football games, and try to recover from their Christmas holiday hangovers. But, for many people it is a day to remember the past and to dream about the future. It can be a lonely time."

I agree. It can be a lonely time. Or it can be a time for keeping silence, being calmed in the spirit. I choose to use the moment as an opportunity to celebrate quietness—the tranquility of Mary who listened to the words of the hill-shepherds, watched carefully the wonder and awe of their homage, and "treasured all these things and pondered them in her heart" (Luke 2:19).

Too often we keep a "holy" picture of Mary in our minds. We know her as the Mother of God, but we do not entertain thoughts of her mothering God. Because we know intellectually that no one can mother God, we prevent ourselves from meditating upon the many ways in which Mary must have had a profound influence on her son, the God-man Jesus. We gather knowledge about Mary without giving ourselves the solitude needed to build a relationship with her.

Mary is both mother and virgin. From the beginning, she is a woman of mystery, someone who knows pain and sorrow. Through her willingness, her "yes," she bears a child who comes to give creation all he has, only to be rejected by a world that refuses to accept him. Mary gives birth to a son whose whole mission in life is to "redeem those who were under the law, so that we might receive adoption as children" (Galatians 4:6).

Mary lives in the tension of being maid of Nazareth and Queen of Heaven; virgin and mother; Jewish woman and image of Church, all at once. This is not the stressful state we equate with our modern day rat races. It is the creative tension that underlies vitality. Mary fills all these roles simultaneously in the same way that a diamond's many facets provide its sparkling beauty, a beauty that draws awe and admiration. Mary's dynamism lives in the pull and push of opposite poles, just as we find life in the creative magnetism of being both saints and sinners.

In the sounds of silence, treasuring all that is seen, heard, known, and experienced, we can begin to soak in the truth that our complexity is our beauty. Our grace is mysteriously wonderful. Its fullness is found in our freedom. We can be close to God only to the degree that we are free. To tie ourselves down is to inhibit our proximity to the One who has emancipated us. God refuses to bind us. Instead, God has blessed us with the capability of choice, even to the degree of suffering our rejection!

Mary knew no chains. She lived as God intended us all to live. Mary chose God freely, even blindly. When God called, she acquiesced without fully understanding what was being demanded. She selected her answer without being forced but out of desire. Alone with an angel who spoke of terrifyingly pregnant possibilities, together with Joseph in a cold, uninviting stable, racing fearfully along the road to Egypt, tearfully trodding Jerusalem streets, paining with the sight of Calvary's cross, mourning within Jesus' tomb, bravely present to anguished disciples in an upper room, Mary had choices. She could have said, "No, not this time." She could have opted out of the pain. She could have submitted to numbing denial or given way to terror, doubt, hopelessness, or despair. But, she did not. Mary always chose God's way and trusted.

Her individuality is made credible precisely through her choices. She is not an either/or person but one who embraces both/and. Mary lives the reality of being both maid and Queen; virgin and mother; daughter and bride. She supports us in our quiet presence as well as our active leadership. Mary understands what it means to be emptied out and to be filled. She knows the pain of watching her beloved one suffer and the power of basking in hearing him be praised. Mary is witness to the slavery that fear brings and to the compassion that empowers and transforms that same fear with faith. Mary's beauty is her humanity.

Not just a name, sign, or symbol, Mary is a woman who chose acceptance of God's graciousness, a mother who speaks to us of the goodness and power of her son. She is a homemaker whose hospitality knew no bounds. She is a beacon, lighting the path of God. Mary is sister to all and a human testimony of divine possibility.

More than that, Mary is alive. She is alive in the welfare mother whose poverty crushes her body into a statistic but does not break her spirit. She is alive in the grieving parent whose terminally ill child is wracked with unexplainable pain. She lives in the handicapped person whose perception pierces the complexity of modern sophistication with the clarity of simple wisdom. Mary is alive in all who stand up for justice and peace in a society comfortable with injustice and violence.

Mary's grandeur can be ours, if we choose it. We can allow the Spirit of God to rush through us. We can treasure all things, quietly reflecting on them in our hearts. Recognizing who we are, who we have chosen to be, with one voice, we sing, "My spirit rejoices in my God. My soul proclaims the greatness of the Lord. Holy is his name" (based on the Magnificat).

For Reflection and Discussion

• In what ways have you proclaimed the greatness of the Lord in your life? What things have you treasured, quietly reflecting upon them in your heart? How do you understand and interpret the statement, "We can be close to God only to the degree that we are free"?

Prayer

My soul proclaims your greatness, O my God,
    and my spirit has rejoiced in you, my Savior,
For your regard has blessed me,
    poor, and a serving woman.
From this day all generations
    will call me blessed,
For you who are mighty, have made me great.
Most Holy be your Name.
Your mercy is on those who fear you
    throughout all generations.
You have showed strength with your arm,
You have scattered the proud in their hearts' fantasy,
You have put down the mighty from their seat,
    and have lifted up the powerless.
You have filled the hungry with good things,
    and have sent the rich away empty.
You, remembering your mercy,
    have helped your people Israel—
As you promised Abraham and Sarah.
Mercy to their children, forever.

                       — *A Sunday Psalter: Canticle of Mary*,
           Mother Thunder Mission, Carmelites of Indianapolis

Epiphany of the Lord

Isaiah 60:1–6; Ephesians 3:2–3, 5–9; Matthew 2:1–12

"Magi-cal" moments

Did you ever arrive at a family gathering only to find, unexpectedly, that non-relatives were present? How did you feel about that surprise? In my birth family, those times were rare. Family was an extremely limited and limiting concept. At times, relatives of the relatives were accepted. But, by and large, family meant traceable blood kinship. Family was trusted—and entrusted—with gossip, news, special events, recurring tales. All others were held suspect, guilty until proven innocent.

Somehow that concept crept insidiously into following generations, and family almost became a psychologically incestuous word. If one did not belong to the group, did not have a blood tie, the only alternative was to be considered a stranger, an unreliable foreigner in our midst. "Family, hold back" was no longer the cry to refrain from indulging, to leave room and food to nourish others. It was a warning that others were in our midst, so hold back the truth, keep the cards close to the chest, save the best (or worst) for later when only the family is in earshot. Only the *real* family needs to be privy to the hassles, humors, and mishaps that are part and parcel of growing relationships.

I suspect that same diminished concept of family has hovered over the family of God from its inception. It is interesting to know that the church, consciously or not, places two post-Christmas family celebrations in close proximity. The feast of the Holy Family is followed quickly by the feast of the Epiphany. The one is a portrait of a sainted trio whose life together is interrupted by the presence of Simeon and Anna, both of whom share the same Jewish heritage as Mary, Joseph, and Jesus. The other is the feast that incorporates into that heritage those whose background, understanding, and life experience is quite different. Incredibly, strangers have been invited to the family feast.

When we dare to allow God to expand our relatedness, when we courageously incorporate all God's people into the family circle, "magi-cal" moments are ours to experience and enjoy.

Allowing others in the family circle is never a simple task or an easy one. Lurking among the "Magi-cal" strangers who seek only to share our life and goodness are those whose intentions are far more devious and diabolical. There will be pretenders in our midst whose presence is death-dealing. Like Herod of old, they will take gifts meant for homage and honor and twist them into maniacal weapons of hatred. There will always be people who are not at all interested in observing rising stars, those who fear such resurrection lest it mean their demise. There will always be those whose posture indicates interest in learning and growing but whose hearts are determined to remain closed, and self-seeking. They are unwilling to unveil truth and unable to sustain its revelation. There is no joy for them unless it is the fleeting pleasure found in ruling others.

Knowing this to be true, the family of God must choose to risk awesome inclusivity knowing that it carries with it awful possibilities or it must choose to close ranks in the safety of exclusivity, to diminish vision, and to allow darkness to cover the earth and its people. Will we chance being blinded by light and find renewed sight or stay securely shadowed to find that limited view also brings limitless fear? Such fear prevents our seeing that "nations shall come to your light, and kings to the brightness of your dawn, your sons shall come from far away, and your daughters shall be carried on their nurses' arms" (Isaiah 60:3–4). It constrains our seeing to the point that we are no longer radiant.

Impoverished by our own limitations, we are rendered blind to the gold and frankincense of life and have nothing to offer in praise of God. The question remains: will we chance the experience of "magi-cal" moments or wrap ourselves in "herod-ical" cloaks of pretended homage?

If the choice is to follow the lead of the Magi, a certain awareness is necessary. There will be inquiries to make and people to question. We will need to follow the star given to us, follow it into the black night, going where it points and stopping where it stops. We will seek the advice of leaders while heeding the wisdom of followers. Our search will be diligent and fraught with promise. Ultimately, we will step into the place where both mother and child can be found waiting for our arrival. We will come face-to-face with the opened treasure chest where all are welcome as they are and encouraged to join in the family festivities, not as strangers but as beloved relatives and cherished partners, as "Gentiles have become fellow heirs, members of the same body, and sharers in the promise in Christ Jesus through the gospel."(Ephesians 3:6).

If that is our choice, we will experience magi-cal moments without end.

God's presence in our lives will become an ever more profound epiphany. Divinity will be unveiled in unexpected arenas, perhaps in those held most suspect. People and places once considered to be unworthy, (the least among the "rulers of Judah"), will be noted as ones who are birthing salvation.

Uncrowned and throne-less, they shall shepherd the people of God with authority bred of authenticity. Their rule will be marked with honesty dealt without the benefit of scepters or the bondage of slavery.

Unlike Herod, there will be no secret meetings to plot revenge, scheme murder, or eliminate all who offer opposition or contradiction. Instead, openness to new life will be held holy. Homage to possibilities will be given high rank. All who have decided to follow the path of the Magi will recognize the fact that, despite being the "very least of the saints," we have been graced with the call and power to bring news of the boundless riches of Christ to all, to reveal God's plan hidden in the mystery of universal salvation.

Together we will see and follow rising stars that lead to birth not death. We will stop long enough to praise God and attend to dreams. We will allow ourselves the adventure of different routes home. We will endlessly experience the MAGI-cal moments of Epiphany People, telling our story as we go.

For Reflection and Discussion

- What would you have to do in order to see others as guiding stars or to recognize them as cunning Herods? When and with whom have you had "magi-cal" moments? How did those experiences affect your daily life?

Prayer

Dear God, you have graced my life with many "magi-cal" people and moments. Too often I have overlooked them, unaware that you choose to make your presence known in human epiphanies. I have limited my family, my universe, to those with whom I am comfortable, those who agree with my perceptions and philosophies. Help me to accept the stretching that comes with following your star into unlikely places in the company of unusual people. Let me understand that you really do want nations to walk by my light, the light that infuses me and enlightens me when I choose to journey with "magi-cal" strangers. Amen.

BAPTISM OF THE LORD

ISAIAH 42:1–4, 6–7; ACTS 10:34–38; MARK 1:7–11

Chosen and upheld by a delighted and loving God

In the days when I served the Church professionally as a Director of Religious Education, I was often the one who met new parents for pre-Baptism classes. We interacted on a number of occasions to watch catechetical films, share discussions, and generally get to know each other, so that the upcoming sacrament would be undertaken with seriousness and understanding. What we meant to do was witness to our own baptismal commitment and learn from others the depth of their own conviction. Though the intent was excellent, the process sometimes limped. Undeniably, there was an underlying disbelief that the parents were sincere in their request. Perhaps they were also lacking information or knowledge. Despite any shortcomings, good effects seemed to result. At least no one went away angry, upset, or refused to go through with the celebration.

As I look back with a degree of regret, while admitting that I did not know any better at the time, I wish I had taken the Scriptures a bit more literally, not fundamentally, but literally. I wish I had asked different questions, ones that probed the reality of our human existence instead of concentrating on logistics. Rather than walking couples through the ritual, I wish I had been able to express my own wonderment that I am here—we are here—as servants of God, upheld by God, chosen by God.

We are people in whom God delights. Imagine that!

Imagine a parental God smiling with joy at the wonderful person who is part of divinity. Baptism then becomes a public celebration of the marvelous truth that God delights in having chosen us without partiality. God's divine Spirit is upon us. Like all parents, God has expectations of us, goals and ideals for which we must strive. These are placed before us, not because we are not good enough as we are, but because we are good enough for God's delight, good enough for God to continue upholding us in our ongoing efforts to bring justice to the nations.

We are good enough for God to want to live God's life in us. That is an amazing thought made even more stupendous when we begin to integrate its truth and power into our everyday lives.

At a given point in the Rite of Baptism, the celebrant priest or deacon asks the presenting couple this question, "What do you ask of the Church for your child?" The rite provides a number of responses for parents to make. It also allows parents to create their own response. Obviously, most opted safely for one of the suggested responses. Usually it is to ask for "Baptism." Now I wish I had encouraged them more strongly to think about the words of Isaiah and ask that the Church help this child to bring forth justice faithfully, to be a covenant to the people, and a light to the nations. Ask that the family of God in their particular parish community give assistance, support, and cooperation as we go forth together to open eyes that are blind and bring out prisoners from the dungeons where they sit in darkness.

I wonder if we are ready to hear and heed those requests. I wonder if I really want to live out that kind of baptismal commitment. Are we not more prepared for the rite than we are for the *right* of Baptism?

Entering into our baptismal right carries with it a profound sense that "God shows no partiality, but in every nation anyone who fears him and does what is right is acceptable to him" (Acts 10:34–35). That sense leads to our ever-deepening responsibility to live in a manner that shows no partiality; one that honors, respects, and embraces all who fear God and do what is acceptable to God. Differences and disrespect disappear in the wake of Good News, our preaching and practicing peace. To enter our baptismal right is to immerse ourselves in the process of enfleshing God's word. Its hallmark is our human incarnation of the Christ who cared enough to give us the very best, a share in his own divinity.

Like John the Baptizer, we both admit our lowliness (recognize our imperfection) and yet dare to "baptize" Christ in and for a world sorely needing salvation. We are chosen, called, and upheld for a unique conspiracy of love, a breathing together with God that will inspire creation to grow and glow with divine wisdom. Neither pushing Christ into the waters of humanity nor keeping him from them, we simply respond to Christ's presence and permit Christ to be Savior of the universe. That human action is enough to tear heavens apart. It allows God's Spirit to descend and spread over the whole universe and all humankind.

Bruised reeds do not break in the wind of godliness; they bend with welcoming waves. Dimly burning wicks catch the breeze of goodness, and their flickering flames burst into fiery holocausts. The poor are enriched by our presence. The rich note their spiritual impoverishment and request wealth no money can buy. Those oppressed by demons determined to separate them from their true selves are set free from enslavement. Shalom is in sight. Peace, the product of justice, can be viewed when baptism is a right to live, not a rite of life.

Godliness is a gift, a grace, not a grindstone. It becomes torturous only when we try too hard to control it, channel it, or criticize its presence. It is only when we forget we are divinely chosen, called, and upheld for God's purpose in God's time frame, that our troubles begin and our baptismal right becomes a brazen rite.

We need to remember that we are baptized in the waters of our humanity as well as the spirit of divinity. As divinity was made flesh and dwelt among us, so does our humanness incorporate divinity so that we might dwell with God. We are both baptizer and baptized, unworthy and supremely worthwhile. Called in righteousness, taken by the hand, kept in graciousness, we are beloved sons and daughters.

We are chosen and upheld by a delighted and loving God who is well pleased with all of us.

For Reflection and Discussion

- What in your life is preventing you from recognizing that you are chosen and upheld by a delighted God who is well pleased with you? What is deepening that realization in you? What would you change in your life if you perceived Baptism as a conferring of rights rather than a celebration of a rite?

Prayer

Beloved and loving God, my Friend who is pleased to call me forth, I thank you for my birth into your divinity. Cleansed constantly by the mercy of an immense variety of graceful waters and filled by the unimaginable gift of your Holy Spirit, may I be ever faithful to my baptismal covenant and, as your loyal servant, reveal your presence wherever I am and wherever I go. Amen.

Season of Lent

First Sunday of Lent

Genesis 9:8–15; 1 Peter 3:18–22; Mark 1:12–15

Rainbows for remembrance

Driven mad by misled love, Shakespeare's Ophelia spoke of rosemary for remembrance. Madly driven by divine love, God's people have rainbows for remembrance. Interestingly, so does God. Can you imagine that God needed a reminder? That is hard to believe, yet the Genesis writer records the divine promise as one made to Noah but also to prod and assist God's memory. "When I bring clouds over the earth and the bow is seen in the clouds, I will remember my covenant that is between me and you and every living creature of all flesh; and the waters shall never again become a flood to destroy all flesh" (Genesis 9:14–15).

Forevermore, water will be marked as a tool for new beginnings rather than for destructive flooding—birth instead of death. Watered clouds will bear rainbow promises that pierce the heavens and are made visible in the light of the sun. All that was gray and depressingly bleak will brighten with color. And all life will now be seen through that prism.

Too often Lent is viewed solely as a sackcloth and ashes time, six weeks set aside for fasting and denial. Actually, it is a season to remember rainbows. Lent affords us the opportunity to savor the salvation frequently taken for granted It gives us the chance to recall Baptism "…not as a removal of dirt from the body, but an appeal to God for a good conscience through the resurrection of Jesus Christ" (1 Peter 3:21).

Lent is a time we give ourselves to seek and see rainbows, divine arcs of triumph, offered for remembrance.

Remembering can take place only when we make room for the memories. Remembering necessitates silent stopping, a kind of spiritual cardiac arrest. While we are running to keep apace of our daily busy-ness, our mental arteries are being clogged. Plaque accumulates until we are unable to recall. The race disengages us from the reality of reminiscing. True, we might call to mind facts and figures and label them memories, but serious recall demands a concerted effort. It needs our total concentration, as well as our desire to search the past existing in the present and to prepare for the future.

In order to enter Lent with any degree of preparation, it is helpful for us to recapture the fact and faith of our Baptism. Obviously, this does not mean that we haul out old photo albums to gaze at the faces of our parents, godparents, friends, and family. Nor is it simply a fingering of yellowed lace or the lighting of a baptismal candle. At the same time, we cannot summarily dismiss those things. The images and stories create a rainbow of remembrance that might trigger a deeper understanding of the day on which faith was claimed and proclaimed. What we want to bring more profoundly into consciousness is the power of our baptismal commitment, power divinely given and humanly received.

As Jesus arose from the baptismal waters of the Jordan to see the heavens torn apart and the Spirit descending like a dove on him, so do we when we arise from the waters of our own Baptism to accept God's call. Reflecting upon our lives since the chronological moment of being baptized into the people of God, we see a rainbow of possibilities becoming a highway of grace. Little by little, with each subsequent event and experience, we hear God's voice saying, "You are my Son, the Beloved; with you I am well pleased" (Mark 1:11).

Remembering serves to empower and impel us more deeply into God's presence. Filled and refilled with God's Spirit, we are then driven, as was Jesus, into life's wilderness where fear is forged into faith and faith is purged of fearfulness.

Providentially, Lent affords the people of God a unique opportunity to follow God's spirit into a divinely ordained desert experience—a prayerful wilderness. Unlike any locale we might choose, this place is not plagued with insidious aridity but blessed with healing heat. It is not devoid of water, but bears selected oases that can be found only with careful search and keen vision. Thirst is quenched neither easily nor quickly. This desert is a spot where cacti bloom delightfully but unexpectedly. It is a place where contrasts serve to build character, enforce preparedness, and empower interdependency. Hot days abruptly give way to cold nights. Sands shift to blur the way. Without assistance or guidance, one can easily become lost in desert places.

Yet, here—day by day in this lunar landscape—each of us discovers the Son, our personal Savior, our individual mode of salvation, our unique witness, as we conspire with God in the work of divinity. Day by day, all of us in community collaborate in that same work. Both alone and together, we live with and battle the wild beasts of avarice and greed, jealousy and envy, pride and covetousness, lust and sloth, anger and apathy. Alone and together we discover that angels wait on us as we wait on and for each other. In the process, we become the patient people of God.

Every once in awhile we stop to remember. Each remembrance refreshes, renews, and offers a rainbow of recollections. Each remembrance is also an opportunity to re-member our personal brokenness and to be re-membered into the wholesomeness of the Body of Christ. It is a chance to repent and to appeal once more to God for a good conscience.

To seek and receive a good conscience that incorporates weakness with strength and success with failure is the tremendously good news wrought in those journeys into yesterday, if not yesteryear. God does not ask that we mire ourselves in the muck of sin anymore than we ought to get stuck in superficial sanctity. God only offers rainbows set in clouds, mixed blessings with colors that marry into the wholeness of holiness.

God provides the Good News that rainbows are for remembrance.

For Reflection and Discussion

- What in your life has to be re-membered this Lent? How do you understand the quote from 1 Peter 3:21 regarding baptism: "...not as a removal of dirt from the body, but an appeal to God for a good conscience through the resurrection of Jesus Christ"? In what ways might you practice remembering so that your gratitude may deepen and grow?

Prayer

Dear God, so often I forget who I am, whose I am, and where I am going. I get stuck in those clouds of forgetfulness and do not see the rainbow that dwells in the midst of that fogginess, the rainbow that comes when I allow your Son to shine through my life. Help me to become aware of that bowed beauty. Let me remember that we are together in this vision. Let me deepen my belief that you will never flood me with more than I can bear or destroy my life. You will only place rainbows of remembrance in the skies of my faithfulness and find joy in the sight. I am grateful that you are my God and you have chosen to live your life in me. Amen.

Second Sunday of Lent

GENESIS 22:1–2, 9, 10–13, 15–18; ROMANS 8:31–34; MARK 9:2–10

Let's give it up for God

Comedy Central's parting line for each comedian is a request for the audience to "Put your hands together and give it up for…!" Clap those hands in applause. Open up your cache of compliments. Give the guy or gal a break. Move from being a harsh critic to a hearty appreciator.

Sometimes that is extremely difficult to do. When the comic is less than clever or hard to take or too sarcastic for words, I want to shout "Boo! Get off the stage!" I only want to "give it up" on my terms, my time, my evaluation.

God is scarcely a comedian. Sometimes God is not on my center stage. However, the request remains the same. Divinity demands that we "give it up, for God." I don't know about you, but I am reluctant, at times perhaps far too often, to give it up for God. I am not interested in experiencing the pain involved with sacrifice. I do not have the faith of Abraham who apparently overcame all parental angst in his willingness to give up his only and beloved son for God. Isaac, at the same time, offered no resistance or questioning. He quietly allowed his father to bind him and place him on an altar of wood without uttering a word of protest. Father and son are presented to us as the epitome of sanctity—unwavering, unquestioning obedience.

Is that the truth of the matter? Is it my observable reality, and yours, as human beings? Are we all lacking in faith? Or is it that we have not yet recognized that we and God are in the same spot? Is it not more true that the divine I AM, the essence of all that is, is speaking to the I AM who is the core of my being? The transcendent, untouchable, immutable, unknowable God who is so far above me that I'll never reach the heights of divinity is speaking to the God who dwells in me and is closer to me that my own breath and heartbeat. Separate and one, as the Trinity is separate and one, God above seeks to be united with the God within and asks that all else move aside to let that happen.

When Abraham responded to God's call with the words, "Here I am," he was echoing God's own words to all of us. "Here I am! Here I am, with you, in all the mess and muddle. Here I am, in the midst of the pain and problem. I am giving it up for you at the very instant and in the very instance that you are giving it up for me."

God and I are in the same boat. God and you are in the same boat.

God and all of us are in the same boat, together!

"If God is for us, and with us, who is against us?"

As my children like to say, "What a concept!"

God is not asking us to do anything that God would not do, has not already done, for us. The God who gives all to us empowers us to give all—not so much in return as in response. And blessings result, blessings beyond our comprehension.

For me, this is a mind-blowing reality. It will take me a lifetime to digest, if not understand. I am really not doing anything on my own, no matter how individualistic it may seem to be. I am always being and acting in God. God is being and acting in me, in you, in us, in all humankind! And it is God's choice that it happen this way. God is sacrificing divinity to make holy our humanity. God is giving it up, for us.

We can do nothing more or less than to imitate God's way of being. When Abraham offered Isaac, God was acting in him. When Peter, James, and John followed Jesus to that high mountain, God was acting in them. When Jesus was transfigured on the mountaintop, God was acting in him. When Peter, recognizing the power and grace of transfiguration, pronounced the goodness of the place and the experience, it was God acting with astounding creativity.

Like Peter, we scarcely know what to say or do about this kind of life—a life transfigured by God-in-us, living divinity in us. We want to capture it. At the same time, we have an innate feeling that we can't remain there. We are simultaneously filled with trepidation and tremendous excitement. Fear and faith collide in creative tension.

Interestingly, Peter mentions only three tents, one for Jesus, one for Moses, and one for Elijah. He offers no suggestion of a fourth tent for himself, James, and John. Somehow, Peter knows he cannot remain at the heart of sheer divinity. Divinity's dynamism scares him. It scares us.

The truth is that the recognition of transfiguration is a terrifyingly beautiful realization, perhaps too terrifyingly beautiful. To be changed by God's presence, to be changed into the presence of God, is an unspeakable grace. God's choice to live God's life in us is an overwhelming power. God-in-us gives only one affirmation and speaks only one command: "This is my Son, the Beloved; listen to him"(Mark 9:8). Those words turn our mountaintops into plateaus from which we must descend or die. They also give us a companion whose divinity is replete with humanity; whose humanity is completely divine.

God is giving it up for us magnificently in offering Jesus, Son of God, Beloved One, as our brother. God is expanding the divine trinitarian union to include all of us as the family of God. To listen to God's Son is to listen to our brother, our fellow pilgrim, as well as our resurrected Lord and Savior. God gave it up for us. God's clapping hands affirm our goodness, transfiguring our faltering and failings into faithfulness. God's profound solicitude for our well-being and wholeness is evident in life's numerous blessings. "He who did not withhold his own Son, but gave him up for all of us, will he not with him also give us everything else?" (Romans 8:32).

In light of all we have received, we applaud the unknowable, believe the incredible, and rejoice in the ineffable. There really is only one appropriate response.

So let's give it up for God!

For Reflection and Discussion

- What do you think and feel you need to do to surrender finally, decidedly, and fully to God? What happens to you when you hear God say to you, "Here I am"? How do you feel when you hear God pronouncing these words, "You are my beloved son. My beloved daughter"?

Prayer

Here I am, Lord. I am here, my God.
Present, accounted for, and ready to trod
The path you choose, the way you lead.
Wherever you go, I am with you, indeed.
I want you to live your life in me
Daily, wondrously, within hardship or glee.
My desire is only that I will hear your voice
Telling me that I am your choice.
I am your beloved, your darling one.
I am your daughter. I am your son.
Amen.

THIRD SUNDAY OF LENT

EXODUS 20:1–17; 1 CORINTHIANS 1:22–25; JOHN 2:13–25

Saints in the hands of a jealous God

I am a fairly volatile, first-generation Italian-American who storms through life—sometimes with grace and ease, but always with grand fervor. Perhaps that explains my ability to empathize with an angry, whip-lashing Jesus whose fury was unleashed in the Temple-turned-marketplace. Surely, it underlies my secret joy in seeing the bad guys, at least some of them, finally getting their due.

When my emotions are in high gear and I am boiling with the need to address apparent injustices, I can easily relate to the impassioned overturning of tables and deck-clearing that Jesus accomplished. There is, however, a major difference between the two of us. Jesus acted solely out of an all-consuming zeal for God's house. Often, I react with quite mixed motivations. It happens insidiously. Instead of remembering that God is my essence, my all, I idolize my own perceptions, take control of the situation, and change places with God. Despite my best intentions, the decks I clear with great facility can, sadly, become yet another temple, another marketplace, another possibility for buying and selling.

So, I sit back in my soul and take another look at the scene. What is God trying to tell me and you about divinity in the words, "Zeal for your house will consume me" (John 2:17)? Then it comes to me. Unlike the fire and brimstone fear promulgated by the eighteenth-century philosophical theologian Jonathan Edwards in his famous sermon "Sinners in the Hands of an Angry God," this story of a fiery Jesus is one told to comfort as well as challenge saints in the hands of a jealous God. That is who we are. People of God, we are saints in the hands of a jealous God, a God who so zealously loves and guards us that the fire of ardent love is palpable.

We are the temple that God is cleansing of all ills, because God's zeal for us is all-consuming.

God cannot and does not want to watch the divinity housed in the temple of humankind endure thievery. God will not allow us to be robbed of our godly essence in the name of efficiency or economy. Worse yet, God cannot permit the continuing ravages of treacherous legality. Jesus the Christ, Son of God, is also our brother, savior, friend, companion. One of us, he is enraged at what he sees happening to and in the human temple, God's house. I cannot help but believe that this narrative of Jesus' outrage in the Temple of Jerusalem is the story of saints being given sanctuary in the hands of a jealous God. At the same time, it is truly a tale of overturned tables, of pietists who are unmasked as thieves seeking to rob the poor of their right to worship freely.

We have been sent a Messiah, anointed to assist us in realizing how precious we are to God. This historical Jesus who died for us is risen from death to inspirit us with God-sight. Power, possessions, prestige, the idols we revere, are costly. They tear at the fiber of our being and devalue God's dwelling within us. Inappropriate use of our time, energy, and talents is no less a disgrace than finding "people selling cattle, sheep, and doves, and the money changers seated at their tables" (John 2:14) in the Jerusalem Temple. The fact that they were present in the Temple is not detrimental as much as it is that they were there to cheat and gouge, to take advantage of piety, to play havoc with the powerless poor. It is no wonder that Jesus made a whip of cords and drove them out. It is God's grace that Jesus continues to "whip us into shape."

Jesus' zeal for God's house, God's people, consumes him.

Amazingly, at the same time, we are becoming more cognizant of our own worth and value as God's family. Brought out of the house of enslavement, led from the aridity of desert life, God is ever more real and present to us. It makes little or no sense to continue to bow down to idols that do nothing more than diminish our goodness and bind us tightly to their increasing demands. The money changing we must do is to change monetary surplus into mandatory service. It is to use whatever we have to enhance the temple of God, not the building, but the people God has called to be family.

Interestingly, as I continued to reflect on the Scriptures and meditate on their meaning, I was distracted by the sound of the television. Leaving my computer to investigate, I discovered that the Rosa Parks story was being aired. Promptly, I sat down to watch. It was as if God had put me in front of the set to see the Temple story come alive again. I was astounded to watch the unveiling of zeal for God's house as it consumed Rosa. She risked her life, her husband, and her family, in an unceasing quest to see justice done. She willingly and willfully allowed herself to be used by the NAACP as a poster woman for all who were weary of being downtrodden and oppressed.

Deep in her heart, Rosa Parks knew that human beings—all human beings—are God's dwelling places. None are more or less worthy than others to be a divine habitat. One day, believing this truth, she simply sat still in her bus seat. By refusing to move, Rosa Parks overturned age-old tables of injustice. Making a whip of the cords of past abuses, she drove her people to nonviolent action. She helped them demand their civil rights as human beings, as

Americans. Rosa Parks took her ability to lead and teach, not as a professional but as a person in whom God lived, and used it to empower others to do the same. Rosa was a saint in the hands of a jealous God. So are we.

God's all-consuming desire for us—God's possessive and zealous love—commands us to embrace divinely each and all in a massive hug of humanity. For our good, we are told to spend serious time contemplating the sanctity we share as a result of the holiness of the One who is always with us. Leave the workaday world behind, at least once weekly, to bask in the wonder of God and to recognize the power of our weariness. Be consecrated in the sacredness of those moments and uncover your own magnificence. Give honor to those who have offered you birth, those whose parenting is an ongoing process. Honor them and discover your own exaltedness.

Let nothing interfere with that resolute love. Neither murder nor steal nor lie nor misuse God's holy name. Do not fall prey to the false idols cloaked in covetous feelings that can easily override goodness with lust. Be consumed with zeal for the house, the family, the people of God. Be as consumed with zeal as was Rosa Parks, as was Jesus.

Be saints in the hands of a jealous God.

For Reflection and Discussion

- In what ways do you see or feel the Holy Spirit cleansing the temple you are, way down deep, even in your unconscious self? As a mature Christian, how are you living and speaking God's reforming truth in your world? in your church? in your family?

Prayer

Create a clean heart in me, O God. Let me not remain stuck in my own ideas or allow me to pray only in the pews of my own desires and fancies. Inspirit me with God-sight. Give me a vision of the divine kingdom I am uniquely called to serve and empower. Show me the way to go home to you in the company of the saints you have placed along my path. Give me the courage to accept, receive, and integrate the gift of consuming zeal for your house, your people, your reign. Help me as I strive to be a saint in your hands, my jealous God. Amen.

FOURTH SUNDAY OF LENT

2 CHRONICLES 36:14–16, 19–23; EPHESIANS 2:4–10; JOHN 3:14–21

Remembering to see beneath the surface

How often have we heard the adage "Remember the past so that you won't repeat it" only to go right on forgetting it and repeating our mistakes? Remembering is fast becoming a lost art. Worse yet, traveling down memory lane has become a source for manipulation by the unscrupulous who unleash false memories that cause pain and sorrow. We have become a consumer society that uses and throws away everything, including remembrances. The resulting deprivation has not yet touched our hearts, possibly because it is only beginning to reach our pocketbooks.

It is a problem that echoes through the ages of human existence. Grumbling Israelites who found desert harshness to be less desirable than Egyptian bondage forgot their desire for freedom. Despite the encouraging presence of their leader Moses, they no longer remembered the reason for their march nor did they recall the God who walked with them. They refused to be religious people. No longer were they people who, in the words of Richard Rohr, OFM, "believe that all authentic religion is an issue of radical participation. Participation in another and larger life than my own. A life that can bear both the burden of sin and the weight of glory at the same time" (NCR, 2/15/02).

To remember those words, to be re-membered in them, is to see beneath the surface and to live in liminal space.

Princes of Judah, priests and people alike, all forgot the subject of their worship. Somehow, life had ebbed from their Temple rites, leaving only deadly rituals in its wake. Despite their bereavement, known or hidden, at the loss, people in their midst tried to awaken a sleeping sense of remembering, recalling, and reorienting. But the Israelites "kept mocking the messengers of God, despised his words, and scoffing at his prophets, until the wrath of the Lord against his people became so great that there was no remedy" (2 Chronicles 36:16).

We are equally shortsighted today. It is far more comfortable, far easier, to cease remembering than to risk the danger of radical religion. It is less taxing to live in the space of religiosity where camaraderie poses as community and control is perceived as virtue.

For many, Church is often just a building and a weekly obligation. This kind of religion is less concerned with relationship than it is with rules and regulations. Certainly, it cannot be mixed with politics, even in casual conversation, without causing great consternation. Justice becomes a great idea for action, if it can fit into an already crowded schedule of activities. Truth is spoken, until it becomes inconvenient, and, as a result, we become unpopular. Unheeded, God's messengers and our prophets are shunned and isolated, if not exiled, from the community. We look for facile answers everywhere, fearing the cost of the cross that we know is found at the core of trust.

If the story were to end here, it would not be a Lenten tale preparing us for paradoxical resurrection living. It would not urge us "to see beneath the surface." Anthony Padovano once wrote, "Jesus always saw beneath the surface, to how deep and infinite humanity is. He saw more than sight could offer. He saw wine in water, an apostle in a fisherman, a saint in an adulterous woman, a missionary in a promiscuous Samaritan. He went to the heart, the core, the essence.

"He found forgiveness for executioners and learned to trust as death approached. On the surface, things appeared desperate and impossible. But Jesus did not dwell there. Were Jesus here, he would see more than the surface flaws and failures of a perennially imperfect world" (Padovano, NCR, 2/28/97).

Jesus saw the world as God sees, beneath the surface. What was apparent in the days of the Chronicler were the unfaithful princes, priests, and people. As in the days of the Exodus people, evil continued and multiplied, but God never surrendered his clarion call to covenantal relationship. Despite the mockery and complaints of his people, God refused to give up. Instead, God saw beneath the surface and deepened and toughened his love for them. Allowing a temporary conquest by the Babylonians to be a period of purification, God then remembered the promise given and intervened through Cyrus, King of Persia, to bring his people home and back to life.

Our God is a God who remembers. Our God sees beneath the surface.

Rich in mercy, God continues to bring us to life, even while we are sinfully dead. That is the promise of our remembering/re-membering God. Our "deadly" existence is only the surface. God sees beneath it to the covenantal life given us in love. God sees eternal life, quality life free from corruption and decay, in us. God sees our truth and beauty and goodness. God loves what God sees wherever it is.

It is time for us to lift up the Son of Man so that all might see him and receive the eternal life God freely gives. Now is the acceptable time to speak of an uplifting Savior. Now is the time to use the body language of people who are committed to raising rather than razing. It is time for us to be rich in mercy. It is time for us to avoid condemnation, to act in truth, to come into the light, and to be clear that our deeds are done in God.

It is time for us to remember and see beneath the surface.

It is time for us to recognize "There is, you see, grace everywhere—visible, palpable, not far from the surface, out of sight but not beyond reach. In the tangled complexity and dispiriting debris of modern life, we strive to make life better. A time for grace has come. A time to see the grace sacramentally hidden beneath the surface of the commonplace and banal, the hostile and the seemingly irredeemable" (A. Padovano).

Our Lenten message and challenge is a simple one: See, love, and remember as God does—beneath the surface—to discover the heart of life.

For Reflection and Discussion

- When God looks beneath the surface what do you think God finds in you? In what ways have you embraced the darkness rather than the light? How have you brightened your world and banished darkness from the lives of others?

Prayer

God of remembering, I am sorry for the many times I have refused to remember the good and to re-member my brokenness and that of others. I know that these failings are times when I have forgotten you and all that you have done in, with, and through me. I have not recalled my giftedness nor helped my brothers and sisters to realize theirs. I ask forgiveness. I ask that I might see beneath the surface of your creation and discover the goodness that awaits discovery and sharing. With the help of your Son and Spirit, I know your vision will become mine. Amen.

FIFTH SUNDAY OF LENT

JEREMIAH 31:31–34; HEBREWS 5:7–9; JOHN 12:20–33

Troubled souls with hearts of love

I have just returned home from a meeting of persons dedicated to the service of God's people. One would expect that there, as in no other place, there would be the greatest commitment to charity, the most intense covenantal love. And there was, until a discussion of law began. Almost immediately, the tenor of the group changed. Some remained silent as tombs. Quite literally, they said nothing from beginning to end. Nor were they even asked to express their opinion. Others were both loud and vociferous. Vehemently, they stated their points of view, convictions, suggestions, and demands. Tension grew proportionately. Rising tempers were thinly veiled, though grand attempts were made to cool down and listen. At least for the time being, these men and women were troubled souls with hearts of love. It was not a happy time.

As I write, I am reflecting on what could have been, might have been, needed to be done to evoke charity in the midst of change. What came to mind, first and foremost, was that none of us asked to have the meeting begin with prayer, though praying had always been our starting point. Committed, covenanted people, we forgot who we were and fell into the powerful hands of efficiency and time management. The agenda seemed to revolve about a compulsion to get quickly to the business at hand. In so doing, we truly forgot the heart of the matter—and became troubled souls. The room became a graveyard of distress.

From that moment onward, it was a downhill slide. Business continued to be addressed, but it was done with anger and angst. It became ever more clear to me that law, when it is not written on the heart, is nothing more than binding, enslaving legalism. Each person at that meeting slavishly and sharply presented an individual viewpoint, a particular perception. No soft words were in evidence. Some feeble attempts were made to listen. However, they were quickly supplanted by an overriding need to establish laws—rules that would cover as many possibilities as could be foreseen. I could see the life of the group being lost in the generating of laws. It became much more important to teach one another with forceful authority than it was to recognize compassionately our collective mission as people of God.

We were troubled souls who had forgotten our hearts of love.

My gut reaction was to beg, "God, save me from this hour." I was ready to quit. Give up. Walk out of the room and go home. In fact, I actually had to hold on to the chair to prevent my exit. At this age and stage of my life I did not need any more nit-picking over rules and regulations. Nor did I wish to quarrel over words and phrases. I just wanted to be part of a simple little group of people committed to service. Leaving would have been the easy way out.

Then, bubbling up from the depths of my troubled soul, I heard the answer to my prayerful plea: "No, it is for this reason that I have come to this hour. Father, glorify your name" (John 12:27–28). I heard God telling me that I needed to see clearly that God is married to us, even while we are married to the law. Stay with the group. Find God in the midst of all the wrangling over policy and procedure. Recognize that life is not easy, but it is always worthwhile. Do not remember the faults and failings of others, as if I have none of my own. Instead, begin to realize that all know God, from least to greatest. Learn from them. Learn with them to see Jesus.

If our desire to see Jesus is heartfelt and sincere, all laws will break open to love. But it will take a trip to Calvary before that vulnerability happens. Even among the most committed people of God, there will be a scourging, a crowning with thorns, a bloody walk to death. Each of us will carry a heavy beam, the wood of our own crucifixion. Like Simon of Cyrene all of us will also be called upon to bear the burden of another's cross.

If I am as committed to service as I proclaim, I must also know there will be haggling over my garments. Bids will be cast to see who gains ownership of my possessions, my place in life. I will endure mockery and dismissal of my very person. Anguished, I will offer up prayers and supplications, with loud cries and tears, in the radical belief that I will be heard and healed in the very heart of my hardship.

I might be a troubled soul, but I will also have a heart of love.

Lenten journeys never take us down easy pathways. They are always reminders that life and death are intimately entwined. Life and death spin and twirl in a paradoxical dance of victory. Strangely, each mirrors and completes the other. Jesus expresses it succinctly for us. "Very truly, I tell you, unless a grain of wheat falls into the earth and dies, it remains just a single grain; but if it dies, it bears much fruit" (John 12:24).

None of us relishes the fact that we are like grains of wheat that must die in order to live. Yet all of us have come face-to-face with that truth. It is our life experience. We bury seeds, only to watch delightedly as they sprout and grow. Each tiny green leaf is acclaimed. Vitality is applauded. God is praised. When maturity is reached, and fruits and vegetables are ripe for picking, we pluck them from the garden of their being, and enjoy the lush wonder they provide. Harvest time is not an ending but a beginning. Eating the produce is not a completion but a continuation of the life process. In much the same way, we move and grow as human beings. We "die" to pleasures in the discipline of "duty first." We bury the desire for "me first" in order to open the graves of those we have killed with our self-centeredness.

Inch by inch, moment by moment, we become people who are dying to live. Troubled souls with hearts of love.

For Reflection and Discussion

- What experiences of life have sprung from any recent evidences of your "dying to self"? In what ways have you come to know and realize the words of Jeremiah, "I will be their God and they shall be my people" (Jeremiah 31:33)?

Prayer

My God, desire of my heart,
I want to follow you, at least to start,
From morning to evening and all night long—
To see your face and hear your song
In all the people whose paths cross mine
And learn to wonder, not to whine.
My heart is right, my head is true,
Yet I often choose myself, not you.
Implant in me a broader hope, a deeper trust,
That your promises are truly gold, not rust.
Do not save me from my hour of pain
But let me know it is not loss, but gain. Amen.

Passion/Palm Sunday

Isaiah 50:4–7; Philippians 2:6–11; Mark 14:1—15:39

Palm-wavers on passion's path

I find it both interesting and unnerving to note that the Roman Catholic Church, for a number of years, had been embroiled in a raging revelation of its pedophilia cover-up. For a while, it was not unusual to see daily articles on the subject in our local newspapers. More remarkable is the fact that I live in the Bible belt South where Roman Catholicism is growing but still a minority denomination.

Each day my e-mail was clogged with forwarded copies of similar articles from newspapers, magazine, and journals scattered nationwide. Each day I became more and more convinced and more and more confused. I love Roman Catholicism dearly. It is my home, my family, my way to God. It is the place where I used to prance in a parade of palms as a professional religious educator, lector, and dedicated parishioner. I held my children in its baptismal waters and sent them to its schools to be educated, as I had been, from elementary school through college and graduate school.

For me, the Church (and I use the capital letter with purpose) was the place where priests and nuns had been given, as Isaiah writes, "the tongue of a teacher that they might know how to sustain the weary with a word." And I listened. I knew, "the Lord God has opened my ear, and I was not rebellious, did not turn backward. I gave my back to those who struck me and my cheeks to those who pulled out the beard. I did not hide my face from insult and spitting" (Isaiah 50:4b–6). In other words, I equated the Church with Christ. It was easy to wave palms in that parade. My part was to do nothing more than to pray, pay, obey—and wave those palms with jubilation knowing that I was a loyal follower of Roman Catholicism.

I was not yet fully aware of an important reality. The palm-waving parade was walking a path leading to passion and death.

While those days of innocent joy are not over, they are now inseparably intertwined with nights of darkness and denial. The Church—my Church, the people of God—has entered a time that will test and try our holiness in the crucible of doubt. There will be more questions than answers, more probing than polity. Calvary looms large on a horizon too close to be avoided. Somehow, in the midst of the terrible turmoil, freedom will surface. Resurrection will be found in reformation, the re-forming of the *Church* into the Body of Christ, instead of the other way around.

It is so difficult to sort out the various components and seek accountability, so easy to point at others with fingers of blame. I vacillate. At times I am the woman with the alabaster jar whose only thought is to break it open, pour the ointment over the head of the Church, and anoint it for burial, in the hopes that what I do will be told as good news. At other times, I am Judas looking for an opportunity to betray this Church that would be Jesus because it is not what I believed it could and should be. Or, I am like the disciples, scattering just far enough away not to witness the mess created by the striking of the shepherd.

Sometimes I am Pilate. I seek the easy way out, looking for a scapegoat: anyone, anywhere, who will end this terrible trial. To short-circuit the process is my goal. I would rather an obstruction of justice than an observance of it. So, I put up smokescreens and facile solutions. Instead of facing the complexity head on, I try to bring things to the least common denominator by repeating, "This too will pass." I want to believe that problems within the institutional Church can be traced to and remain with a few bad apples in the barrel. I do not want to admit that the barrel itself is badly in need of repair and reconstruction. Wishing to satisfy the crowds who refuse to be discomfited, I wash my hands of the matter and hand over the Christ to be flogged and crucified.

Most often, I guess I am Peter. Perhaps most of us are. Boldly brazen, we boast our belief when it is convenient to do so, when crucifixion is not yet a clear and present danger, yet fail to remain awake, even for one hour, in prayerful discernment of God's will. Our spirits are willing; our flesh is weak. Our fear is so great that we deny affiliation with the Christ *en route* to crucifixion. We want an easy Jesus and a comfortable Church where bad things do not happen to good people. We want a priesthood without problems and ministry without mishaps. We want to wave palm branches in celebratory joy without recognizing or realizing that the path we walk must lead to passion and death before it can take us to the splendor of resurrection.

Though it may frequently be against my wishes, I am compelled to carry the cross of Christ. Carrying it to the crest of Calvary, I am forced to see a bloodied, beaten Messiah whose only desire is to love us and bring us home. I am compelled to watch as he is derided, taunted, mocked, and scorned. I cannot turn my head from the sight. I am unable to block my ears from the plaintive sound of his anguished psalm, "My God, my God, why have you forsaken me?" (Mark 15:34). His groan mingles with mine. We both give out a loud cry and breathe our last breath.

It is ended.

Can this be the tale of God's people suffering today? Can we resonate with the experiences of those who are memorialized in the pages of Scripture? Can we accept our responsibility as well as our reward as members of the Body of Christ, the Church? Can we give this model of Church permission to breathe its last breath? Can we allow it to die, so that it might truly live?

The answers to these questions reside deep in the hearts of believers. To find them we need only watch and pray with Jesus, "Abba, Father, for you all things are possible; remove this cup from me; yet, not what I want, but what you want" (Mark 14:36).

Watch, wait, pray. Then act as a renewed and renewing people of God. Be palm-wavers on passion's pathway, people on a death walk to impassioned resurrection.

For Reflection and Discussion

- After reading the Markan passion narrative, with whom do you most identify? Why? What does that identification reveal about your inner self? Put yourself in the place of Jesus on the cross. From that vantage point, what do the world, people, friends, family, look like?

Prayer

How painful is the cross you bear, my God and Savior Lord.
It hurts to see you hanging there, your side pierced by a mighty sword.
Yet, I, in my own humble way, would take your place and cry,
"My God, you have forsaken me and I do not know why!"
I ache with sorrow, fear, and dread as dying draws me near.
Your cross is hard to bear.
And I am just a tiny one, with little courage left to spare.
Come to my aid, increase my love that I might fully care
To follow in your way and bring with me
All those whom you have called to be
Kingdom dwellers, lights to the world, people of God
Who pray as they play; sing as they trod
Home to you, our Savior God. Amen.

Season of
Easter

EASTER SUNDAY

ACTS 10:34, 37–43; COLOSSIANS 3:1–4; JOHN 20:1–9

Magdalene's memories

Sabbath rest—aach! Who could rest on this Sabbath? I know I could not. I did not! So much has happened. There is so much to tell. Where do I begin? How far back do I go to find the starting point? I don't even know! But, sit, sit down and let me talk. Sometimes things unravel and make sense when I do that.

It was just a few weeks ago when I first got uneasy feelings that something terrible was going to happen. There were rumblings in the street that the Pharisees and Sadducees had found someone else to bicker about. At first, I thought that it was the usual philosophical arguments they shouted at each other. But, this time I noticed that they did not end in arm waving and a mutual agreement to disagree. This time there was a growing animosity and ferocity. I got scared. Trouble always happens when those two join forces.

I tried to warn my Jesus that he was becoming too powerful for them. "No good will come of this," I said. He just smiled in response, gave me a reassuring hug, and continued on his way. I knew a woman could do little, in public view, to change a man's mind or course of action. I also knew that she could quietly do a lot to affect a man if she stayed her course, remaining in the background but never disappearing. So, I decided to make certain that I went wherever he did.

That's how I got to be in the Upper Room with him and the Twelve as we celebrated Pesach together. In fact, I helped Peter to get things ready; then arranged and served the meal. There was such a silence in the room. I shivered. *Was this what Moses felt at Sinai?* I wondered. "Ah, you are such a fool, Magdalene," I said to myself as I tried to shake my fears away. The meal continued, its pattern broken only by Judas' sudden leaving. This was of little concern since he was rather a strange person, anyway.

Even Jesus' request for us to come with him to the garden to pray did not startle me, for we had often gathered in prayer together. Suddenly Judas appeared with armed men who grabbed my Jesus and arrested him. I bit my tongue to keep from screaming. Everything became so clear to me. This was the "end" he had been trying to tell us about. I was filled with all sorts of conflicting feelings. One thing was sure. I was not going to leave him now when he needed me the most. But, I must first run to tell his mother what had happened. She would be sorely pained, and I had to help her as well. Each of us would sustain the other.

So many confusing events occurred from that moment on. I still have not sorted them out. All I know is that it seemed we were next walking along the streets of Jerusalem, pushing and shoving our way through the crowds of curious onlookers. We got to the hilltop in time to hear agonized grunts escape from Jesus' lips as the nails were pounded into him. Then that cross beam was put in place and dropped into the earth. I never thought I would feel such pain.

The worst was yet to come. Mary, his mother, and I held each other. We prayed for the end to come swiftly. Each minute was agony. We watched. Even tears would not come to soften our suffering. Why should they? Tears did not wash my Jesus' face. One last cry and he was gone. Now we cried. We keened our pain. Pesach was over. Our lamb was dead.

We hurried to do what all women do when their men have died—prepare the burial. But even this solace was denied us. It was the eve of Preparation Day and little time was left. Thank God, Joseph of Arimathea arrived. He had heard of all that happened and managed to convince Pilate to have Jesus' body given to him. Quickly, we wrapped Jesus in a linen shroud, and Joseph laid him in a tomb he owned.

Just as quickly, we rushed home. Mary came with me. I insisted that she should not be alone this night. At first, we spoke tenderly of all that Jesus meant to us. Then the words became swords ripping us to shreds. In our grief, silence reigned. We tried to sleep because we knew that would be good for us. Perhaps we did fall into a fitful sleep, I do not remember, but rest was not ours. The night was simply time to let pass until we could get to the tomb in the morning and do what we could to anoint our Jesus as was proper. Though it seemed never to come, the dawn did break. I waited for no one. While it was still dark, I rushed to the place of the tomb. When I got there, I saw that the huge rock had been moved away, and I knew immediately that Jesus was not there. Fresh pain seized me. He was not there! Where had they put him? Who had taken him? Was there no end to this dying?

I was wrenched with the pain of my loss. My whole body ached. A piercing emptiness begged release, yet I could not cry. I could not allow the void to disappear. I was angry. Why had Jesus done this to me? I had begged him to speak more politically. I had reminded him that the terrible envy of the Temple authorities was going to bring him trouble. Yet, he continued to do what he always did. Didn't he love me at all? Didn't he love his own mother? How could he do this to us?

And I was frightened. He was gone. What would happen to the rest of us? What did all of this mean? I ran to tell Peter and John about the empty tomb. Clutched by the ambivalence of belief while still wrapped in the arms of disbelief, they had to see for themselves. They, too, ran to the place and saw the emptiness.

It was then that my tears came. I stood there weeping. As I wept, I felt that I had to take one last look. I stooped to peer inside, and there I saw two angels in dazzling robes. They asked me why I was weeping. I was confused. Didn't they know? "Because the Lord has been taken away, and I do not know where they have put him," I told them.

No sooner had I said this, than I felt a presence, was moved to turn around, and I saw yet another man standing there. I thought he was a gardener who might know where my Jesus had been taken. When I asked him the question, he simply said, "Mary." At the sound of his voice, my heart raced. All my questioning melted into an overwhelming feeling of such deep love. Everything was all right. I did not understand, but I knew.

I knew.

My Jesus lives!

Pesach is over.

In the darkness, I have seen the Lord.

In the light, I will always remember.

For Reflection and Discussion

- What mini-resurrections have you experienced? How does this story of Magdalene's memories affect you? In what ways is it your story as well?

Prayer

My God, how often I have felt like an empty tomb. I have felt devoid of emotions, bereft of those good feelings that often propelled me into active prayer. Tears would not come to cleanse my spirit and soothe my aching soul. Yet, I remained steadfast in my sorrow. So, I praise and thank you for the grace of determination, the gift of endurance. I praise and thank you for being in the garden of my agony, the graveyard of my desolation. I praise and thank you for calling my name and letting me know that you are always with me. Seen and unseen, known and unknown, you are my God and I am your beloved. Amen.

Second Sunday of Easter

Acts 4:32–35; 1 John 5:1–6; John 20:19–31

What the world needs now is love, sweet love

The song may strike us as sentimental, but the idea—no, the ideal—is right on target. What our world needs now, and has always needed, is love, sweet love. It does not call for a saccharine substitute that provides the sweetness artificially, but the genuine goods. We need a love that challenges as profoundly as it comforts; that disturbs and demands as deeply as it delights. To love is not easy, but it is worthwhile.

Anyone who has parented a child, anyone who has been a friend to another human being, certainly has experienced the difficulties that accompany true love. True love has but one mission, and that is to empower healing and holiness. Loving persons want nothing but what is best for those they love. Loving people are believers who are of one heart and soul. None claim private ownership of any possessions, but everything they own is held in common. There are no needy people where love is present, for all that we have is distributed to each as any have need.

"Whoa!" you say. "This is an impossible dream. No one is going to live up to such a fantasy." Admittedly, it sounds as if it can never happen. But it has occurred. It does take place. It is a reality, however imperfectly achieved. The fact is that each and every one of us—trusting in the God who loves us first, always, and in all ways—has both the means and the might to go wherever love is needed. We are sent into a ravished world as messengers of peace and love. Ours is an inspired mission of conspiracy. We bear and share divine breath. At the same time, we are conspirators, breathing with God's own Spirit and collaborating in God's own plan of salvation.

As a result, we have the power and ability to stand in the midst of those who are imprisoned behind their closed and barred doors of fear. We have the stamina to pronounce that "shalom," holy wholesomeness, is right here with us, if only we will open our eyes to see its truthful presence.

All we have to offer this needy world is who we are, wounded healers with bodies and spirits torn and tattered, but alive in the goodness and grace of God. Who we are is recognizable to those whose lives are equally scarred and shattered. We are believable because we have been raised from our many deaths and are willing to share the process with those who seek a similar resurrection.

True love acts fearlessly in the face of fear. True love offers whatever is necessary to assist another to be whole and therefore holy. We who wish to be God's people are called to be authentic in our loving. Our life is one of giving and forgiving. If someone cannot move from denial and avoidance without a physical touch, without seeing the nail marks of suffering in our hands, without putting a finger into those marks or a hand into our slashed side to authenticate the pain we have sustained or are yet enduring, we willingly acquiesce to their need. Though strong, we become vulnerable so that the vulnerable might become strong. This kind of "for-giveness" is the great power with which we give testimony to the resurrection of Jesus. It is the vehicle by which intellectual thoughts and dogmatic statements are enfleshed and take root in the heart.

When the people of God can see that there is not a needy person among them because each one has distributed to all from their bounty, the sight will also magnetize many who live in doubt and fear. When the people of God recognize that their bounty is not only found in an abundance of material goods, but also in time and talent, energy and enthusiasm, awareness of need in their own communities will become ever more visible. While the aphorism "One cannot give what one has not got" is verifiable, it is also true that one cannot receive what one has not been offered.

The disciples cowering in a locked room for fear of crucial consequences could not give anything but fear to those around them. That's all they had to offer. When Jesus came into their midst brandishing shalom, they apparently did not receive it or understand it. All they could do was to rejoice in his presence among them and hope that everything would go back to normal again.

No matter what Jesus said to those followers, no matter how well he delineated their commissioning to be sent into their world as he had been sent to them, no matter that they had been empowered with the privilege and responsibility of forgiving and retaining sins, they did not respond proactively. They stayed where they were and as they were until a doubter called their bluff. Someone who had left the community for reasons unknown except to himself and thus had missed what occurred now returned to the group. He returned to listen, learn, but also to be honest in stating that he needed a personal experience of resurrection before he could truly accept it as truth. Thomas who was called the Twin is indeed our twin, and we are his.

If we are honest with ourselves, we too demand proof before we will take action. No one really wants to be a fool, even if we are called to be fools for Christ. Thomas' authenticity, expressed in his demands to seek the mark of the nails, to put his finger into those marks and his hand into the side of Christ, is also critical for the quavering disciples who spoke of a joy they could not express publicly. Thomas' response far outweighed a simple expression of delight. His was both an astounding discovery and a profound belief. His expressed needs melted away in the power of awareness that his friend, this Jesus, was Lord and God.

As he professed what he realized, the others were affected. Their fears collapsed into his freedom. As he saw deeply, their sight intensified. Their world needed the kind of love only authentic doubters can give. Our world today, twinned as we are with Thomas, needs that same kind of love, a love that blesses both those who must see to believe and whose who are able to believe without seeing. We can give the world what it needs right now, if only we will unlock our doors of fear and let Jesus stand in our midst to gift us with a shalom that can be and must be shared. With the sharing comes believing. With believing, we have life in God's name.

Ah yes, what the world needs now is love, sweet love!

For Reflection and Discussion

- How aware and responsive are you to the needy near you? Who, and by what means, has recently filled your spiritual, psychological, and physical needs? Do your Sunday acts of worship give you a taste of "upper room" experience? If so, why? If not, why not? When have you only been able to offer God your negative feelings? How have you discovered a transformation in the giving?

Prayer

Open to me the gates of righteousness,
  that I may enter through them and give thanks to the Lord.
This is the gate of the Lord;
  the righteous shall enter through it.
I thank you that you have answered me
  and have become my salvation.
This is the day that the Lord has made;
  let us rejoice and be glad in it. Amen.

— Psalm 118:19–21, 24

THIRD SUNDAY OF EASTER

ACTS 3:13-15, 17-19; 1 JOHN 2:1-5; LUKE 24:35-48

When miracles are not enough

In our small faith community we enjoy sharing our thoughts on the Scripture readings. Each of us brings to the table a unique insight and understanding that delights and often disturbs the group. Among us is one member who is usually silent and might well—but quite erroneously—be perceived as one not greatly touched by the offerings. During a particular gathering, he blurted out, "I don't understand these disciples. There they are, right in the midst of all those miracles, looking at everything Jesus is doing and hearing all he is saying, and they still don't believe. If I had seen everything they saw and heard what they heard, I'd surely be a believer."

Then, he paused a moment before continuing. "But it sure gives me comfort to know that people like them, people who were right there with Jesus, had a hard time believing. It helps me when I have a hard time with it, too."

He said it simply and surely. None of us disagreed because all of us were in the same boat. We were—and are—persons who possess belief that disbelieves and disbelief that believes. Each one of us could easily point to times when miracles were not enough to solidify our credibility or make it permanently stable.

My husband plants a tiny seed in an indoor pot. He waters it faithfully, turns it daily so that it will not be lopsided as it bends in the direction of the sun. He comments on that bending process that occurs even when no sunshine is visible to our human eyes. One day, a bud appears. He has watched and waited for that to happen, and yet his first and most profound response is always the same. Without wavering, he says, "I can't believe it. It's a miracle."

Now, I know that he is really saying, "Wow, what a miracle of life! I can scarcely contain what I have seen." The second statement signifies his human reaction to the incomprehensible wonder of birth, the magnitude of life that causes one to pause and ponder with awe.

I suspect that is the case with all of us. Even when we are together in a community that has just been gifted with the peace of Christ, total shalom, we are somehow caught unaware. Like the disciples of old, our tendency is to react rather than respond. Startled and terrified, we think we are seeing a ghost. Fear strikes at our faith to splinter and shatter it. Doubts arise in our hearts as our heads cannot comprehend the radical newness of this miraculous presence. Can this Jesus, the Risen One, be real?

Even our joy at the sights and sounds of goodness, even our individual witness and confession to the fact that Jesus is right here, right now, is not sufficient to dispel the disbelief that lingers to tinge all credence with wonderment. This Jesus, the Anointed One and resurrected Messiah, is more than we can fathom. His presence among us is more than we can digest.

Rather than watch us choke on our battling emotions, Jesus does what he always does. Jesus comes to us where we are. Jesus takes his presence and makes it palatable. More than that, he makes it recognizable. Jesus asks if we have anything to eat, so that he can demonstrate to our unseeing eyes that what we have and are is much more than we realize. He takes whatever morsel we possess and consumes it. Jesus takes us into himself in ways that make sense to us.

At the same time, his actions trigger memories we had buried lest they resurrect the pain of crucifixion and the loss of an empty tomb. As Jesus takes the piece of broiled fish and eats it, something visceral happens, not simply physically but spiritually as well. Another meal shared in another place and time comes to mind. A commission is recalled: "Take and eat…take and drink. Do this to remember me."

The tiny seed of faith planted in the potting soil of our souls, watered with the blood of Calvary, watched with anguished eyes from atop that hill, is now leaning toward the Sonlight and beginning to bud. Memories that once plagued us with hurtful sorrow now re-member us with salvific healing.

Each of us has missed the mark in life at one point. Each of us has failed to do good. All of us have sinned in one way or another. We have handed over and rejected holy and righteous ones. We have asked for the release of murderers rather than face the pain of coping with the message of prophets. We have chosen pious platitudes in lieu of profound prayerfulness. We have spoken with anger and steeled ourselves against truth. We have killed those who would bring us into deeper life, not with weapons of war but with the insidiousness of superficial peace. Sometimes we have acted in ignorance. Other times, it has been with full knowledge. No matter, the fact remains we have all done that which we did not will to do and have not done that which we wanted to do.

We are not perfect. That is true. However, we cannot, we must not, stop dead in our tracks because of that truth. We need it as the engine to move our train of thought, our vehicle of transportation and transformation.

Miracles are not enough!

What is needed is an open mind and suffering heart. What is needed is a profound understanding of the Scriptures. Information about God is only a starting point. The knowledge we gain must penetrate all the layers of our being. It must be integrated with every muscle and fiber of our personhood. It must cut to the core of self until there is no longer a separation between the God I know and the God whose image I am.

Miracles are not enough, unless they become permanent marks to be touched and seen. Miracles are not enough, unless they are proof for us that God is not a ghost without flesh and bones. God is real, alive, dwelling in our presence, and asking if we have anything here to eat.

For Reflection and Discussion

• How would you answer Jesus' question, "Is there anything here to eat?" What is your understanding of the need to have an open mind and suffering heart? How have you responded recently to the gift of shalom?

Prayer

Creator God, you have already miracled me with life and love more generously than I deserve. You have given me the power to release people from bondage, and I have not always used that power. Instead, I have held them bound. I have controlled the lives of my family and friends, manipulating them to believe as I believe. Your miracle was not enough for me because I did not see it or appreciate its worth. Help me to become ever more aware of life and love. Help me to share generously that gift and know that I am loved, warts and all. Amen.

Mothers, God, and cornerstone questions

My experience of motherhood—and I do not mean to limit that reality to the physical process of giving birth—certainly revolves about and evolves from questioning and being questioned. Memories of my earliest parenting days resound with interrogations: "Where are you?" What are you doing?" "Have you washed your hands?" "Did you say 'thank you'?" "What did you say???" I am sure that my children thought of me as the Grand Inquisitor.

At the same time, I often felt that I was under someone else's microscope with my parenting skills and style being questioned and judged: "Why did you let him do that?" "Are you sure she should be going there?" "Whatever made you think dancing lessons would help?"

I recall one incident that stands out in my family's memory bank and is brought out for inspection at each gathering of the clan. The story goes like this. I am out in the front yard of our fairly new residence in a somewhat upper middle class neighborhood. Obviously, my children and I are trying to fit it, yet I am not dressed as the other mothers in the area. Because the ground is still wet from recent, unrelenting rains and I don't want to damage my good footwear, I am wearing a pair of old shoes. In fact, they were my husband's and were slightly too large. As I am toiling to get the lawn into nearly decent shape, a neighbor walks past and asks, "Are you Paul Salone's mother?"

Now, I have only the one son and he had not had an unblemished school career. His days were spent mainly in the corridor outside the classroom. Distraction was his middle name. Obviously, he also was the brunt of many a youngster's teasing. His antics frequently kept the family under siege and on the alert.

With this background coloring my disposition, I responded to the questioner with another, quite defensive, query, "Why do you want to know?" I needed to surface her motivation, to discover if anything devious lay beneath an apparently innocent inquiry and, perhaps, to deflect her direct probing. Happily, the neighbor had nothing more than sincere interest in mind. Subsequently, she became a friend to the whole family and remains one to this very day.

In retrospect, I realize this was the moment when I began the long, slow, painful process of questioning how I was to shepherd my children with goodness. My neighbor's question triggered a new beginning to my own beleaguered parenthood. To say that I would lay down my life for my children is both too easy and too difficult. The ways in which I would be called to do that kind of dying are more important. So many questions come to mind.

How will I recognize the wolf coming to snatch and scatter my children? Would I be alert and awake enough to act appropriately? What about the others, those who are not directly related to me yet are part of my extended family? How do I attend to their needs, protect them, give them comfort and consolation? What happens when my children have children of their own? How well will I have taught them to shepherd beyond their own flock?

Then I think about my church family and its extensions into the larger church community. I hear the call to lay down my life in that arena as well, and I find myself enmeshed in more complex questions than ever before.

I know that Christ is not the kind of shepherd who simply herds flocks into a pasture to watch passively as they eat, frolic, and play. Christ is alert to their every need and danger, always calling their names, always looking out for their betterment. There is no relaxing of effort nor resting from the task at hand. I know also that each of us is to be that kind of shepherding leader, no matter where our lives take us, even if it kills us.

And I am frightened.

My fear is not that I'll be unable or unworthy to respond or attend to the vocation of shepherding. I am afraid because, deep in my soul, I know that the call is also a command to be a cornerstone in the same way that Christ is cornerstone of his church. Unknowing builders could not, would not, see the value of that stone. They rejected the kind of foundation Christ offers, the compassionately challenging leadership Christ commands. If I choose to be a shepherd leader, a building block of committed love, I will be rejected as well. I can feel the pain of that isolation even as I type these words.

And I am even more deeply frightened.

I do not want to be a prisoner of my own commitment. I do not want to be encircled by those who want only to pummel me with statements that intimidate, confuse, and diminish my spirit. I am uneasy with interrogations that question the good I try to do. I do not like hearing intimations of evil motivation. What I really want is to be a good shepherd with and for all people—and to be accepted and respected as such.

But shepherding, like parenting, is cornerstone living. It does not come with ease and guarantees. It arrives only with profound hope and faith. It involves Spirit-power and empowering spirits. Respect and acceptance are not given by outside forces but are a matter of one's own integrity and authenticity as I lay down my life and take it up again, over and over.

What is true for me is true for each of us. We all have the power to lay down our lives and take them up again. We all have the potency to be strong cornerstones of faith communities. We all have received this command from God who is the ultimate Parent, Shepherd, and Cornerstone of our life.

Of this, there is no question!

For Reflection and Discussion

How do you see God's presence in your life as a

- cooperative coworker?
- compassionate companion?
- comforter?
- conscience of the community and church?
- consciousness raiser?
- cornerstone of church, family, neighborhood, workplace?
- challenging communicator?
- commander-in-chief?
- committed lover?

How has the laying down of your life been followed by the taking up of your life?

Prayer

The stone rejected by the builders has become the cornerstone.
O, give thanks to the Lord, for he is good;
 his steadfast love endures forever!
It is better to take refuge in the Lord than to put confidence in mortals.
It is better to take refuge in the Lord than to put confidence in princes.
I thank you that you have answered me and have become my salvation.
The stone that the builders rejected has become the chief cornerstone.
This is the Lord's doing; it is marvelous in our eyes.
Blessed is the one who comes in the name of the Lord.
We bless you from the house of the Lord.

— Psalm 118:1, 8–9, 21–23, 26

Fifth Sunday of Easter

Abide in fear or abiding faith?

I guess that each of us, at one point or another in life, has had to make the crucial choice between fear and faith. More importantly, we have had to opt for an abiding faith even if we are sometimes afraid. We cannot serve two masters. We will either elect to abide in fear or to have an abiding faith.

The choice is not always clear or comfortable. Fear is a powerful factor in our decision-making. I know that I am often afraid. I am especially afraid of telling the truth when I know it will both involve and evolve into communication that might well be confrontational. When I sense things are going in that direction, I somehow manage to practice avoidance and denial with great aplomb. I take evasive tactics. I manage to convince myself to take the route of the five most dangerous words in the world, "Maybe it will go away!"

The fact is that it won't go away.

Until and unless each of us addresses the fear factor in our lives, until we begin to realize that faith cannot flourish in the midst of fear, until we understand that fear deals a fatal blow to faith but faith will always conquer fear, we cannot be disciples. Clinging to the vine of Christ is not enough. We must be fruitful branches, or we will be pruned from the tree of life.

This is serious stuff. And it is scary.

I know that I do not wish to be thrown away. I know that God does not wish to throw me away. Nor does God want that for any of us. God's desire is our abiding faithfulness. God's desire is for us to be more than clingers on the vine. God's wish is for us to be active participants in the mystery of life.

To be that kind of person—vitally vibrant in my Christianity—calls for community, cooperation, and compassion. Abiding in faith cannot be a solitary endeavor. We need each other as companions on the way. We need to empower each other to live courageously in our faithfulness.

It is interesting to read about Paul, the great Apostle to the Gentiles. His conversion experience powerfully and radically changed him from being a persecuting Pharisee to a demanding disciple. Yet, even though he had been speaking boldly and fearlessly in the name of Jesus, he was neither universally nor quickly accepted among the corps of followers. Paul was bearing the fruit of faith on the vine of Christ, but the other branches wilted with fear of him. He needed help. He needed the assistance of a spokesperson who could plead his case and break the barriers of fear that kept the disciples from extending their faithfulness to include a former enemy.

Paul needed Barnabas in his life. He needed a spokesperson who would witness to his authenticity and commitment. The disciples needed Barnabas in their lives so that their fear of Paul could be transformed. Within a faithful community only one kind of fear would be allowed to rule their lives. This is the fear that abides in awesome wonder of God's majesty and power.

We are equally needy today. We seek charismatically prophetic individuals who will speak the truth that heals and frees us. We are on the outlook for those who "love, not in word or speech, but in truth and action" (1 John 3:18).

We search for those who will label our goodness, witness to our discipleship, empower our continued faithfulness, be companions journeying with us on our life pilgrimage. We need a Barnabas—or many of them—to attest that we sometimes forget or neglect our ability to speak boldly in God's name.

I know that my Barnabas lives in many places, not the least of which is my own home. Whenever I seem to incur fear or disbelief in a group because I am saying something that is hard to hear, my husband becomes my Barnabas. Gently, but forcefully if needed, he begins, "What I think Fran is trying to say is…". His rephrasing and powerful affirmation removes my dismay and soothes me. At the same time, it allows the group time and space to assess and internalize what has been offered to them. Additionally, he has served as example for me. When my adult children are in their own unique circumstances of fearful disbelief, I tell them, "You are right. I believe in you. Go for it."

In similar fashion, I both hear and heed the voice of Barnabas in the Scripture groups I facilitate as well as in our small faith community. Reciprocally, I am Barnabas for them. In every case, all of us become Barnabas for others. And, in the comfort of the Holy Spirit, little communities everywhere increase in numbers. Pebbles thrown into small ponds have a ripple effect mysteriously discovered in larger and larger masses of water.

Each individually, and all of us communally, begin to leave our abodes of fear to abide in faithfulness. No longer do our hearts condemn us. We now have boldness before God. We receive from God whatever we ask because we obey God's commands to believe in the name of Jesus Christ and love one another. In other words, abide in Christ as Christ abides in us. This is what pleases God. This is the meaning of faithfulness.

So, how does Christ abide in us? Christ is within us through thick and thin, good and bad, repentance and regression. Christ is forever faithful, an "always presence." Christ is the power behind our potency, the electrical current that energizes our brilliance, the wind beneath our wings. Apart from Christ we can do nothing.

We can deny him as Peter did. We can sell him for blood money like Judas. We can run, with the other disciples, in terror from his crucifixion. We can weep, like Mary, at his empty tomb. Still, he will always be in our midst, never leaving us alone. Christ will forever be the central vine for our feeble branches. No one can remove Christ from us. Not even our own willfulness can do that. All that we can manage is to deal ourselves a mortal blow by cutting ourselves out of Christ. To lose that vitality is to deny divinity, ignore immortality, abide in fear and ultimately die.

Christ will never move away from us. It is we who choose to move from Christ. That is hell. That is what burns us up.

We have a choice, both as individual believers and as faith communities. Our choice is simple yet profound. It is also integral to our very existence. The choice is dangerous because it will not go away. We have placed before us life, a lifetime and lifestyle in which we abide in faithfulness or death, an abode of fear. God begs us, "Choose life!"

Do not wither and die in fear. Abide in faithfulness.

For Reflection and Discussion

- In what ways have you experienced the awesome wonder of God's majesty and power? Over the past week, how have you labeled someone's goodness for them? How were you a companion, a sojourner who empowered faithfulness with another person on the Way?

Prayer

My God, I know you are near. But I need to see you, touch you, feel your presence in my life. In my need, I beg you to send me a Barnabas to be my companion as I journey. Let me, also, be that kind of sojourner with others. Help all of us to understand, remember, and live with the deep belief that you are our vine, then we, the branches, will live well in you. Show us that you are choosing to live your life in us. In your name, O Christ, we pray. Amen.

SIXTH SUNDAY OF EASTER

Acts 10:25–26, 34–35, 44–48; 1 John 4:7–10; John 15:9–17

The joy of being only mortal

Some of the most comforting phrases in Scripture are those that indicate God's love for us—particularly the magnificence of a God who loves us as we are, only mortal.

While I was doing my rounds as a hospital chaplain one day, I visited a patient in the Intensive Care Unit. He began to tell me his story of various experiences with heart problems, beginning with the one that most affected him. It was the first surgery he underwent, one that included seven by-passes! As he spoke, his face changed. He was going back in mind and memory to the evening before surgery when he lay awake in bed, filled with the anxiety and terror of the anticipated procedure. The hospital chaplain stopped by and prayed with him. As the gentleman recounted his story, his countenance changed. Wrinkles seemed to disappear. He told me, "I stopped being afraid. It was like having a heavy load lifted from my shoulders. And, you know what? Everything went perfectly. I didn't even have much pain and I healed quickly and got back home to exercise and eat properly."

With the assistance of prayer, the gentleman in that bed learned what each of us must discover. We are only mortal, and that's enough for God.

How often I mess life up when I try so hard to be more than what I am—only mortal. I do not even love myself because it is not enough for me to be only mortal. If I cannot love myself as I am, then how can I love anyone else who is only mortal? It is such good news to know that our God loves us as we are—made in a divine image and likeness.

Basking in the warmth of that love, I can be who I am, mortally wounded yet marvelously healed. Through the healing powers of my woundedness, I am empowered to love others as they are, persons who await healing from their own mortal wounds. I can experience the joy of being "only mortal."

Some might view the phrase "only mortal" as a cop-out, an avoidance or denial of reality, or an excuse to do nothing. Far from avoiding vitality, this is a journey into its depths. It is neither apology nor explanation. It is the experience of being real.

In the once popular story of *The Velveteen Rabbit*, to be real was described as having one's hair completely rubbed off with the wear and tear of loving and being loved. Shel Silverstein's *The Giving Tree* tells us that life is nothing more or less than the total offering of self. From the start of the story to its finish, the tree loved. The tree loved a boy who became a demanding adult. He took and took all that the tree had to offer until finally he sailed away on the bark provided by the Giving Tree. All that was left of the tree was a stump. After a long time, he returned a tired old man who just needed a quiet place to sit and rest. The tree stump was just enough. "An old stump is good for sitting and resting." So, the boy/man sat and rested. And the tree was happy.

There is such joy in being only mortal! But there is more than joy. There is growth. We grow to understand ourselves and others more deeply. We grow in compassion for each other. We intensify our ability to listen attentively and respond more carefully both to what is said and what remains unstated. The sword of mortality pierces through to all that is hidden in the heart, releasing it both for healing and for help.

Strangely, though I believe with all my heart in all that I have written, I yet find I am amazed at the power and potency unleashed when I am most human, when I am sheerly mortal. It always surprises me that being who I am is good enough for God. Equally astounding is the fact that pedestal people seem to have limited influence. They are too far removed from my state in life to be meaningful. Worse yet, proximity ruins the picture of their perfection. With clay feet unexpectedly revealed, I am distracted and dismayed. Having placed them beyond the ken of mere mortals, they are now marked with mediocrity. I can find no joy in their mortality, and neither can they.

When he first met Peter, Cornelius fell to his feet and worshiped this man of God who had arrived at his home. "Stand up; I am only a mortal," Peter told Cornelius (Acts 10:26). Being placed on the pedestal of perfection was not to Peter's liking. He knew his own humanity and vulnerability only too well and had come to understand the joy of his being only mortal. His mortality had brought him pleasure and pain. It caused his spontaneous outbursts of faith. It was the seat of his outrageous fear. It evoked both adventurous plans and pleading avoidance. Peter's mortality took him to mountaintop experiences of transfiguration and valleys of desperate denial. It walked him atop sea waves and ultimately led him to the very death he would have spared his Lord and Savior.

Peter's mortality taught him what our humanity teaches us. To be good enough for God is the lesson of a lifetime. It is also a precious grace. When we unwrap that gift to become truly charismatic people, we will truly begin our understanding "that God shows no partiality, but in every nation anyone who fears him and does what is right is acceptable to him" (Acts 10:34).

All who hear and heed God's word will feel God's Holy Spirit falling upon them. The charism is unrestrained, freely given to be freely received. There is but one qualification: to be only a mortal.

So empowered and inspirited, there can be only one response: to return freely what one has received. Given life, love, acceptance, I now reveal and share life, love, and acceptance. I am now able to shower all wounded mortality with the balm of those gifts. Realizing my own giftedness, I now assist everyone to recognize and make real their own bounty.

No matter how painful it will be to be rubbed raw with requests for loving responses, no matter that I will become a stump of my former self, all the hurt involved in being human will never harm me. It will, instead, be a valued venue. It will be my way to learn the wonder and worth, the joy and jubilation to be found in being only mortal.

For Reflection and Discussion

- How do you feel about the call to be used like a giving tree worn out in loving? What life experiences have convinced you that God thinks you are good enough, just as you are? How do you think others view you: as a pedestal person or a mortal one? How do you view Jesus: as a pedestal person or a mortal one?

Prayer

Pedestal high, I falter and fail
Having gone far beyond my pale
Trying to be what others see,
Denying the beauty of my mortality.
Pedestal God, of you I beg and pray
The grace to be who I really am this day.
Let me grow in constant awe
Of the wonder I am, despite any flaw.
Let me learn to be the one you love and treasure
And share that gift beyond all measure
With those who also live on pedestals high
That they might know that mortal joy is earth not sky. Amen.

FEAST OF THE ASCENSION

ACTS 1:1–11; EPHESIANS 1:17–23; MARK 16:15–20

On being lifted up

To understand ascension is quite difficult for me. I have visions of magical levitation taken to its ultimate with a body riding an invisible elevator into a cloud mass that eventually swallows it up until it completely disappears. Somehow, that image does not speak effectively to me. It does not affect my faith or my faithfulness as much as it intrigues me and gives me more questions than answers. Perhaps that is the point. Perhaps the celebration of Christ's ascension is meant to be the vehicle by which we ask questions, ponder the impossible, wonder about our participation in this journey from birth to death to renewed life.

As the Lucan community states, the first accounting of our lives probably deals with all that Jesus did and taught from the beginning until the day he was taken up to heaven. Carefully, we stay on that earth, allowing ourselves occasional glimpses up into the cloudiness of discipleship. Crucial though this sojourn may be, it is also a comfortable one. It allows us to reminisce more than re-member, to relate good news more than to be people of the gospel.

The result is that we continue asking the wrong questions, looking for facile answers, diligently guarding our ignorance, and retaining both denial and avoidance of the real truth. Like the disciples of old, we speculate if this is the time when we get to be the sole owners of the kingdom. Firmly planted on the ground of our finite faith and limited vision, we just don't grasp the boundlessness of God's salvation plan.

Our quest for concretized blueprints blurs the deepest reality of gracious living. Both our time and tempo as Ascension People are temporary. It is life lived in between times. It is both presence and promise, already here and not yet complete, clearly evidenced and cloudily evoked. Lack of faith and stubbornness, because I do not believe those who see God's action, Christ's presence, keep me from ascending to heights of credibility and descending to the inverted mountaintop of credulity.

To understand ascension is difficult and complicated. I can only comprehend it metaphorically.

I know what it is like to ascend from the depths of dark discouragement and find hope in the smallest rays of sunshine. I understand the hard work and discipline involved in climbing each day's mountain of chores. I also have witnessed the joy of completed efforts.

The power of ascension became a clearer reality on the day we had a number of huge hardwood trees cut down and removed from our property. There was a degree of pain involved because my husband and I truly love trees. However, the power of hurricane winds that had already ripped through their branches, weakened their hold on the earth, and threatened the safety and security of our dwelling necessitated the move.

Monkey-like, a slim, strong young man ascended to the top of the nearest tree. With a swift, decisive motion, he started his chainsaw and cut carefully through each selected branch, slicing his way down the tree trunk until only a stump remained. Tree after tree was ascended in this manner or via a motorized bucket. As he moved upward from the earth, gained height, and defied gravity, we watched. Looking skyward, we gained a certain sense of renewed capability. Even his coworkers stood straighter, taller, in the light of this one man's ability to scale those verdant heights. They, like my husband and I, were onlookers. Watching, we were also absorbing abilities to leave our own individual grounds of fear. We were being empowered to aspire to faithfulness. Eyes to the sky, we were becoming believers that all is possible with God.

The ascension that happened in our backyard enacted a whole new view of a nearby creek. It also opened the vista to a renewed sight of our neighbor's workshop, not the prettiest of scenes. This ascension created delight in the newness of our yard, as well as additional tasks to be accomplished. It did not bring an ending, only a new beginning to life lived in the meantime.

First of all, there was a mess to be neatened. Wherever cutting occurred, there were twigs, leaves, stumps, stubble scattered about. No matter how carefully the chopping was done, no matter that everything was dropped to the ground with planned precision, the aftermath was messy and needed to be raked, gathered, and cleaned up.

Branches eaten by the massive grinding mechanism became a mountain of mulch to be spread over the newly exposed area. Hardwood logs would be cut, aged, and used for firewood. Perhaps some of it would be transformed into artwork or furniture. Everything was gone. All was changed. Yet, nothing had completely disappeared. It would return another day, another way, to assist and accompany us on our journey through life and death.

We will tell this story over and over. It will become a saga of spirituality, an epic description of our ascension from persons who looked fearfully to the skies of our own limitation only to discover the futility of that action. The clearing of our land, made possible only by the ascension of one man who was willing to climb to greater heights than we would dare, created new life, new vision, new possibilities, renewed labor. Hopefully, our narration will inspire other tales of faith, other visions of glory, experienced here on earth.

We won't be left to stand staring at an empty sky and wondering what has happened to our Savior. Nor will we be concerned about the present or future events of our lives. Instead, the vigor of a certain peace has descended in the aftermath of ascension. Enlivened, we can mount molehills and know soaring faith. We can aspire to heights of glory as we tread upwards, always upwards. Scrambling for handholds, tackling difficulties, surmounting sadness, ours is an ascension from living to dying and dying to living. It is an ascension into eternity that can only begin when we climb the tree of life.

For Reflection and Discussion

- In your life, what trees can you climb both to scale the heights of your faithfulness and trim the branches of fear and doubt? How have you been an onlooker to that process? In what ways has that action been fruitful, and in what ways has it been a hindrance?

Prayer

Dear God, so many days I find that I am simply staring at the sky in a futile attempt to see where you have gone, to discover your hiding place. I feel hopeless, lost, and even abandoned. Yet, deep within my spirit there is a sense that you have ascended to heights I will one day reach. You have left me, not to my own devices but to empower yours. I know that you are here in me and in others. I believe that, even when I cannot see it. I believe it because I cannot see you clearly. Help me to climb the tree of life. Help me to trim its branches. Give me the grace of a renewed vision of life and love, truth and justice, so that I might speak of that sight to my world each day. Amen.

SEVENTH SUNDAY OF EASTER

ACTS 1:15–17, 20–26; 1 JOHN 4:11–16; JOHN 17:11–19

Witnessing to resurrected life

Every time I read about Judas I feel so sad. Here, numbered among the select group of Twelve, was an intelligent, forward-thinking, compassionate man. It appears his life goal was to help the helpless. That purpose is both valiant and virtuous. So, one wonders, where and how did he go astray? When did he stop being a witness to life and start down the slippery slope to despairing death? Why did he feel so unforgiven and unforgivable that the only solution was suicide? For me, the questions remain hanging in the very air of our faith life. They are questions to be asked without answers, save in the complexity of God's will and plan for human salvation.

In pondering them, however, one thought continues to surface. Could it be that Judas, in the face of all the death surrounding him, found it impossible to maintain his steadfast witness to life? His solutions did not seem to match those of his Savior, the Life Giver and Master he had chosen to follow. Though he must have known the Talmudic adage, "God's kingdom is the world turned upside down," Judas could not face the kind of topsy-turviness Jesus was advocating. He could not see a kingdom there, or any substantive life. For him it was a continually festering wound with no salve or balm to ease its pain or prevent its ultimately fatal end.

Judas, it seems, found no joy—only pain—in the process of resurrecting life.

There are days when I am just like Judas. In fact, I remember well the months of anguish endured when the Roman Catholic priesthood, and the Church itself, was roiling under the ongoing scandal of ephebophilia and pedophilia. Cries of anger and anguish commingled with commands for silence and strict obedience. Dissent was brazen betrayal; challenge was heretical obstinacy. E-mailed articles from newspapers nationwide flooded my inbox. I read and read until the type blurred before my eyes. As I pondered the words, I began to feel terrorized and horrified. This was not my concept of church. This was not the way I wanted to live as a Christian. More and more deeply, I experienced the pain involved in the process of resurrecting life out of this death-dealing mess.

Where had all the idealism gone? Where was the voice of God to be heard? How had a divinely founded and grounded community dwindled to a small, select few who refused to allow God's Spirit to flow freely and freshly among the many? Who was asking for the fulfillment of Scripture in our midst? How could God's abundant and overflowing love for us ever be evident in a shattered, scattered, sorrow-filled people?

People everywhere were irate. My own children were fuming. Questions abounded for which I had no decisive or clear-cut answers. Reform was the cry! Reform the church! Would this mean schism, more scandal? The suggestion was simple. The process could not be simplistic.

It would have been so easy to sell it all for thirty pieces of silver. It would have been a simple solution for me to turn aside from my understanding of ministry and service, my grasp of wisdom, my faith in the true meaning of church and "go to my own place." And I almost did.

I nearly gave away all the coins of radical optimism I had been given and received over my then sixty-four years of living to dwell in bleak, unfeeling death. No, I am not speaking of following Judas into suicide—unless one considers the taking of life to be a refusal to continue living with the sharp sword of justice piercing one's heart. For me, to give up, to stop trying, is to die. And I almost did. I nearly died carrying the burden of black despair.

But, I guess in the end I am more like Peter than I am Judas. In the face of crisis—despite my moments of denial, rushes to judgment, and temporarily triumphant marches to mountaintops—I stand up among the believers to seek God's will. Somehow I know that it is still going to be a matter of casting lots, putting my faith in God's presence among us and mustering onward, come what may. Positive action enacted in and through prayerful discernment is the only way I can go.

If I am not witnessing to resurrected life, I am empowering resolute death.

None of us can be or do anything more or less than God intends. We are purveyors of divine truth. We can only witness to resurrected life by seeking truth, hearing truth, being truthful, and speaking truth. To be anything other is to die and to bring desiccation and death wherever we go.

The words are harsh. The message is hard. But there is joy at the heart of it all because we are engaged in a mission of love. Our challenge and commission is to scrape away all the putrefying infection that deadens the flesh of the people of God. It is to open all wounds to healing Sonlight. It is to refrain from the temptation to bandage the ills, covering them up without permitting the healing process to begin or continue.

To do this, we must stay in the world of the dead and dying. Jesus is not asking that we be removed from the messiness of mortality. What Jesus is asking is that we be protected from any evil that might stalk us. In our name and for our good, Jesus prays, "Sanctify them in the truth; your word is truth. As you have sent me into the world, so I have sent them into the world" (John 17:17–18).

As Jesus was sent, so are we. And Jesus was sent that we might have life and have it in abundance. There is our mission and our message. It is our plea, prayer, and promise: *"L'CHAIM, to life!"*

God's name is spread and accepted where life is experienced. All the hows, whys, and wherefores disappear in generous life. It is compelling, even overwhelming, and seductively salvific. God has put before us life and death. It is up to us to choose which way we will go.

I am convinced of one reality: If I am not witnessing to resurrected life, I am empowering resolute death.

For Reflection and Discussion

- In the midst of our topsy-turviness, when and how so we see Jesus' kingdom breaking in? In what ways have you seen resurrected life coming out of what looked like ashes in your life? What did you do to keep yourself encouraged and able to see the "upness" of Christ in those down days? What are you doing to reform and re-form the temple that you are, the church you must become?

Prayer

Dear God, you have given us the resurrection of a topsy-turvy world. Yet, we are often people who refuse to live in that kind of upside-down truth. We see only the visible realities and are blind to the underside of life. Continue to bless us with radical optimism and renewed vision. Continue to present us with opportunities to look beyond the dying embers of life to see flickering flames of truth awaiting your inspiration and our breath. For this grace we pray, with all our hearts, through the intercession of our brother, savior, lord, and companion, Jesus, the Christ. Amen.

PENTECOST SUNDAY

GENESIS 11:1–9; EZEKIEL 37:1–14; JOEL 3:1–5; ROMANS 8:22–27;
JOHN 7:37–39

Renewing the face of the earth

As I remember my high school days, both as teacher and student, I recall the wonder and lightheartedness of Spirit Week. This was the time set aside for the entire assembly, faculty included, to "get into" school spirit. It was not that we lacked it so much as it was that each and all of us needed a specific time and place in which to focus on the essence of our togetherness in the whole process of education. We needed to remind ourselves of our spirited presence lest we become dispirited when challenges and obstacles arose.

Spirit Week served us well. It roused us to a sense of community. It renewed us as people as well as persons. Within a short seven-day period, our identity intensified to a fierce fidelity and concentrated charity.

I noted a similar "in-spiration" as I listened to my daughter Jeannine's friends speak of their imminent departure to Guatemala for the adoption of their seven-month-old daughter. Having entered the critical age for childbearing with no apparent "success" in conceiving, their alternate hope was both palpable and scriptural. Blindly optimistic, both husband and wife fairly oozed these words, "Now, hope that is seen is not hope. For who hopes for what is seen? But, if we hope for what we do not see, we wait for it with patience" (Romans 8:24–25).

Elliot and Mary were obviously inspirited individuals. Hope in their unseen daughter was evidenced in faces that shone as if lit with interior tongues of fire. When they spoke of their imminent trip to Guatemala, joy sparkled their words with graceful glitter. Laughter rang, filling my daughter's house like the sound of a violent wind. At the same time, there were inner groanings. These were the labor pains of anticipation.

Jeannine's friends had come to visit her the evening before she was to undergo surgery. They could have remained at home harboring their own multilayered emotions, but they chose to be with her. They elected to share their spirit of happy anticipation tinged with hesitant anxiety as she, in turn, became partner in hope for the healing removal of what she could neither see nor feel, a possibly cancerous growth. All three knew the common need to enjoy the momentary delight of spiritual fireworks as preparation for the hard work that lay ahead.

I watched the trio and marveled as I saw the Holy Spirit renewing the face of our piece of earth on Putnam Street, Columbia, South Carolina.

Mary, the mother-to-be, spoke of hope's challenge. She told stories that demonstrated how hard it was for her to concentrate at work. Her mind was on the baby they would welcome into their lives. It also embraced a certain hesitancy, a "hoping against hope" that accompanies all pre-birthing experiences. At her behest, neither she nor Elliot would speak the baby's name until she was physically present in their arms. They would await her adoption with forceful love. They also anticipated the redemption of that little person from her captivity in the Guatemalan "prison" called foster care. Theirs was a radical hope against all odds. It is the rooted optimism that marks the people of God.

Thirsting, they had come to God to drink, and were satisfied! God's Spirit was renewing the face of their earth, and they knew it! Their unity as a couple was not a false one. Mary and Elliot did not seek to build a city for themselves alone. Their home was not to be a compound designed and designated for two. Nor did they wish to spread their individual names and fame. The common "love language" they spoke was not a case of exclusion but a cause for expansion. It was communication that would stretch limits and make boundaries become borderless horizons.

God came to see what they were building and was pleased with the sight. It is so easy to build for ourselves. It is easy to construct a false unity. We can look united when we are simply similar in appearance. It is not at all difficult to misuse unity by making it uniformity. Too quickly we dissolve into groups where like-minded folks seek those who hold identical ideas and thoughts. It is easy to applaud the fact we are all speaking the same language, singing on the same page of music, and label it unity. In fact, the label is itself a towering Babel.

True unity happens when each speaks to all, as the Spirit gives ability! When each individual proclaims the truth God has given, a bewildering sound is heard. Gasping breath gives witness to our astonishment at the unexpected results we see. Our messages are understandable, credible, and transformational. We can remove barriers. We can promote the common good and see it achieved. Renewal is apparent over the entire face of the earth.

Dry bones now come to life. Sinews and flesh grow over our formerly bare-boned existence. The thundering voice of God's presence deepens to a rattling noise as bones join bones, and a divine spirit renews the face of our earth.

These bones are the entire people of God. We had been saying, "Our hope is lost and we are cut off." However, when we pronounce God's truth—each of us as we have been given ability—despair is replaced with radical hope, fear is supplanted by faith. Closed ears open to hear God's promise: "I am going to open your graves, and bring you up from your graves, O my people, I will put my spirit within you and you shall live, and I will place you on your own soil; then you shall know that I, the Lord, have spoken and will act" (Ezekiel 37:12–14).

"Then afterward I will pour out my spirit on all flesh; your sons and your daughters shall prophesy, your old men shall dream dreams and your young men shall see visions. Even on the male and female slaves, in those days, I will pour out my spirit. I will show portents in the heavens and on the earth" (Joel 2:28–29).

From Spirit-ed songs that inflame a school with loyalty and pride to the inspirited laughter and love of parents-to-be, resurrection is complete and visible. Babel towers no more. Together we continue to build the city of God.

For Reflection and Discussion

- Where, when, and how do you see the Spirit acting in your family, your church, your communities, your daily life? Think and recall moments in your life when you heard "the wind," saw "the fire," and felt God's inspiriting presence. Give thanks and praise for what happened.

Prayer

O Holy Spirit, beloved of my soul, I adore you.
Enlighten me, guide me, strengthen me, console me.
Tell me what I should do.
Give me your orders.
I promise to submit myself to all that you desire of me
    and to accept all that you permit to happen to me.
Let me only know your holy will. Amen.

– Author unknown

The Holy Trinity

When is God?

Frequently my husband reminds me that I am not asking the right questions. It is not enough to ask where is God, what is God, or who is God. I need to ask "When is God?" The idea is not originally his. He learned it from reading Rabbi Harold Kushner's book *To Life!* Whatever the source, the question is a sound one.

Neither you nor I nor anyone else will be able to "acknowledge today and take to heart that the Lord is God in heaven above and on the earth beneath" nor be able to proclaim "there is no other" (Deuteronomy 4:39) until and unless we begin to see *when* God is. As Kushner says, "Statements about God, then, do not describe God. They describe how we and our world are different because of God. An old rabbinic text reads, 'God is like a mirror. The mirror never changes, but everyone who looks at it sees a different face'.

'When is God?'—that is what has to be happening to us and around us for us to recognize the presence of God" (Kushner, p. 149–150).

The Scriptures clearly state when God is. They tell us that God is when the statutes and commandments of the Lord are kept. God is when long life is experienced. God is when we remain in the land God gives us. God is when we live according to the Spirit of God. God is when we cry out "Abba! Father!" God is when we witness to the fact that we are children of God, heirs of God, brothers and sisters of Christ. God is when we suffer with Christ, and when we are glorified with Christ. God is when we "go, and make disciples of all nations, baptizing them in the name of the Father and of the Son and of the Holy Spirit" (Matthew 28:19). God is when we remember that we are never alone. God is when we keep in mind that Christ is with us always to the end of the age.

Those Scriptures, however, need to be unwrapped in our daily lives, both as individuals and as communities. We need to look into the mirror of all life to see when God is. In particular, we need to see when God is Creator, Father/Mother/Parent, when God is Brother/Son, when God is Spirit. In other words, when is God a most Holy Trinity within us?

Each of us must seek and see for ourselves when God is before we can proclaim when God is in the presence of others.

When is God for me?

God is when my granddaughter Audrey phones me to tell my how sad she was that I could not be with her at the celebration of her First Eucharist. She also tells me that she understands I had to be with my own daughter, her aunt, in the aftermath of surgery. Then she shares as much as she can of the experience, repeating the reading she did so that I could "be there" in a different manner. She mentions the fact that she did not really feel like this was a *first* eucharist for her. Pausing a bit, she says, "Maybe it was because I was really nervous about reading. Next time, will really be my First Communion."

Listening at the other end, from miles away, I hear a little girl's authenticity. I marvel at her ability to accept herself as she is, nervousness combined with courage. Audrey's honest assessment of her spirited self brings me face-to-face with God's evaluation of me, acceptable as I am, warts and all.

God is when I speak to my daughter and son-in-law, encouraging and supporting them as they face a difficult encounter with a particular teacher. Little disturbances at school have mounted. What had been a tiny ant hill now looms large in their parental perspective. E-mails fly back and forth between Connecticut and North Carolina. Lengthy phone conversations take place. As a result, anxiety is diminished to anticipation; blaming individuals changes to naming obstacles. My love is tough, but its challenges are heard deeply. Through the shared difficulty, our intimacy grows and deepens. As God has called, so do I call them by name. As they are God's, so are they mine. The bond is forever.

I hear the breathless tone in the voice of my pastor-friend who is racing from one state to another as he tends to the needs of a cancer patient. He is multitasking to the hilt—yet takes the time to respond to my phone call regarding chaplaincy. No argument is given for the interruption in his routine. Only laughter and joking is shared to break the tension of his stressful journey. Each of us eagerly assists the other without question or comment. And I know when God is.

By the same token, I also see those times and events that defy the question and deny God. I hear about the meeting of a small, faith-sharing group in a local congregation. One day a newcomer sought to join them and was refused admission because: "We are limited to twelve participants and the group has already melded and shared intimately. A new person would be an intrusion." And I ask myself, "When is God in this church?"

I take note of people who hear the voice of God speaking out of the fire in their lives. They hear and heed divinity in the midst of inflamed isolation—out of the fiery cauldron of prejudice—despite the hot, lashing tongues of gossip. When no one will accept them, when they are punished with unholy excommunication for being authentic to their discerned and discernible calling, I demand to know, "When is God in this rigid legality?"

I watch denominations crumble into choirs of competition as they attempt to make all nations into their own disciples, while insisting it is a mission that comes from and leads to God. I am left to wonder, "When is God in this work?"

When is God?

God is when two or three are gathered in Christ's name, when terrifying displays of power lead us out of fearfulness into freedom and fidelity, when we remain in the land of the Lord and allow all to enter it, when we permit ourselves to be Spirit-ed away into paradoxical suffering and glorious transformation. That is when I begin to understand there is no definitive answer. There are only descriptions that place a mirror before the question, reflecting it back to me as a life quest. I will have glimpses of God along the way, but they will emerge only if the question is kept alive and vibrant. If I am to know God, I must continually ask myself. I must always inquire, "When is God?"

For Reflection and Discussion

- Before bedtime tonight, look over your day and ask "When was God" in my life today? How have you or how can you make the Triune God a living, pulsating person in your life, someone closer to you than your own heartbeat, rather than a cold dogma to be recited in a creed?

Prayer

God of my longing, you have spoken to me in the midst of fiery infernos of undying love and fearsome remembrance. You have freed me to be and become the person you knew from before time began. You have summoned me to mountaintops of exultation and impelled me into valleys of enervating fearfulness. And always you were there. In all ways, you were with me. Creator, Redeemer, Nurturer, Sustainer, Sanctifier God, I only ask one thing of you. Please allow me to recognize when you are here with us. Permit me to praise your presence both in the ways I can and those I find difficult. With profound joy, may I always proclaim that you are God and there is no other. Amen.

BODY AND BLOOD OF CHRIST

EXODUS 24:3–8; HEBREWS 9:11–15; MARK 14:12–16, 22–26

On giving-living

For many people retirement is volunteerism. Days and evenings are parceled into allotted timetables for civic or religious organizations, hobby groups of all sorts. Time, talents, energy, and finances are universally shared. Workshops are attended to attain more information to be distributed among all the organizations that have staked their claim on us. We feel both stretched and fulfilled, but also and often somewhat frazzled. One can almost hear the sighed statement, "It is better to give than to receive."

Lots of motivations come into play, I am sure, not the least of which is the "cramming for the finals" attitude that compels so much of our charity. Days seem to grow shorter, time flies faster, and some of us worry that we have not done enough with our life. So, we plunge headlong into "good works." It is as if we were at the base of Mount Sinai with the people of Israel, crying their words with them: "All the words that the Lord has spoken we will do" (Exodus 24:3). Somehow, deep in our hearts, however, we know that we have the message confused. The "works" are more for us than for others. The "gain" is our tally sheet kept for possible reward. Even more importantly, we have not stopped to ponder if our action is what God has told us, or if it is our own doing.

Claim it though we will, the choices we made are really not for shared life!

The feast that commemorates the Body and Blood of Christ, however, is all about life shared and sacrificed for others. It is about life given without reward, offered without recompense. It is the Easter life of a Eucharist people who know that resurrection can only happen after death. It is learning each day that we do become what we eat. We consume the Body and Blood of Christ to become the body and blood of Christ, now empowered to share the body and blood of Christ with the entire body of Christ.

I learned a great deal regarding the reality of giving during a nine-day vacation spent with our granddaughter Audrey Elizabeth when she was still a tiny tot. Audrey daily awakened with an agenda which could be summed up in one word, delight. Everything was fresh and new and ready to be explored. Questions abounded from early morning until forty-five minutes after she was supposed to be in bed. "Mist, I can have breakfast?" "Mist, where is Scrapper?" "Mist, I want to," or "I don't want to!" Day broke on the word "Mist," and night fell on the same intonation.

Gone were my leisurely morning trip through the newspaper, my favorite television programs, the book I had started. Chatter, explanations, distractions replaced quiet. I began to understand once again what it means to take the bread of my life, bless it, break it, and give it. All these little routines, pleasures, desires that nourished me and continued to make me who I am were mine to give away. It meant taking the cup of loving sacrifice and giving thanks for the opportunity to replace my wants and needs with those of another. I did not do it perfectly or permanently. I only began to learn again what it is to be Christ with another Christ.

That's all right. Moses and his people did not do it perfectly or permanently; nor did the Twelve. The only one who did was the Lord Jesus. He modeled for us the way of "giving living." Suddenly, I began to notice that the verbs associated with accounts of Jesus in Scripture are active ones: Go. Follow. Say. Get ready. Audrey was teaching me that I am not the one to choose the time or place or person or event. I am simply to go, follow, and say. I am to get ready and be ready to be present to the call of covenantal relationship.

All that Audrey really wanted was me to be Mist, her very own grandmother who would bond with her in ways that only she and I could do. Others were in the house. Others could answer her calls, but Mist was the one called. Mist was the one who had to respond with her life. At this time and in this place, nothing and no one else would suffice.

At day's end, when all has been said and done, there is a reward. I learned that from Audrey, as well. There is a hug that brings tears of joy. There is a look that pierces my heart with delight. And there is one simple, profoundly moving statement, "I love you, Mist." I can only reply, "I love you, too!"

What I heard Audrey saying those many years ago, echoes in my heart as the voice of God. I hear God saying, "I love you, Fran." I can only reply, "I love you, too." The words are powerful. They impel me to go out into my corner of this vast universe. They help me to follow in the footsteps of my Savior. They enable me to say what is right no matter how wrongly I am treated as a result.

My belief in the God who loves me first, last, and always allows me to get ready and be ready to respond to the call of God's people. It prepares me in ways mysterious to hear the voice of God asking me to take, bless, break, and give the bread of life and the cup of love to one of the little ones.

Audrey's call reflects God's call to "giving living." Offered and perfectly enfleshed in God's only begotten Son, it was then commissioned to the disciples. The command continues to resound through the hearts and lives of all those who hear, listen, and respond.

Each of us is what we have eaten—the body and blood of Christ. We are filled with the God who loves us. Energized, we answer God's call to "giving living."

For Reflection and Discussion

- For what reasons do you value your participation in the Mass, the Christian Eucharist? How do you try to be Eucharist for others? In what practical ways might others see you as one who is saying, "Take and eat, this is my body, given for you"? When have you deceived yourself and confused doing good works with "being Eucharist"?

Prayer

Jesus, Best Friend,
    may your soul give life to me,
    may your flesh be food for me,
    may you warm my hardened heart.

Jesus, Best Friend,
    may your tears now wash me clean,
    may your passion keep me strong,
    may you listen to my plea.

Jesus, Best Friend,
    may your wounds take in my hurts,
    may your gaze be fixed on me,
    may I not betray your love.

Jesus, Best Friend
    may you call me at death's door,
    may you hold me close to you,
    may you place me with God's saints,
    may I ever sing your praise. Amen.

             — Inspired by the prayer, "Soul of Christ,"
from the book *Draw Me Into Your Friendship*, by David L. Fleming, SJ

Ordinary Time

Second Sunday in Ordinary Time

1 Samuel 3:1–10, 19; 1 Corinthians 6:13–20; John 1:35–42

Latter Day Saints and the Lamb of God

I have facilitated a weekly Bible study group in a little Southern community for fifteen years. Comprised mainly of senior citizens, Wisdom folk who are truly latter day saints, the gathering is both lively and challenging. A while ago, one of them asked, with a smile that spoke more than her words, "Why don't you ever write about us?" I did a grand dodging step, but I heard what she said and let it reverberate in my being. If we are all brothers and sisters, daughters and sons in the family of God, why, indeed, had I not written about these members of the family? Were they merely sitting on life's shelf awaiting demise with dimming eyesight, deafened ears, and diminished capacities? Or was it that I had forgotten that I was ministering to the Lord under their direction, learning from their wise experiences? Was I ignoring the fact that the lamp of God in their life had not gone out? They were still "lying down in the temple of the Lord where the ark of God was" (1 Samuel 3:3).

As I reflect upon the time we spend together, I begin to discover that it is they who are Eli to my Samuel. They are the ones who help me to discern God's will and mission for me, as much as I try to do the same for them. Ours is a mutual pilgrimage to the God who calls both directly and indirectly, the God whose message frequently needs translation, whose voice is heard both in solitude and in solidarity.

When any of us stays too much alone, even with God, our vision tends to become skewed. We too often view and hear only the divinity created in our own image. This image seeks directions with which we are either comfortable or familiar. It remains securely fastened to our own perceptions, which are always accurate though may also stand in need of correction. We see and hear what we want to see and hear, not necessarily what we need to see and hear.

Even Jesus did not remain a solitary figure. He chose solitude when necessary, but he spent the majority of his time with others who helped him hone his prophetic stance and honor his mission. As a carpenter in the company of fishermen, a rabbi who ate with tax collectors and women, a young man traveling with older folks, Jesus recognized the value of differences. Others assist us in separating the noise of our own desires from the stillness of God's demands. They help us to perceive the difference. Together we are more apt to garner truth and gain trust that God is calling. Together we grow in courage as we listen to God's voice, not our own. Together we dare to risk silence, to cease frenetic activity, to lie down in the stillness of our being. Together we are are able to respond, "Speak, Lord, for your servant is listening" (1 Samuel 3:10).

As I write these words, I see the faces of those marvelous men and women, and I see God. I see the God whose head lowers ever so slightly to hide the smile caused by my fumbling and foibles. I notice laughing countenances wrinkled with divine delight at my stories. I learn to slow my pace as God does, walking slowly with those whose arthritic limbs are crippled with age. I find that my God, our God, bends down to hear our slurred, stroke-diminished speech. Through the Searchers of Scripture, as they have chosen to define themselves, I continue to discover that our God speaks with joyous glee as well as serious challenges. I do what we say we are, persons who search the Scriptures—the holy books of our lives as well as the Holy Book that lives.

Together we unveil an amazing truth, one found only in community: "All things are lawful for me…for us…but not all things are beneficial" (paraphrase of 1 Corinthians 6:12). Alone it is nigh impossible to differentiate between that which is lawful but not beneficial and what is beneficial but not lawful. Without a real faith community, a group that challenges as it comforts and comforts as it challenges, we might find ourselves in the dilemma Thomas Hardy described as being "alone and lonely in a world we never created." Arm-in-arm with Emmanuel, the God who lives among us, we are empowered to recreate a world beneficial to all. At the same time we are also re-created in the understanding that our bodies, each of us and all of us, are parts of the Body of Christ. To harm one is to hurt all. To hurt all is to create a wound in the Body of Christ more devastating than the sword thrust into Jesus' side as he hung dying on humanity's cross.

Latter day saints are acutely aware of this reality. I know that the Searchers of Scripture are certainly attuned to it. We are not standing idly on the corner of life, indifferently watching God's world go by. Gathered in groups of believers, we are watching with interest to see if Jesus will appear. We are eager to get a glimpse of God. Suddenly someone in the group who is brave enough to speak the truth exclaims, "Look, here is the Lamb of God" (John 1:35). It is a clarion call to action. To recognize the presence of God is to respond. And we do, to a degree. We follow in Jesus' footsteps, perhaps with more curiosity than commitment, until Jesus turns around to face us with ourselves and to ask, "What are you looking for?" (John 1:38).

There it is. Life's most basic question, "What are we looking for?"

If our answer matches that of those who are disciples, it is "Where are you staying?" (John 1:38).

That is the quest of discipleship, to discover where Jesus is staying. That is the quest of our little Bible group. It is, or should be, the search of the larger church community, the heart of evangelism, the core of Christianity. All of us are looking for the place where God is staying, where God is constantly in residence. We want to know where the Body of Christ abides. Or do we?

Interestingly, Jesus tells us only to "Come and see" (John 1:39). No specific direction is given or indicated. Come and see. Enter into the process of following Christ. Keep looking for the Lamb of God. Come along with Jesus and see where he lives. Amazing things will happen to us when we begin to see that Jesus lives everywhere and in everyone. To our own wonderment, we may even start to exclaim, "Look, here is the Lamb of God." Not once will we say it, or twice, but over and over again as each member of God's family enters our view.

Our desire is to stay a while and be renewed, reclaimed, and renamed—as latter day saints, lambs of God who have come to live in the company of the Lamb of God.

For Reflection and Discussion

- Who are or have been the "Elis" in your life, your mentors? What have they taught you and where have they led you? Deep down inside of you, what are you looking for?

Prayer

Lamb of God, you take away the sins of the world, have mercy on us. Have mercy on my failure to look and see that you are here, living your life in me. Have mercy on my refusal to respond, "Here, I am" when you have called. Have mercy on my inability to recognize you in the many people you have sent to assist me on my way to you. Have mercy when I do not ask you to speak to me, or listen when you do. Lamb of God, I believe that you do take away the sins of the world, my sins, and that you do grant me peace. Amen.

Changing the mind of God

I recall having been told that prayer does not change God's mind. It changes ours. Prayer changes our hearts and minds. Prayer empowers a different viewpoint, another perception of reality that more closely resembles God's view. All of that may be true, but there is also the possibility that God's mind can be changed. It is comprehensible that God offers us second and third chances; in fact, countless opportunities to engage in our mutual relationship to open the doors to newness. God's mind can be changed in response to our continued movement toward divinity.

That is both a comforting and a challenging thought. I am comforted by the fact that God always calls us, never forgets us, will not leave us forsaken and lost. At the same time, I recognize that this is a challenging comfort. If God does not leave us, neither does God leave us alone. God persists until our resistance is worn down. Certainly we have the freedom to continue rejecting God, but it is almost as if God were causing us to experience such fatigue that we say yes simply because we are tired of saying no.

Whatever the case may be, we move from passively sitting, from being reluctant prophets bound by the status quo, to people of action. The word is heard. Get up! Go! We are awakened to our need to participate in God's world and spread God's message. Though the task may seem incredibly huge, totally intimidating, we need only decide to begin. Success is in the beginning. As the slogan states, "Just do it!" and let God take care of the rest. Most assuredly, God will. Amazing things happen, even with the first step, the first day of this lifelong journey.

All change evokes mixed emotions, fear being a major factor. Humanly we are loathe to try what is new, whether it is food we have never before tasted, a country we have not visited, a job with which we are unfamiliar. It is so much easier to stay put, to befriend the devil we know lest we find an even more powerful Satan in the unknown.

So, what is the secret behind the success found in starting? I suspect the key that opens that door is authenticity. When we speak truth, God's truth, people hear us, no matter who we are or where we go. The message supersedes the messenger. Jonah, Scripture's reluctant prophet, set out and went to Nineveh, "according to the word of God" (Jonah 3:3). The people listened because his mission was imbued with God's word, not his own. The people listened even though the message was one of doom and disaster, even though there was a time limitation. They listened, believed God, and acted on their belief. They proclaimed a fast. Everyone, great and small, put on sackcloth, and God was impressed with their attentive response.

Can we change God's mind? We change and God responds to the positive movement, the committed repentance. God cannot and does not punish those who have exchanged bad for good, who have unveiled the latent goodness they have kept hidden in evil.

So, what are we waiting for? Why do we deprive ourselves of the opportunity to change God's mind? The only time we have is now. Now is time for all good men and women to be who they are called to be, to do what they are chosen to do. We have only the present, and that is rapidly passing away. Our choice is simple: Repent and believe the Good News of our salvation or stay as we are and know only bad news.

It has been said that an optimist is one who sees opportunities in difficulties and a pessimist is one who sees difficulties in opportunities. By the same token, a faithful person is one who sees that the dominion of God is near and is unafraid; a faithless person is one who sees the dominion of God is far away and is trapped in fear. Lest these remain aphorisms, what are we to be? What are we to do? What, in fact, is our journey, our Nineveh?

I suspect that our commission differs little from that heard by Simon and Andrew, James and John. As they were told so are we. We must fish for human beings. We need to leave our controlled, little lives that bind us in the mundane "busy-ness" of life. We need to enter the business of living, the enterprise of love. We are to set out bait, not to entrap but to entice. How to do it? A good start would be to leave our nets and follow Christ. Stop mending nets that are uselessly binding us, tying us into knots of complacency. Get out of the boats called comfort, security, mediocrity. Go a little farther than we dare. Take a tiny chance, but do it now. Act immediately, before it is too late. Change God's heart by changing our own. Follow the Messiah of Messiness, the God who challenges our comfortableness and shakes our security. Follow—and lead.

Leaders are followers who believe.

Their faith lies in getting up and going. Where and how are not their questions. Asking who leads them is their only discernment. To follow God's lead is to be who we really are. It is to know that others will follow our lead. No major life adjustment is discernible. Seen only is a radical change in attitude.

As a result, we discover we must follow in companionship, like the creatures in Noah's ark, two by two—coupled with God and each other. Followers know the need for community. They recognize the imperative for faith groups to keep us from returning to our confining nets and constricting boats, our entanglements and securities. We begin to recognize that leaders have a sense of immediacy. They quickly and consciously leave what must be jettisoned and keep that which must be treasured.

What is of major importance is that God's dominion has come near. All else flows from that reality. Repentance and belief in good news emanates from the nearness of God's reign. We cannot simply bask in the glow of God's presence. We are not people of the aura. We are people of the hour. It is ever more evident that piercing requirements are made of faithful followers. All who are called to lead fearlessly are also called to continued growth.

We who are follower/leaders are asked to change, not for the sake of change, but for our sake and God's.

For Reflection and Discussion

- In what ways and for what causes have you heard God say to you, "Get up and go"? How did you respond? Where are your "Ninevehs"? What is netting you in fear and preventing your move to evangelize or minister? Describe the means you use to discern where the Spirit of God is leading you.

Prayer

Beloved God, you never cease to call me to join, ever more deeply, in the loving, creative building of your kingdom. Loosen the nets that still hold me and prevent me from getting up to follow wherever you lead me. Make me your leader by showing me how to follow you. Empower me with the help of your Holy Spirit to become the "me" you have called me to be. Grace me so that the fraudulent me melts and is molded into the me who resembles you. I believe you can do this, so I pray with confidence in Jesus' name. Amen.

FOURTH SUNDAY IN ORDINARY TIME

DEUTERONOMY 18:15–20; 1 CORINTHIANS 7:32–35; MARK 1:21–28

Life is beautiful. Why choose death?

Sometimes prophets take strange shapes. I know that I was surprised to find such a person in Guido, Roberto Benigni's character in the movie *Life is Beautiful*. Judging from the rapid demise of the movie, despite the many awards it won, the surprise was ill received, misunderstood, or marginally acceptable. As all prophets are. The movie has been entombed, perhaps ensconced, in the racks of video stores to be viewed by aficionados of foreign film. To this day, its effect on my spirit remains awesome.

Guido, like most of us, was an ordinary person with humanity's usual faults and foibles. He also possessed a great imagination, extraordinary insights, and the faith to make them real. For him, and thus for all who were in his company, life was nothing less than beautiful. The vital sincerity of his conviction offered impelling authenticity and powerful appeal to his prophetic stance. No one who met him was left untouched. Yet, Guido was just a waiter, a bookstore owner, a bumbling charmer, a loving husband and father, a friend to all. The ordinariness of his life was exactly the surprise.

Sometimes, prophets take strange shapes.

Raised up from his kinsfolk, Guido's higher status of joy empowered him to be enraptured by the sheer marvel of creation. God's creative force was his—integrated with humor, demonstrated in love. For him, all the world was not a stage; it was an opportunity to surface beauty, even in ugliness. This was the message of God to which he gave voice.

To the confines of a small village, he brought largesse. Where other businesses bore signs banning Jews and other "ugly" people, his bookstore was open to all and everything was half price! If there was to be any exclusion, his was limited to mythical beasts or clans long dead. Always, the prime motivation was to unveil beauty for his son and imbue him with that vision. Some might have called it senseless game playing; others, serious denial. Both would have been in error. Guido's life was not a meaningless game. It was a marvelous gamble on God, a God who was never called by name. That was not necessary for Guido. God and he were one on the playground of creation.

Guido spoke God's word. His message was profoundly simple and simply profound. It was a message that baffled and caused problems for most who would not hear. Guido proclaimed with all his heart, "I want you to be free from anxiety" (1 Corinthians 7:32). In every way he knew, Guido's intent was to liberate others from excessive worry. Clearly, Guido had learned that anxiety bound people, chaining them with cramping pettiness. It forced them to think small, be wary, become blind and deaf to oppression. So, he told stories, altered circumstances, caused distractions—taking the worry upon himself and transforming it with the grace of comic relief. Guido did not put any restraint upon others but only promoted "good order and unhindered devotion to the Lord" (1 Corinthians 7:35). In a word, Guido was about the business of saving people from themselves.

As is too often true, perhaps always, there was opposition to this vitality. People do not like or want to hear the voice of God when it impinges on their selfish desires. There is quick reprisal, fearsome, cruel, and unwarranted. The excuse for retaliation, in Guido's case, was his Jewishness; the perpetrators of that evil were Nazi Germans. Despite all efforts to silence and contain the prophetic voice of God, Guido continued to be who he was.

Guido entered the synagogue of life—the village where his family resided, the place where his business was done, ultimately the camp designated for his imprisonment—and "The people were spellbound by his teaching because he taught them as one having authority and not like the scribes" (Mark 1:22). Guido taught with a smiling heart. His passion was to free all, especially his son, from worry and to certify his conviction that life is beautiful. It was a magical liberation of the spirit that empowered bodies to continue in the face of danger, burdensome labor, and imminent death. There was nothing that Guido would not attempt in order to achieve the goal of certifying the beauty of life.

In this prison camp synagogue were unclean spirits. These men and women trivialized life and showered people with death. Guido banished them with the vitality and authority of his new teaching. Though they continued walking and talking, barking orders, and issuing fatal sentences, they truly ceased to exist in the minds and hearts of those who had chosen to see differently. What was real was the beauty of life. Death and destruction were the games!

The price of this vision was costly. Guido willingly paid dearly, giving up his own life.

Some might think it was an exercise in futility, but they are the ones who closed their eyes to the stars shining in the eyes of Guido's son, Joshua. When the game was over and the enemy had finally left, Joshua emerged from the hiding place in which his father had placed him. Slowly, carefully he walked. Intently he looked for signs of triumph and listened for the sound of victory.

In the distance, at first, he heard an indistinguishable rumble. As the noise neared the enclave where death had momentarily ruled, Joshua saw the fulfillment of his father's promise become real. There could be only one response to the completion of prophecy and he made it, for all of us. Eyes wide open with astonishment, the words rushed from Joshua's heart: "It's real!"

Guido's efforts and determination to speak a prophetic message found success in the wonderment of his son's belief. The stories of beauty and birth were true. Conviction had given birth to commitment. The authority of the person and the authenticity of the message were wed. Worries were dispelled; restrictions were removed; good was promoted—all through the life, work, and ministry of a strange sort of prophet.

It's real. It's true. Life is beautiful. Why, then, are so many so intent on choosing death?

For Reflection and Discussion

• In what ways have you made life beautiful for others? When only darkness could be seen, how have you brought light? When unclean spirits have taken hold of you or of others, how have you commanded their dismissal? Describe the ways in which you see yourself as a prophet.

Prayer

Lord, increase my faith and trust in your good intentions for us. Help me to go about my life confident that whatever happens to me will ultimately work out for the best, and help me to praise your goodness in all times and places.

— *All Will Be Well*, Ave Maria Press

FIFTH SUNDAY IN ORDINARY TIME

JOB 7:1–4, 6–7; 1 CORINTHIANS 9:16–23; MARK 1:29–39

Ya gotta do what ya gotta do!

A friend of mine who is also a pastor frequently asks, "Where is the Good News here?" He insists that we look for and uncover the good news of the Gospel message, especially when there is apparently only not-so-good news to be seen. His "take" on life is that we are frequently too enmeshed in the bad news. Immersed in negativity, we totally miss the positive goodness inherent in life, both ours and God's! It seems that sometimes we are hard-pressed to find good news in the day's routine or in its surprising twists and turns. (Certainly it was not good news for me that my computer froze in the middle of this very reflection I was writing and had not yet saved!)

Surely I do not turn to the Book of Job when the sky is gray, the atmosphere heavy with cold dampness, and my saturated sinuses cause my eyes to ache. I feel as if I already have a hard service on earth and my days are filled with futile laboring. Daily, a bulletin flashes before me, a broadcast of information complete with its neon lights that blind and illuminate simultaneously. I begin to see that, despite all the nocturnal tossing and turning, the endless days and eternal nights, "Ya gotta do what ya gotta do!" Now, who wants to affirm that depressive thought?

So, where is the Good News?

I guess I'd say that the Good News is "Ya gotta do what ya gotta do!" Both my prize and my commission is to do what God impels, as God impels it, in God's timeframe. That is not always an easy task, though it is always a rewarding one. We need only to look at the life of Jesus of Nazareth to discover the degree of difficulty.

Jesus and his disciples were always on the go. Though their activity was never frenetic, it was continuous. They were not retirees who chose their arena of interest with the announcement that their dues were paid, once and for all. Their response was not a statement that they would no longer do what was demanded and distasteful. Nor were they upwardly mobile with decisions based on what would improve their status in life. Neither were they "stay-at-homes" whose doors were closed shut against the claims and clamor of needy outsiders.

The Nazarene and his troupe simply did what they had to do, daily and consistently. This was especially true for Jesus. Wherever he went, he was presented with problems to be solved, people to be seen, illnesses to be cured. Called to serve, he served—and that was good news for all. More than that, his serving became a lifestyle to emulate. Once uplifted by Jesus, the one who was formerly ill or infirm, ailing or unable responded by doing as Jesus did. Each began to serve the others. True for the people of Jesus' time, it is equally real for us today.

Sometimes it may seem as if whole cities gather around our doorway. People and situations of all stripes beg for assistance. The need to be served as well as the need to serve can appear overwhelming. It may have been that way for Jesus, as well. However, he managed—and so do we—by curing, healing, empowering, strengthening one person at a time. Never looking at the mammoth mound of responsibility, Jesus did what he had to do. He simply picked up single stones, one by one—and the whole mountain moved.

Jesus did not allow the demons of distraction, negativity, and opposition to speak. Nor can we. He did not permit any expression of radical pessimism to deter him from his messianic message. Jesus came to save people from themselves, their worst selves. To stray from that path would be disastrous, for us and for him. We are called to follow in those anointed footsteps.

The way of the Lord is a mixture of aloneness and community. It is a desire to be with friends and family as well as a need to commune in solitude with God. It is a pilgrimage into prayerfulness that is both peopled and private. "In the morning, while it was still very dark, he (Jesus) got up and went out to a deserted place, and there he prayed. And Simon and his companions hunted for him. When they found him, they said, 'Everyone is searching for you'" (Mark 1:35–36).

It was obvious that, for Jesus, this was not to be a moment of quiet, alone with the Alone. Though humanly he may have both needed and wanted that kind of time to spend with his Father, it was not what was in God's mind for him—at least not here, not now. This was to be action time. The people were ready to listen, to attend to his words. He had to put aside, momentarily, his own proclivity for silence and contemplation in order to do what he had been sent to do.

Jesus, Paul, Peter's mother-in-law, you and I, all of us are asked to become slaves to all so that more might be won to God. We are not asked to be enslaved by all. Nor are we asked to acquiesce to abuse or treatment like doormats meant only to be stepped upon. That kind of masochism serves no purpose. Ours is to offer, voluntarily and deliberately, the service only we can give. It is for us to choose to become, as Paul puts it, a Jew for the Jewish people. It means we are to become persons who adhere to the law for those who dwell in that state of consciousness. To the weak, we are weak; for the strong, we are strong. All is done with a profound understanding that, for the sake of the gospel (and only for that reason) we "have become all things to all people so that (we) might by all means save some" (1 Corinthians 9:23).

When we do what we "gotta do," everybody wins. We are victorious because we begin to know what it means to share in the gospel blessings. Those we serve are also victors because their dis-ease is healed. All that bedevils them disappears.

True enough, we will probably still experience nights of angst and days of distress. The difference is that our attitude toward the struggles begins to change. With a new heart and a renewed mind, the months of emptiness apportioned to us take on new meaning. Instead of remaining simply trials and tribulations to be endured, they become challenges and adventures to be experienced and enjoyed. The shortened span of life is no longer a gasp for oxygen, but the gift of breathing. Tasks move from being onerous to becoming opportunities.

And it is all because "Ya gotta do what ya gotta do!"

For Reflection and Discussion

- How have you changed your attitude toward life from its being a drudgery to being a delight? For the sake of the gospel, in what ways are you a person who is weak with the weak and strong with the strong? How do you see yourself as one for whom everyone is looking?

Prayer

Dear God, some days I feel so bedeviled I can do nothing more than exist. There are so many needs and so little time and energy. It really does seem s if my life is nothing more than a drudgery and I am filled with restlessness and dismay. Help me to remember that my happiness is not a product I can attain or earn. Let me realize that I am already filled with all that I need to be a happy, useful, necessary part of your creation. I am already good enough to be good news, offered freely to all whom I meet. Let me be the healer they need, the helper they seek, so that your will may be done. In the name of my brother, companion, and friend, Jesus the Christ, I pray. Amen.

Sixth Sunday in Ordinary Time

Leviticus 13:1–2,44–46; 1 Corinthians 10:31–11:1; Mark 1:40–45

Imitation is the highest form of praise

I can remember being greatly perturbed, well, angry actually, as a young child when my younger sister imitated me. I wanted to be an original, one who stood out uniquely in my world. And there she was, mimicking my every move. Naturally, I voiced my complaint loudly, only to hear my mother replying, "Imitation is the highest form of praise." Comforted little by that observation, I grew more deeply annoyed with the mirror image who was following me everywhere.

Now that I am much older, a mother and grandmother to boot, I am beginning to recognize the profound truth of my mother's statement and am humbled by any imitation. I also realize that my mother, unwittingly, was mouthing the words of Paul to the church at Corinth—words to be heeded in church communities today. " Be imitators of me, as I am of Christ" (1 Corinthians 11:1).

Imitation is, indeed, the highest form of praise. The modeling is itself glorification given to the one who offers example. Ultimately, adoring adulation is given to the Creator in whose image we are all made and whose life is lived in us. If this is true, why did my sister's mimicry bother me so much? Why did it take me so long to appreciate its value?

I suspect the answer is that I am yet a fragile human being who questions her own value and worth. Such questioning leads too quickly to competitiveness. Instead of recognizing the kudos there is only a feeling that I must out-match the tag-along sibling imitator, or any other who dares to ape me. At the same time, I listen to the admiration spilling from my daughter's voice as she tells me stories of her daughter watching and imitating every maternal move. Donna walks a power walk; Audrey's arms swing in unison. There is no competition here, just a profoundly compassionate understanding that imitation is the highest form of praise.

As quickly as we humans demand that those who bear scabs of sin, pustules of imperfection, or blotches of faultiness dwell apart from us and make their abode outside our camp, God is swift to will that they be cured. Even more,

God stretches out to touch them. The outstretch of divinity makes a physical contact that sears the spirit and inflames it with the wholeness of holiness.

God stretches. So must we. To imitate God we need to expand our limited understanding of sin and sanctity. We need to broaden our beliefs to embrace those who are different and have lived in isolation, exile, and alienation outside the camp of our own particular creed.

God wills to cure all. So must we!

The proof is in the pudding. Healing happens. It cannot be denied. It is evidence of God's presence. We waste so much time arguing the details. Who did it? How did it happen? Was the person worthy? Will it last? Heated discussions lead to heavy debate and we skirt the real issue in the process. We do not question our attitude toward the leprous members of the Body of Christ. More importantly, how do we view our own leprosy, our own scabrous sanctity?

Are we truly imitators of Christ to be imitated as Christ?

No doubt, the questions are disturbing ones. They poke and prod at the ease with which we treat dis-ease. I can recall many loud conversations evolving from and revolving about the topics of terrorism, terrorists, and terror. The range of views ran from "Kill 'em dead" to "Be totally nonviolent." Feelings of angst, agony, and anger permeated the atmosphere. All of us in the room considered ourselves to be good people who were steeped in our Christianity, yet our thoughts diverged quite dramatically and drastically. All of us were quite sure we knew how those terrorist lepers should be treated. None of us was completely accurate. We had all stopped at the juncture where healing might happen. We were all keeping the lepers out of our camp, whether it was violently or nonviolently. Distance, if not death, was still the remedy.

Healing begins to happen as soon as we remove the bars from the gates of our communities. When we open wide the doors to Christ, all peoples sense the welcoming invitation to imitation. The scales and scabs of sinfulness are less prominent, both ours and theirs. Simultaneously, the wholesomeness of holiness becomes every more visible. "Outsiders" can appreciate the model of Christ that "insiders" offer because we, in turn, appreciate the model of Christ present in them. No offense is given to anyone while each of us seeks not our "own advantage, but that of the many that they may be saved" (1 Corinthians 10:31).

What is essential to modeling Christ is that we spread our arms horizontally, exposing our vulnerability and accessibility in a sign of the cross. That posture is a difficult one to maintain, even physically. It is tiring and pains the muscles. It is, however, crucial to our growth in godliness. It is a nonverbal statement of unconditional acceptance. Outstretched arms move us from holding tightly to ourselves—our personal wants and needs, opinions and biases. Outstretched arms empower our ability to touch others, healing them with palpable presence.

As we touch, so are we touched. As we seek to heal, so we are healed. Once again, imitation becomes the highest form of praise. Imagine a world where people say to each other, "If you choose, you can make me clean" (Mark 1:40). Imagine each of us making that statement to our families and friends, our acquaintances and enemies alike. Imagine that kind of outreach, that kind of open embrace, that admission of interdependency. Imagine it. Imitate it. Be people whose highest praise of God is evidence in imitation of divinely universal healing!

For Reflection and Discussion

• In what ways can you be a healing touch for those who have been declared unclean and are alienated and ostracized from the community? How can you be that same touch for the community? When and where have you told the story of healing and being healed?

Prayer

O Lord, I am not worthy that thou shouldst come to me.
But speak the word of comfort,
My spirit healed shall be.

And humbly I'll receive thee,
The Bridegroom of my soul,
No more by sin to grieve thee
Or fly thy sweet control.

Eternal Holy Spirit,
Unworthy though I be,
Prepare me to receive him
And trust the Word to me.

Increase my faith, dear Jesus,
In thy real presence here,
And make me feel most deeply
That thou to me art near.

—"O Lord, I Am Not Worthy"

Belonging to the clean slate club

There is nothing sadder than people who cannot let go of past offenses, whether real or perceived. How many families remain shattered and scattered because one relative or another holds tightly to hurts experienced long ago? Sometimes, the schism remains intact right up to and beyond the death of the victim or that of one who delivered the injury. Despite the heaviness, the aridity of this wasteland of memories, we seem so reluctant to forgive and forget, to bury the negative and give birth to the positive.

In the face of this human "foot dragging," we have a God who begs us "Do not remember the former things, or consider the things of old" (Isaiah 43:18). Instead, God pleads that we choose to concentrate on a new occurrence. God speaks to us with the gentle but strong command, "I am about to do a new thing" (Isaiah 43:19). Obviously, the edict is delivered not to have us concentrate on novelties—situations, experiences, thoughts, and ideas that are coated with newness for its own sake. It is not required that we become "pious Pauls or Pollyannas" who step over harsh reality and label the movement holiness. Nor are we to look askance at the imperfect, disdaining its presence in our life.

Clearly, God is asking that we look anew, gaze at life through a divine prism rather than solely with human spectacles. Erase our "life-slate"; remove all deprecating scribblings that prevent sharp vision and cause blindness. Start again with a desire to belong to the clean slate club. In other words, keep looking for God wherever we are, wherever we go. After all, God is the one who firmly establishes us in Christ. God is the one who anointed us and has sealed us, depositing the Spirit in our hearts. All that is needed is acceptance.

To do that, we cannot remain stuck in the past. Breaking free from its clutches, we must also incorporate it—not with vicious virtuosity but with a keen sense that each of us is shaped by our experiences, good and bad, individual and communal, past and present.

I guess what we all need is a lesson in how to get through the crowds of things, events, commissions, omissions, people, and places in order to bring ourselves to Jesus. It is not that those crowds are necessarily evil. It is just that they, like the scribblings on the slate of our spirit, are clouding our vision. They are obstacles that prevent us from reaching and touching our center-point—a closer encounter with Jesus. How do we make room—not for Jesus, but for us—in the midst of those crowds? What are we to do?

There is a marvelous story in Scripture that gives a helpful example, if not advice. Word got around that Jesus was at home in Capernaum and everybody gathered around him. The numbers grew until there was no longer any available space, even around the door. There is the scene. It was more crowded than a theater with standing room only!

Into the picture comes a paralyzed man. Complication number one. How is someone who has no mobility going to be able to approach the star of the show, an individual who is apparently inaccessible? Worse yet, room was needed not just for the one, but also for the four others who were carrying him. The mob refused to budge. Shoving and pushing was not going to be effective this time. The past was crowding out the present, never mind any possible future. Something creative had to be done. With ingenuity born of new vision, "when they could not bring him to Jesus because of the crowd, they removed the roof above him; and after having dug through it, they let down the mat on which the paralytic lay. When Jesus saw their faith, he said to the paralytic, 'Son, your sins are forgiven'" (Mark 2:4–5).

When those four friends wiped clean the slate of impossibility, they were empowered to see new ways to achieve entry into Jesus' presence. But, Jesus did something even more astonishingly life-giving. Based on the faith of the paralyzed man's friends, Jesus forgave the sins of the paralytic!

Incredibly, no one but Jesus seemed to notice the prevailing power in that strain of goodness. Friends were curing friends of their spiritual ills by being faithful to each other! Jesus noted and authenticated that potency. A person paralyzed by his own inability to envision newness was given a new lease on life simply because his friends wanted him to have the gift. They were willing to open up a spot for him so that he could be brought to Jesus. They would chance the anger of the householder, the fury of a crowd, even possible rejection by Jesus. Nothing was going to deter them from purposeful love.

The idea was not novel. It was simply newly perceived. Newly executed, it was also newly rewarded. Those who were stuck in the quicksand of the past could only concentrate on the blasphemy of this fresh approach to life. For them death was better than this kind of dishonor. They were more concerned about Jesus' audacity than with his authenticity. How dare he act like God! How dare he utilize the divine spirit with which he had been endowed! How dare Jesus affirm the faith of those who would chance "raising the roof" to get to God's healing power!

By the same token, how dare we do as Jesus did! How dare we challenge, confront, question, and upset the powers that be or the people in the pew. How dare we raise the roof, opening holes in legal exclusivity to make room for others to enter the presence of God.

The boldness we demonstrate when we select membership in the clean slate club is disturbing, to us and others, as well. Those who see and serve the "freshness deep down things," as Gerard Manley Hopkins phrased it, are people who are awestruck by the divine power they possess as gift. With clean slates affording clarified vision, they are, hopefully we are, folks who spend their days and nights giving praise to God by exclaiming, "We have never seen anything like this!" (Mark 2:12).

For Reflection and Discussion

- In what concrete and specific ways can you put "feet to your faith" by helping and healing those in your circle of family, friends, and acquaintances? How do you score on forgetting as well as forgiving? What means do you use to work through the crowd of distractions and obstacles that block your journey to God? When have you witnessed others working miracles for you?

Prayer

God of Miracles, work your wonders through me
Let my life be a witness of faith all might see—
Trust that moves mountains and raises the roof
To open wide spaces for wisdom and truth.
When I need to be carried on litters of hope
Give me friends to bear me beyond my small scope
And fill my empty heart with eager delight
For all the newness and promising sight.
Let me pick up my mat of dismal despair
And learn that you offer much more than I dare
To acknowledge and accept, but know that I must
If I wish to rise up and walk in the newness of trust.
Amen.

EIGHTH SUNDAY IN ORDINARY TIME

HOSEA 2:16–17, 21–22; 2 CORINTHIANS 3:1–6; MARK 2:18–22

The spirit gives life, the written law kills

Two companion phrases we most frequently heard as our house construction got underway were: "We never did it that way" and "We always do it this way!" With those verities ringing in the air, my husband, the idea person, and our "local boy" contractor went amicably to their respective corners. The verbal sparring began. Each was determined to convince the other of the inherent value of his belief. Foreign newness was waging war by impinging on accepted custom. The strangeness of the one encountered the solidity of the other. Something had to give. More to the point, someone had to give way. One had to make room for possibility without losing the power of past experience. The other had to admit the wisdom of the tried and true without denying creativity. Compromise would not accomplish the desired results. Consensus, however painstaking, would.

So, the conversations continued. Jean would present his theory. Richard would respond negatively. "It can't be done!" His answer came quickly and easily—based on those two timeworn axioms— "We never did it that way, We always do it this way!" Jean persisted, questioning the rationale and requesting a detailed explanation. Invariably, they agreed to "sleep on it." Overnight pondering led to Richard's broadening his limited outlook. "I believe I can do it, if I do it this way." The process was repeated with each phase of the construction, in the face of every "different idea." In the meantime, the house continued to be built—well, creatively, solidly—and in a manner that had never been done that way before, at least in this neck of the woods! With any luck at all, the new concepts will not be concretized, or permanently ensconced into those same two axioms to be repeated for yet another client who has an alternate idea!

All of us find such difficulty in changing our viewpoints. Having struggled to arrive at an understanding, we want to settle into it. Set in our ways, we find that newness is intimidating. It forces us to rethink what we believed had been fully revealed, discovered, analyzed, synthesized and completed. List makers suffer the most. I know because I am one of them. There is such glee and sense of achievement in checking things off. At day's end, "Done" is benediction as well as valediction. If a new idea crops up, all the "doneness" disappears. With it blessing leaves, taking along the sense of accomplishment and success. I can still hear an insidiously fatalistic message bathing me in uncertainty. "Just when you know the answers, they change the questions." Never ending is the name of the game. Process can be unnerving, annoying, and downright frustrating. So are those who keep changing the questions!

Yet, Christianity is all about new wine and new wineskins. If the equation is altered, both are negatively affected. Put potent new wine into the "same ol', same ol' "cracked, desiccated wineskins and there can only be loss, both of wine and skin. Creative, vital life suffocates in an atmosphere of negativity and denial. In order to survive and grow, it needs the oxygen of continued transformation and radical rebirth. Loss or gain is in the balance. There is no space for stagnation or margin for mediocrity, no room for rigidity.

Christians are new wineskins bearing the powerful new wine of inspirited life. They are called to be letters of Christ written by the Spirit of the living God, letters written on tablets of flesh. Everything Christian must ring and sing of life. There must be about us an aura of vitality. Breathing, beating, pulsing hearts full of life must be ours. It's a dangerous, exciting, exhilarating way to live. Vulnerability and sensitivity are necessary. We must chance the rigors of breathing too hard, having our heart beat too fast, our pulse race with compassion.

No matter how scary, our belief, our faith, tells us that the fright will not be lethal. Only the written law kills. Only adherence to old wineskins and tattered pieces of the past, held tightly with fists clenched in trepidation, can be the fatal flaw. We need to ask ourselves why we are holding on, and to what? Are we fasting simply to retain and maintain the familiarity of past traditions? If that is the case, we are denying the Spirit who gives life. We are refusing to feast on God's presence. The problem lies not with tradition, not with customs and habits that evoke memories and promote gracious action. The fault is not with the "stars" we have observed for guidance; it is with the "starts" we are obstructing, the growth we are repressing.

Christianity's ultimate "test question," its evaluative tool, is: "Are we giving life in the Spirit or killing it with the written law?"

We cannot be stuck in a quagmire of rules and regulations and call that posture Christianity. Heart must speak to heart, and listen with love. Our Bible must not be made of poisonwood— causing undue pain and suffering, allowing life to ooze out and death to take hold. Not only do we have the Word of God to guide us, we are the words of a living God, a loving God who impels with passion. Never a compelling force or a dictating person, our God gives us freedom and offers us choice. "Our competence is from God who has made us competent to be ministers of a new covenant, not of letter but of spirit; for the letter kills, but the Spirit gives life (2 Corinthians 3:5–6).

Where is God's word heard? Most clearly, we hear it when we are led into the deserts of life. Listening is enhanced in those dry, arid, empty moments when our emotional sand dunes seem to undulate ceaselessly, leading nowhere. Distractions disappear. Only barren wastes remain. Emptiness awaiting fulfillment. Familiar tracks are erased. New roads must be carved in those shifting sands, roads which will last only for a time before they too are swept away in the Spirit's wind. It is then and there that God can speak, Heart to heart.

Listen to the word of God that gives life. Life is a gift for receiving and giving. Heed it and respond. Embrace the spirit of the living God and become new, fresh, young, liberated from the killing field of rigid legality. Become a people who are just, loving, merciful, faithful. Come to know the Lord. Hold fast to God's word and feast on it. Become a people who are wed to God, not married to the law.

Live in the Spirit of God. Do not kill it with the written law.

For Reflection and Discussion

- How do you read the law of God in your life? With whom do you discuss and share it? What new roads have you carved in the shifting sands of legalism? When have you experienced those "roads" being swept away in the Spirit's wind?

Prayer

Dear God, so many times I have tried to pour new wine into the old wineskins of my belief, my understanding of the customs and traditions of my faith. I have watched helplessly as the wineskins burst under the pressure of such newness and have wondered what I should do to mend them. I am so grateful that you are teaching me to amend my way of life instead of trying to mend its skin, its covering. Thank you for the courage of my family, my children, my friends who have dared to speak their truth to me and waited for me to hear it. They have stood watch while my heart of stone melted into one of flesh and have rejoiced with me in the process. Let me be that kind of friend, that sort of family member, to those whom I meet as I travel through my desert times and theirs. Amen.

NINTH SUNDAY IN ORDINARY TIME

DEUTERONOMY 5:12–15; 2 CORINTHIANS 4:6–11; MARK 2:23–3:6

The worst defense is offense

It seems that we humans are always asking the wrong questions. If not the wrong ones, then we pose the right ones for the wrong reasons. Our intent is not to learn, grow, gain wisdom so much as it is to prove a point. It is to make certain to all that we are correct. Our accuracy automatically makes the other person wrong. So chilling is the discovery of our errancy or the inadequacy of what we believe that we avoid it at all costs. The best avoidance is attack. Fear of having that one domino fall to the detriment of all the others, makes us throw out questions to which we really do not want answers. Use any means for entrapment.

Most often the difficulty lies in the fact that we have strayed far from our original understanding. Perhaps, we never possessed that understanding in the first place! We never really knew why we believe what we do, nor did we have the courage to seek the truth. We did not integrate or transform facts into faith. As a result, our belief remains superficial, easily disturbed, and indefensible. Deep in our being we realize the lack and it scares us. So we react. In a state of fear, the best defense is offense.

I often recall vignettes from my first teaching job. Young, inexperienced (having only been in a private school environment) and armed with a liberal arts education that was heavy on content and light on methodology, I walked with great trepidation into a public high school classroom. After I stopped my knees from shaking, I assumed the stance of a seasoned teacher—or so I thought. In reality, I was choosing and using sarcasm—offense—as my best defense to deflect any notice of my inadequacy. I learned the hard way that it doesn't work! There might have been a short term effectivity but in the long term both teaching and learning suffered.

One of the braver students, Diane, a young woman whose honesty I shall always remember, responded to my sharp tones with silent glares. Finally, I noticed her anger and asked her to remain after class. With as much hostility as she could muster and demonstrate, she shuffled up to my desk. I asked her why she had given me looks that could kill, if only I had the sense to submit.

Because she believed that her spirit was being destroyed, she spoke out. Her response continues to echo in my head and hurt my heart. She said, "You are so sarcastic. All you do is make fun of us and hurt our feelings. And you don't even care!" Fearfully inadequate for my task, I had not simply whistled a happy tune so that no one would know I was afraid. Feeling incompetent as a teacher I was unable to let light shine out of the darkness I had perceived in my students. Instead, I uttered derisive words. I stripped dignity from them so that I might appear to be sharply witty and in total control.

Thank God, I heard and listened to Diane's hurt. Heeding her words, I began the slow process of integrating the facts I had gained through all those college courses into the faith necessary for education to happen. I resolved never again to resort to using sharp retorts as a defensive tactic. Sincerely asked and truthfully answered, the response to the question, "Why?" had started the long and arduous journey from my head to my heart.

Who is correct is no longer the issue. What is righteous becomes important. Caring for others is essential when religion and faith conflict. "The sabbath was made for humankind, and not humankind for the sabbath" (Mark 2:27).

When we question the veracity of those statements are we not touching the pharisaical side of our human nature? Are we not running from truth in order to hide from responsibility? If our response is based on legal permission without regard for others' needs, we have completely missed the point of godliness.

When someone is hungry we must provide food. Nourishment is crucial. Propriety, law, tradition, customs are secondary. Even things that might, at first blush, appear to be sacrilegious are actually holy when viewed in the light of profound human need. David knew this and gave his men the holy bread which only the priests were permitted to eat. Without a second thought, David defied law, tradition, customs, propriety in order to feed his men. I suspect that David believed it would be wiser to apologize for his actions than to ask permission and risk denial! David held the same philosophy and ethic that Jesus demonstrated in his time and place. Only to ask "Why?" was never appropriate. The interrogation they conducted was meant always to surface issues of life or death. Will my action or inaction bring life or impose death? Am I a life-preserver or a death-dealer? Those questions become guiding principles and motivating force.

Jesus responded to the questions with action, upfront and challenging. He returned to the "scene of the crime"—the synagogue where law was taught, discussed, analyzed, and interpreted—and acted out the essence of law: compassion. He asked those whose vocation and godliness centered in legality to confront themselves with the obvious conflict between love and law. "Is it lawful to do good or to do harm on the sabbath, to save life or kill?" (Mark 3:4).

Silence followed. No answer was given. They had closed their minds against the truth because it was so difficult to bear.

We are as blameworthy and close-minded as were the Pharisees of Jesus' day. Perhaps we do not leave our "synagogues of legality" to plot the destruction of Jesus. Or do we? Do we not keep a wary eye on Christlike individuals and communities, watching to see if we can find anything to hold against them? Do we not seek to persecute those who ask us to look deeply into the law and act with love? Do we not sit in silent obstinacy when we are brought face-to-face with the necessity of freeing ourselves and others from every form of servitude?

My student, Diane, bolstered her courage and spoke out. I was given the opportunity to rise above the legal limits that would not have excluded a bit of sarcasm now and then! She helped me to focus on the essentials— saving life or killing it. She saved my life when killing was within her grasp. In the mystery of providence, I was empowered to preserve hers when I could have continued to destroy it. Taking care, we were keeping holy the sabbath. We were giving rest and freedom to each other— preserving the gift of life we had already received from God but had neglected in the labor of daily existence.

For Reflection and Discussion

- Describe incidents where you have been confronted with a choice between someone's need and a prohibitive law. What assisted you in making your decision to act, react, or ignore the situation? How have you empowered others to choose life rather than to destroy it?

Prayer

Dear God, I beg you to speak to my heart. Let me hear your word in the midst of the many words that fill my life and mind. Allow me to recognize those times when I must fast from my own desires and needs to be emptied enough to realize the ways in which I might meet the needs of others. I know it is so much easier for me to point to a rule and regulation and call it religious behavior. Help me to be a person of faith who will see the value to which the law is pointing and to live it so profoundly that your word and mine will speak in unison. Amen.

TENTH SUNDAY IN ORDINARY TIME

GENESIS 3:9–15; 2 CORINTHIANS 4:13–5:1; MARK 3:20–35

Redemptive suffering is the wheel of life

After an exhilarating round of feasts from Easter to the Solemnity of the Body and Blood of Christ, we are again in the ordinary time of the year. However, the readings are far from ordinary. They plunge us directly into the paradox of living the Christian life that we proclaimed so mightily during the many weeks of Paschal celebration. The Scriptures confront us with the reality that life, after all, must be lived, tested, and examined if it is to be something more than existence. So, we begin our corporate life story in the Garden of Eden with the "proving" of the most precious gift God has given us—our free will.

As a woman I am, at first, bothered by the recorded details. The emphasis seems to be on the "sin" of Eve whose seductress image has endured the ages while Adam is nothing more or less than a passive participant. But, a second look reveals a totally different picture. First of all, there are no names given here—just the man and the woman. Already the sense of individual blame is softened. Second, there is no mention of sin. At least the "sin" is not what we might imagine it to be, one of massive disobedience. Instead, it is fear of being naked before God. The "sin" is lost innocence, but it is not irretrievable. God still called to the man and asked him where he was. The response indicates that the man is not totally alienated or insensitive to God, "I heard the sound of you in the garden and I was afraid because I was naked; and I hid myself" (Genesis 3:10).

Fearless communion is supplanted by fearful concealment.

From this point of fear-filled hiding, they fall down the slippery slide of blaming and irresponsibility. Lost is the perfect harmony between man and woman; humans and God. History's first recorded coverup narrates the human experience of misplaced trust and misperceptions. It is our history of mistaken choices as we second-guess God and discover the meaning of mortality. The Buddhists understand this to be Samsara: the wheel of life. They also accept that all life is suffering.

That need not be a negative or pessimistic statement. After all, to live is to choose. Choices are always painful because they entail leaving one thing, person, place for another. To live is to enter that adventure, to test our free will. In this view, the woman, Eve, is not the villainous seductress of the piece, she is the curious heroine who has opened the door for humanity to recognize the price of freedom.

In this older creation story, there is no mention of humans being created in the image and likeness of God. It is only through the action of the woman who sees that the tree of the knowledge of good and evil bears good fruit, then takes and eats it, that humans are able to see the truth: they are images, likenesses, not equivalencies of God.

Eve is, indeed, the mother of us all. She is the kind of person with whom Jesus of Nazareth later chose to spend time. Does she not remind you of Peter with his impetuous behavior? Perhaps you can see Paul with his bold convictions and dramatic blindness. Yes, she ate forbidden fruit. She consumed it because she thought it would be wonderful to be wise. Her concentration was not on direct disobedience, but on a quest for the wonder of wisdom. Her first response was not one of sinful selfishness, but of saintly sharing. What she did not know and could not have understood was that overstepping boundaries and crossing limits carry consequences. Having eaten the fruit, both man and woman know, for the first time, what it means to be naked before God. And it scares them. The primeval couple's dream of unlimited knowledge and independence is shattered. Their eyes are opened but they do not see God; they see only their own "dis-ease" with God and each other. They see their nakedness and judge themselves through the eyes of another.

And so begins the pattern of human behavior and our endless struggle to understand why evil is chosen over good time and time again. The real punishment of the Eden event is the knowledge God discloses to the first couple. What they have "bought" with the eating of the forbidden fruit is the foreboding lesson of opposites and judgments; separation and death. Freedom to choose is not synonymous with choosing well.

All life is suffering!

Jesus' family experienced an identical truth but could not seem to accept its deep meaning. In their fear, they tried to extricate Jesus from the pain of his messianic process. The Scribes were equally at sea. They could only understand him in terms of possession by Beelzebub because he spent time with sinners. It seems that we find it so difficult to recognize Christ when he walks in the garden with renegades, leaves the sanctuaries of security, and marches headlong on a collision course with the "powers that be." That kind of suffering cannot be life-giving. Or is it that we have eaten the wrong fruit?

Eve ate forbidden fruit and discovered limitations. She "grew up" and left home. Jesus accepted the consequences of that action, transforming it into a life lived as boundless adventure for God not an addiction to safety, security, or social acceptability. Jesus made it possible for us to grow up and come home!

"So, do not lose heart. Even though our outer nature is wasting away, our inner nature is begin renewed day by day because we look not at what can be seen but at what cannot be seen; for what can be seen is temporary, but what cannot be seen is eternal. For we know that if the earthly tent we live in is destroyed, we have a building from God, a house not made with hands, eternal in the heavens" (2 Corinthians 4:16—5:1).

Turning the wheel of life, we learn all life is suffering. We can choose to make it redemptive or ridiculous! Life or death.

For Reflection and Discussion

- What experiences have you had where you or someone you know has felt unforgiven? How did you handle those feelings? What did you learn from them? In what ways do you understand that life is suffering?

Prayer

God of my suffering, come near to me. Let me feel your presence. I try not to lose heart, but I get so discouraged and feel so vulnerable. There are days when redemption seems to be a far-fetched idea and doing your will appears but an elusive dream. I feel as if I am standing naked before you and the sight is less than acceptable. Out of those depths, my God, I cry to you and beg you to hear my voice, hear my cries, heed my supplication. I know I can and will find forgiveness with you and my suffering will be redemptive not ridiculous. Amen.

ELEVENTH SUNDAY IN ORDINARY TIME

EZEKIEL 17:22–24; 2 CORINTHIANS 5:6–10; MARK 4:26–34

We walk by faith and not by sight

It is so easy to say "Trust in the Lord." It is especially effortless to pronounce those words to another when all is well in our world and everything is upside-down in theirs. But trusting in God, walking blindly in faith on a daily basis when there is no clear vision of right and no real indication of wrong, is not an easy voyage. Yet, this is the call and claim of God's reign. It is the true sign of discipleship in the kingdom of God.

When we first bought our property, a lovely lot that bordered a tidal creek, multitudinous trees had to be removed to make space for our home. Lovers of God's creation, our hearts ached with the loss. As soon as the building became a reality, my husband scoured the nearby woods for cedars that would serve as house-side sentinels. They were the tiniest of sprouts, no bigger than a large tomato plant, but both indigenous and large enough to promise us a verdant future.

With that belief firmly entrenched in his being, he patiently planted them. One after another, they marched in a perfect row of boundary bushes. He watered them occasionally and watched them often. As is the case with human beings, both he and I soon grew accustomed to their presence and gave them little heed. Despite our lack of intent interest, those cedars grew and grew.

Beyond our wildest dreams, they grew. They became signs of God's grandeur we could scarcely ignore. We had taken a chance that the sun and rain would nurture them into maturation. We had planted them with faith and limited sight, never really believing, but hoping against hope that they would attain the beauty and height of a veritable forest as they do today.

As we aspired and trusted, believed against disbelief that those scrubby specimens would take root, live, and grow, so does God take a chance on us. We are divine mustard seeds, tiny specks of hopefulness scattered across the universe, implanted in cleared lots and living in untouched forests. God plants us where we are needed as sentinels, as replacements for others uprooted along the way, as signs of beauty and promises of future growth. God plants, watches, and waits to see us absorb both rain and sunshine. God waits for our response to all that comes our way, all that is given us to encourage progress.

Never absent from our midst, but always leaving us room to grow, freedom to spread our branches, to form shady nesting places that give rest and safety, God is our master and masterful gardener.

With time, our cedars grew taller than the house itself. Their branches brushed against the rooftop. Gentle breezes and gusty gales alike, bent those feathery fingers until they caressed the shingles with an acid touch. Day by day, the uncontrolled growth became a deadly gamble. Left alone, to their own devices, those cedars would eventually wear holes into the housetop, allowing rain water to penetrate its shield and rot the interior frame.

Trimming and pruning was necessary for life. At stake was not just the life of the cedars but the vitality of all they touched. Active watching and waiting entailed prudent diligence and patient direction. So, we began the process of creating space for all. We made room for healing sunlight. We created a corridor to allow stormy winds to race and escape without catching vulnerable top branches, lifting them like kites that would strain at their moorings, pull the entire tree from the earth, and cause it to crash and fall to the ground.

The Kingdom of God is all about divine choice. It is a process of election and selection. God is always electing and selecting humans, each and all of us, to care for all creation. The Kingdom of God is a divine gift and a human option. As God acts, so do we. We elect and select God and God's will as both the focal point and goal of our faith journey.

When we choose otherwise, our growth is like the boundless cedar tree that damages rooftops, has too many dead branches, leaves no room for the sun to provide penetrating warmth nor the wind to rush through with energizing vigor. We grow into each other, deny life-giving space, and destroy creative individuality.

The Kingdom of God is truly a mustard seed existence. It is comprised of little actions. It blossoms in tiny moments of goodness and minute manifestations of justice and mercy. It spreads its branches out over a lifetime to cover a universe with gracious plenty.

The Kingdom of God is not a place. It is a way of living by faith and not by sight. It is a lifetime and lifestyle in which God reigns supreme, no matter what happens, not matter how or where it occurs.

The Kingdom of God is invisible to the blinded "I" and acutely visible to the naked "I". When I am most vulnerable and openhearted, I am most apt to see God's reign upon my earth. With the eyes of a believer, the confident vision that defies fear and denies doubt, I will view God's plantings in the tall cedars dwelling on the peaks of mountainous faith. I will also see them in the dark valleys of dread and discouragement. I will know that the tender shoots of fragile faith are the chosen ones. Divinely appointed and planted where the greatest growth can be experienced, they shall provide a home for all who seek shelter, a resting place for the weary, and a space for seers, visionaries, prophets, and all who journey by faith and not by sight.

God will do this. We need only watch actively, wait patiently, and walk hand-in-hand with the God who reigns in our midst.

For Reflection and Discussion

- In what ways have you allowed God to prune, trim, and top the cedars of your faith? How have you experienced Sonlight and the wind of the Spirit as a result? When have you participated with others in God's pruning action to help empower the work of divinity within them and yourself?

Prayer

O God, take the tenderest shoots of my faith and trust;
Plant them where they will grow despite dryness and dust
Into a place of wonder, a spot secure, for all who seek
Rest, reprieve, restoration, and renewal from a life that is bleak.
Trim my crowdedness, top the branches that may cause defeat,
Create in me a dwelling that will warm without the heat
Of anger, jealousy, pride, envy, or greed—
A home where all will listen and heed
Your word as law, your presence in powerful praise
That we might live in ways divine until the end of our mortal days.
Amen.

TWELFTH SUNDAY IN ORDINARY TIME

JOB 38:1, 8–11; 2 CORINTHIANS 5:14–17; MARK 4:35–41

Finding God in storm-tossed seas

I live in the South where hurricane season is well begun. Another five long, anxious months stretch ahead of us. Tornadoes and floods have already wreaked their havoc on other areas of the country and I am immersed in my annual angst. I fear the dread possibilities of storm-tossed seas rising to flood our home or howling winds tearing at shingles, lifting the roof top, and exposing us to a sky-ceiling.

Try though I may to attain and retain a "spiritual attitude," I end up feeling more like Job than Paul. I think I know God. I think I am composed, peaceful, and ready to accept whatever comes my way. But, I know in my heart that I am not ready for disaster. I know that I am still attached to all that I have. So, I question God, whether or not the words are phrased in that manner. This is my seasonal faith testing. It is also a time when I give myself ample opportunity to examine and ponder the whole idea of newness and adventure.

Am I ready to be an adventurer with the Lord? Am I committed to becoming a new person, not once but always and in all ways?

Especially in the Scriptures chosen for this Sunday, it seems to me that Jesus is calling us to that sort of lifestyle. More than that, renewal is the measure of our Christianity. Paul tells the Corinthians and us that there is a big "if" we must face in ourselves and others. That is, "if anyone is in Christ, there is a new creation: everything old has passed away; see everything has become new!" (2 Corinthians 5:17). The way we know and can gauge the depth of our convictions is to examine our newness, or lack of it.

Now, I am really scared!

I know that I am stuck in a comfortable sameness. I like my routine. I enjoy the schedules that afford me a kind of certitude about life and provide parameters within which I can pretend to be quite the adventurer. But during Carolina summers, like Job, I also learn that life happens on storm-tossed seas. I learn that God speaks out of the storm!

When I listen, I hear the questions. "Do you think you know me?" "Are you in charge of the universe?" "Don't you realize who I am and what I can do?"

The answers are not found in books. Job's story makes that clear for us. The answers are found in life experiences.

Those life experiences are both unending and ever new!

Jesus calls us as the evening of our life draws near, as well as when we are in our prime. When he calls, he asks that we leave where we are. Our leave-taking may be spiritual, physical, or geographic. He asks that we go across to a farther shore with him. That is the continuing renewal of our discipleship. We are always to be ready to go across to a farther shore, to stretch beyond our present reach and grasp.

At first, the idea excites me. After all, I am traveling with Jesus. We are pushing off together from the land we know so well. Too quickly, however, I begin to feel an underlying layer of concern eating away at my fearless faithfulness. I begin to smart with the pain of leaving the ease that comes with being part of a crowd. Suddenly, I can taste the reality of my discipleship. I must depart from the cushion of anonymity received as I meld into the many!

Mixed emotions and all, I claim to be a disciple, so I must do as Jesus asks. My trust is in the Lord. This is the message I give to others. It is the message I speak to myself. I hear the words I tell my husband when he worries that the tall pines surrounding our house will topple during a hurricane, damaging or destroying the structure and property. I encourage and comfort those who have experienced such problems. I speak what I sincerely believe. And all is well, until my storm suddenly blows in! It is then that I begin to drown in my own words. It is then that the boat of my faith begins to ship water badly.

All that I can see is the storm. All that I feel is my terror.

I try to hold on to the fact that Jesus is there with me. I know he is, and I wait for him to do something to help me. While I wait, I work. Patience and suffering are my twin virtues. Isn't that what a faithful life is all about? So it would seem.

But, Jesus is calling for newness. Jesus asks that I go beyond those limits and stretch my ability to believe. Jesus believes in me more than I could ever imagine. He continues to sleep, resting on the cushion of my faith, at ease in the boat of my life. Jesus waits for me to admit my need and my anxiety. He awaits my call for help and my questioning of his care for me. "Teacher, do you not care that we are perishing?" (Mark 4:39)

Jesus' response is immediate. He "awakens" to my need and yours and attends to it by calming the storms that threaten faith with fear. Can it be that my conviction is nothing more than sound and fury signifying nothing? What must I do to change direction?

Perhaps the answer is as simple and profound as continuing to ask the question posed by Jesus, the question that we need to keep in the forefront of our life in discipleship: "Why am I so terrified?"

That question will not dispel the storm, but it will cause me to focus on the Lord who sleeps in the boat of my life, resting comfortably on the cushion of my faith. If I can concentrate on the God who believes in me, I will be filled with the spirit of that belief. Overcome with that "awe-fulness," I will be able to enter the adventure of life armed with new parameters that give me peace. I will know, each time as if for the first time, that God speaks to me out of the storms that shake my faith. God will allow the waves to break over me, but not to break me. God is in charge of my boundaries. It does matter to God. I matter to God. I shall not be allowed to drown in my terror.

I cry to the Lord in my distress; from my straits he rescues me.

For Reflection and Discussion

- What storms in your life have caused you to wonder if God cared whether or not you were perishing? At that time, how did you experience God awakening to your need? In what ways have you been awakened to God in the midst of storminess?

Prayer

My God, I fear that I will not survive the storminess that often seems to surround me. I wonder if you are really present in the boat of my life and question your love for me. Do you care that I am perishing? Will you awaken in time to address my needs? Will you rebuke the winds of fear that threaten my faith, create doubts in my trust and swamp my life with discouragement? From the depths of my spirit, I cry out to you. With the slimmest thread of belief, I place my hope in your promise of peace. I am still in your presence. I am in awe of your might. I will no longer be afraid. Amen.

THIRTEENTH SUNDAY IN ORDINARY TIME

WISDOM 1:13–15; 2:23–24; 2 CORINTHIANS 8:7, 9, 13–15; MARK 5:21–43

Fear is useless; what we need is trust

Envy and jealousy plague the lives of good people. Goodhearted individuals try hard to dispel those feelings but they persist in tormenting us, no matter how virtuous we are. It could be that we are troubled by an inability to believe in our own lovableness. Perhaps we suffer from poor self-images.

Whatever the reason, the fact is that we frequently look around, see the luck and fortune others seem to enjoy, and feel a twinge of envy. We crave what they have and long to change places with them. The presumption is that this "good" has come with no cost to the receivers. Sensing our lack, we feel deprived. Deprivation lends itself to jealousy. Anxiously, we hold tightly to our own possessions, gifts, talents, abilities—fearing that sharing them will result in diminishment or loss of what we have and who we are. Erroneous perceptions can lead to needless, death-dealing unhappiness.

In reality, "I do not mean that there would be relief for others and pressure on you, but it is a question of a fair balance between your present abundance and their need, so that their abundance may be for your need, in order that there may be a fair balance. As it is written, 'The one who had much did not have too much, and the one who had little did not have too little'" (2 Corinthians 8:13–15). This is a reasonable philosophy and equitable lifestyle. Why is it that we seem so reluctant to accept and integrate it? Why do we allow envy and jealousy to draw us into the trepidation and possessiveness that eat away at faithfulness, selflessness, "other-centeredness"? Why are we so afraid to act justly and love tenderly? Why do we let fear be our prison when we could be faithful and free?

I do not know the answers to those questions. Old as humankind, they can only be answered individually and experientially as each individual confronts fear and deepens faithfulness. It matters little whether we are richly "educated in religion"—like Jairus, the synagogue official—or simply impoverished, afflicted people, like the hemorrhaging woman.

What matters is that we personally discover, acknowledge, and contemplate the truth in the statement, "Do not fear, only believe" (Mark 5:36).

If we choose to believe and trust God's goodness, those words must be swords that pierce human hearts and affect the very marrow of our being. Contrary to the oft-quoted Mae West comment, "Goodness has everything to do with it, my dear!"

"God did not make death, and he does not delight in the death of the living" (Wisdom 1:13). The divine will is directed to life-giving and lifesaving, to enhancement and enrichment. God does not find joy in our morbid preoccupations. God does not dictate distress, sees no solace in senseless suffering, no comfort in chaos. We need to embrace vitality, especially during times of duress. We need to dispel envy and jealousy, viewing them as enemies that seek to destroy life.

We need to believe as Jairus believed, begging and pleading for Jesus to touch our critically ill "child" and bring us back to healthy living. Even when his household informed him of his daughter's death, Jairus had faith. Even when he was advised not to bother the Teacher further, he continued believing in the power of God.

Jairus could have given up. He could have chosen to listen to and accept the recommendation of his friends. He could have succumbed to his worst fears. He could have been "practical" or "realistic," electing not to hope against hope any longer. Instead, Jairus joined Jesus, disregarding the report he had received. By his action, Jairus expressed the profound conviction that fear is useless. What is needed is trust.

Equally but differently trusting was the hemorrhaging woman. After having spent all her savings searching for a cure, she believed in healing touch and made a crucial decision. Aware of the law, she sought a way to touch Jesus without rendering him unclean. Courageously, knowing that she courted the ire of the crowd, the woman moved closer and closer, until she could touch Jesus' clothing and be cured. It certainly was not easy for her to believe. Nor was it easy for her to act on that belief, but she did, and was cured. "The woman, knowing what had happened to her came in fear and trembling, fell down before him, and told him the whole truth" (Mark 5:33).

Fear is useless. What is needed is trust.

At one time or another, we are Jairus. We are the hemorrhaging woman. Afraid, we fall at the feet of Jesus and make apparently impossible requests. We seek the touch of Jesus for healing. We dare to touch him—ever so slightly, only the edge of his clothing—so that the unrelieved suffering we endure will dissipate and disappear. In desperation, knowing that the "illness" is critical and exhausted with the attempt of handling it all by ourselves, we come to Jesus. Interestingly, we do not come alone, but accompanied by crowds of people eager to see God working in our lives. They want to believe more deeply, too. Our relief is their relief. Our richness is their richness.

Our belief in the uselessness of fear empowers their trust. We are Jesus for each other. Touching and healing, being touched and being healed, we feel Jesus' curative power emanating from us and recognize faith's potency. Undismayed by loud wailings of opposition, we work to see beyond the appearances of death. Dismissing ridicule, we join hands with the poor and needy, the anawim, to help them hear God's gentle command, "Little ones, get up!"

Givers and receivers of healing love, we are not impoverished by the relief others receive. We are only made richer in our own capacity to love. The plenty we presently have does indeed supply others, so that one day they will reciprocate to meet our needs.

Where God reigns there is neither excess nor lack, but equality of justice for all. Alive in Christ, envy and jealousy may still plague us, but they shall not be instruments used to subdue or terrorize anyone. Ours is a radical commitment to the rich and wholesome life of God's people.

We believe that fear is useless. What is needed is trust.

For Reflection and Discussion

- In what ways have you experienced the uselessness of fear? How have those experiences deepened your trust and faith? When did you last make an apparently impossible request of Jesus? What happened to you as a result of that bold prayer?

Prayer

Dear God, with boldness, I come to touch the hem of your garment of grace. I have tried so hard, on my own, to seek a cure for all my ills, all my weaknesses and failures. Now I am too tired to be cautious and careful with my requests. I am dying in my own sinfulness, dear Lord, and I want to live. Hemmed in by all that crowds my life, I finally recognize how much I need you to be my God. And so, I dare to believe that my touch and yours will be effective. I dare to leave my useless fear behind. I dare to trust that you will heal me in ways I cannot even imagine. I dare to come to you for resurrection and renewed life. Amen.

Fourteenth Sunday in Ordinary Time

Ezekiel 2:2–5; 2 Corinthians 12:7–10; Mark 6:1–6

Recognizing the prophets among us

"Leave it all to the Holy Spirit." When I hear these words spoken in church groups, I cringe. Hearing the statement is not my problem. What bothers me is that, too often, those who want to leave it all to God are also refusing to acknowledge that God does ask us to be divine conspirators, to breathe in concert with God's spirit and to act as God's human presence. My recoiling does not reflect disbelief so much as it does my upset with folks who seem not to understand that God's word calls us forth to respond with profound commitment, not to relax in passive complacency.

This is the time when North Americans celebrate Independence Day with parades, flag-waving, and fireworks that light the night skies with explosive brilliance. This day of grand jubilation is an annual commemoration of a moment in time when our ancestors heard God speaking to them. They heard a voice saying, "O mortal, stand up on your feet, and I will speak with you" (Ezekiel 2:2).

When they arose to listen, they knew that life would never be the same again. Never again could they remain in dysfunctional dependence, cowering in the face of injustice and fearful of the consequences of freedom. They knew they would have to resist and rebel. They would have to refuse collaboration with a regal authority whose impudent stubbornness kept their very humanity in chains.

I suspect some opposed rebellion, fearing it would not be successful. Life would then be worse than before. Gratefully, the more courageous ones held forth. Their belief, whether known or not, was based on a basically human and deeply scriptural perspective. This is the creed they must have carried in their hearts, "Like the hardest stone, harder than flint, I have made your forehead; do not fear them or be dismayed at their looks, for they are a rebellious house…Say to them, 'Thus says the Lord God'; whether they hear or refuse to hear" (Ezekiel 2:8–11).

Recognized or not, accepted or not, we must be hard as flint when it comes to speaking God's word. There is the heart of the matter. To be fully human we must take note of the prophets who dwell among us. Indeed, we must attend to the prophet who lives in each one of us.

Prophets challenge our sensibilities, try our patience, and prick our consciousness. When we live a prophetic life, we speak directly to the core issues and, like bulldogs, will not let go. When we are prophets, there is no pretense in us. We have had to come to terms with our own weaknesses. More than that, we are "content with weaknesses, insults, hardships, persecutions, and calamities for the sake of Christ" (2 Corinthians 12:10). We have a keen awareness of the strength to be found in weakness. In turn, a healthy recognition of weakness keeps us from being unduly elated with ourselves and our achievements. It puts things into perspective and gives God both permission and room to assist us.

I have a friend who speaks with the directness of a prophet. It is her gift, and the bane of her existence. On more than one occasion, she has been in tears over the fact that she has been misunderstood. All that she desires is to be helpful, to come to the aid of the powerless, to defend the underdog. And yet, she is pummeled by aggressive people whose verbal attack is no less deadly than a gunshot to the heart. Plaintively, she has cried out to me, "I don't want to hurt anyone. What did I say or do that I shouldn't have? Why do people say they want the honest truth, they love someone who speaks with directness, when they really don't want any of it at all?" Thrown off balance by those who seek and applaud the concept of direct speech only to denigrate the deliverer, she is demolished by the hypocrisy.

Her experience resonates with my own. It also echoes the stories I hear from my own daughters and am already experiencing with my grandchildren. What Jesus told his disciples in Nazareth holds true in our modern-day towns, villages, and cities. "Prophets are not without honor, except in their own hometown,and among their own kin, and in their own house" (Mark 6:4). What is not recorded is the underside of Jesus' statement. For most of us, the only prophetic place we have is our own hometown, among our own friends, neighbors and acquaintances, in our own house! It is prophecy to be spoken to our families, among those who know us best, and least.

If that be true, then we are committed to speak God's word to a people who will not honor us for doing it! This is not a comforting concept, nor is it a gratifying gift. None of us likes to contemplate the reality that our presence, however astoundingly brilliant or beautiful it might be, causes others to bristle with questions.

If the message hits the heart with truth, if the messenger is authentic in weakness and strength, yet both are rejected because authenticity and truth give painful witness to the failings and foibles, sorrows and strengths of humanity, then we know we are in the powerful presence of a prophet.

For the prophet, there is solace in the suffering. It can be greatly eased if we follow the Master Prophet and take nothing on the journey save the staff of service with others. With no money in our belts to buy our way into acceptance or second tunic to cover the nakedness of God's truth, we will discover that prophets are welcome in surprisingly unexpected places. We are embraced by those who know the suffering of injustice. We are recognized by all who dare to name their demons and cast them out. We are comforted by those sickened with the sight of godlessness. Anointing the many who are sick with the oil of compassion, we ourselves are made holy.

We are healed of the ache that comes with being recognized as prophets.

For Reflection and Discussion

- How have you labeled others and yourself, limiting their and your power and ability, denying giftedness and overlooking all as effective prophets in God's hands? Are you aware of others as thorns in your side? In what ways are you a thorn in their side? What measures can you take to change the situation and empower God's work and will in your world?

Prayer

God of my blindness, permit me to see
The wonders you wish to work in me;
To note, as well, your presence in others
So that I might truly regard them as sisters and brothers.
Open my heart to the prophetic message in all of creation
Let me not sit, silent and judging, in my own little station
Of life that is narrow, with limited scope and rigid borders
Instead, help me to follow your will and your orders
As shown in the lives of the simple and plain—
People I need to remember as holy in action and name.
For this I am praying as best I can say
Help me to live as I pray every day. Amen.

Prophetic plumb lines

When I read the message of Amos (Chapter 7, verses 7–8), a big smile broke across my face as I remembered the time when my father and I put a roof onto the carport attached to our cottage. It was a hot summer at the shore and Daddy wanted to finish his project without delay. Lacking a son old enough to assist him, he had to make do with second best, his eldest daughter. I had mixed emotions about the whole deal. I was elated that I was chosen. Obviously, it meant that Daddy thought I had the ability to be his right hand "man." At the same time, there was a certain fear and foreboding. Daddy was a taskmaster perfectionist who could "see" the whole picture in his mind. He had a natural ability to "dope things out," as he was prone to say. I was not so gifted nor did I always understand his commands.

All started smoothly. I began to warm to the task. My five- or six-year-old younger brother, the only son, sat on the sidelines. He was contentedly observing the grand event as he licked his lollipop. Then came the carrying of a huge beam, the load-bearing beam. Daddy grabbed one end while instructing me to do the same with the other. So, I bent and grabbed the wooden piece. Balancing well, we walked it to the drop-off spot. Then the fireworks began. Daddy called out, "Turn it!"

I turned the heavy piece of wood around.

"No!" came the shout. "The other way." And, I turned it another way—only to hear an even more loudly shouted, "NO!" The other way. I gave it a second turn. Obviously, I was no more correct than the first time.

Daddy's voice rose higher. My brother's eyes widened at the sound. He quickly left the scene to find refuge from the brooding storm. As for me, tears began to flow as I tremblingly yelled out my frustration and dismay. "I don't know what you want me to do."

My father's daughter was not the naturally talented son he had imagined and desired. I was equally disappointed that I could not see the plumb line he had in his mind. We tried again, and again, and again. Could there be that many ways to turn a piece of wood? Finally, I got it right. The beam was in place. Daddy was pleased. And I learned how difficult it is to see clearly what is so obvious to someone else. By the time I got to graduate school with its entry requirement of Miller's Analogy, it was obvious from my struggle with the physical analogies of line drawings that I had a perceptual handicap inhibiting my ability to see things spatially. No wonder I couldn't turn that beam on the first try! I still find it a daunting task.

So, why does this scene from my life cause me to smile with remembrance rather than frown with anger at a father who asked of me what I could not do? I guess I am smiling because this was the first of many life experiences that would teach me about the power and pain of being perfected. This was the first of multitudinous events that would bring me face to face with my true self, a self that is able, but differently able. Life teaches me that God, unlike my father, is not going to shout "No!" in frustration. God, however, like my father, is going to impel me to do what I fear impossible until it becomes unequivocally possible. Without the angry outbursts and with the magnificent potency of pure love, God will take latent capability and turn it into undreamed facility.

Like Amos, I could proffer the disclaimer that I am no prophet. And yet I can see God's plumb line, not with my own ability but because God is showing it to me. God is demonstrating for me that there are divine walls built straight and tall that no one can tear down. God's way is a straight and just path made in the midst of the people, a divine line declaring God's perpetual presence. This message I can, I must, and I do speak boldly in the name of God.

Prophets are not disabled, nor are they disabling. They are differently abled because they are called by God. Prophets are people without perceptual handicaps. Prophets have divine vision. Prophets are empowered to point out the elephant, invisible to most, residing on humanity's dining room table.

Perhaps the most difficulty reality of the prophetic vocation is that it is most often a call exercised in the very center of God's people. So incisive and earth-shaking is the message that "the land is not able to bear all his words" (Amos 7:10). Prophets, yesterday, today, and tomorrow are commanded to "go away!" Go somewhere else with your tale of justice and mercy. Tell another group about the need for social justice. Don't bother us with truths we cannot bear to hear.

The worst family secret held by the people of God is the one kept hidden in the closet of pretense. We pretend to be open, caring, hospitable, and gracious listeners to God's word, yet we consistently kill the messengers who carry it into the core of our being. We act as if we want to see more clearly, but we really do not want to pain as we stretch our vision into divinity. We do not want to venture forth with nothing for the journey except the staff of God, the Bread of Life. We do not want to know that there is yet another way to turn a beam of wood. We don't even want the tears of frustration and dismay to flow. All we seem to seek is status quo.

If there are unclean spirits dwelling among us, we'd rather they remain than endure the inevitable suffering caused by casting them out. Sadly, it seems that we prefer perceptual handicaps preventing insight to the vision that impels our journeying into the unknown.

We opt for personal preferences instead of prophetic plumb lines. The Good News is that God continues to set those plumb lines in our midst. God never withdraws from us, or passes us by. Always and everywhere, there is a direct link to divinity, a vertical line crossing our horizontal humanity and fixing it with crucial correctness. Always and everywhere, there is opportunity for repentance and healing.

We need only stop following the flock and begin leading. God's command is simply and direct, "Go, prophesy to my people" (Amos 7:15).

Become prophetic plumb lines with God—and for God's people.

For Reflection and Discussion

- What do you do when you feel that you have words others are unable to bear? How do you convey God's message in those circumstances? In what ways have you been prophetic in your family, among your friends, in your church and social communities?

Prayer

Dear God, you have called me and I am yours. I know and believe this truth but I am often frightened about what you are calling me to do. Even though you are there with me, directing and guiding me all along the way, I fear the unknown, the apparently impossible. I do not know which way you want me to turn the beam of wood that is my life. Often, I think it is nothing more or less than a crucifying timber bearing pain and sorrow. Help me to find resurrection in your prophetic message. Give me the strength and courage to turn that wood over and over again, until it is in place correctly and strengthening all who come under its roof. Amen.

SIXTEENTH SUNDAY IN ORDINARY TIME

JEREMIAH 23:1–6; EPHESIANS 2:13–18; MARK 6:30–34

The miracle of two becoming one flesh

As I sit reflectively with the Scriptures during a long week of rainy days and muggy nights, I am struck by the fact that the depressive, damp dimness I am experiencing is both symbolic and prophetic. My husband, and I along with him, has been in a turmoil for weeks over the fact that his elderly, ninety-one-year-old bachelor brother is ill, living alone in the mountains of North Carolina and persistently refusing assistance. His home is nearly seven hours from us, so frequent visits are virtually impossible. Quickly, guilt enters. Spirituality looms as dire command to serve at all cost. Diagnoses of personal self-concentration, if not downright selfishness, pervade.

With the sound of raindrops softly drumming on my spirit, moistening it to softness, I suddenly see a new message in the Markan words. Jean and I are now members of that motley group of apostles. We gather, with them, around Jesus and tell him all that we have done and taught. We, too, have been coming and going with no leisure even to eat properly. We hear Jesus' words, now addressed to us. "Come away to a deserted place all by yourselves and rest a while" (Mark 6:30). There is such peace in the prospect. We can take a deep breath. Let go. Relax, with our brother's explicit permission!

I am amazed. I had expected to be told to "suck it up and keep on going." I had anticipated a gentle, but firm, lecture on the cost of discipleship and the sin of self-absorption. Instead, I am told, we are told, to come away to a deserted place all by ourselves and rest awhile. Jesus is telling me to go easy on myself. Recognize my own needs and admit my limitations. Jesus is stating that it is not only "okay" but it is necessary to give myself time and space to recuperate and be re-created.

Even more wondrous is my discovery that, though I remain "at sea," inundated with great crowds of plaguing problems or difficulties that simply do not go away, Jesus is the one who goes ashore to meet and greet them! Jesus has compassion on me when I feel as if I am a sheep without a shepherd. Jesus is the one who moors my boat at the dock of discipleship. Jesus is my wholesome and holy peace, my shalom, in the midst of weariness and anxiety.

The words come effortlessly. It is not nearly so easy to live them. Nor is it less complicated to integrate the reality that I am the one who is divided! Each of us bears a certain dichotomy between what we do and what we will to do. We vacillate between burdensome legalism and burgeoning love. We want our obligations and duties to be desires, not chores. We want to like the people we love as well as we love the people we like. Yet, life seems rife with the tension that exists between our loves and our likes, our desires and our duties.

It is so comforting to know that the tension can be creative. More than that, it is creative when we allow ourselves to enter the belief that Christ is our peace. Christ is not just peace between warring factions, differing philosophies, opposing ideologies. Christ is our peace, the peace that patches our inner unhealed wounds into holy wholeness. In his flesh, his perfectly divine humanity, Christ has broken down all dividing walls, internal as well as external. He has expelled hostility and replaced it with hospitality.

Incredibly, Christ has "abolished the law with its commandments and ordinances, that he might create in himself one new humanity in place of the two, thus making peace" (Ephesians 2:15). It is the miracle of two becoming one flesh! Christ became human that we might become divine. Law is recreated with love that love might reincarnate law.

The marriage of law and love is a reconciling force of unimaginable power. Within that family bond there are no longer strangers and aliens, even within our own personhood. Only members of God's household exist, people who are citizens with the saints, God's spiritual dwelling places! My faults are wedded to my faith; my liabilities lie comfortably in the arms of my assets. All are one in me.

Even as I type, I can feel the tranquility of those words. All the hustle and bustle that come with living are manageable. When my troubles arrive ahead of me, despite my best evasive measures and modes of distraction, I can cope. Weariness may dog my steps, but I can continue to walk. Best of all, none of it is my doing. At the same time, all is my responsibility.

It is my "life-boat" a-sail on my ocean. It is my desert place of rest and my town of turmoil. Yet, I am not alone there. I am never alone there. Nor are you in your boat, your desert, your town. It is always Jesus and I, Jesus and you, Jesus and us.

We are the miracles of two becoming one flesh.

When we allow God to gather us up and bring us into the fold of divinity, we shall be fruitful and multiply. There will be a noticeable difference in us, as noticeable as the glow on the face of a happy bride and the beaming smile of a joyous groom. We will be recognized as God-folk, disciples whose weariness is sustained with the warmth of divine love. Fatigue flags in the light of faith and tiredness tumbles with invigorating empathy.

When we get out of the boat of self-absorption, when we depart from the bark of law and limits, people at once recognize our inspirited presence. They note the presence of Christ in our midst. They are free to bring the sick on mats, wherever we are. They are no longer reluctant to "bother us" with pleas to be touched and healed. There are no dividing walls left. Insiders and outsiders are all in one place together. Wounds are healed by wounded healers. Peace comes to those who are far off and those who are near.

The promise is there for each and all of us. To attain it, we need only to come away to our own unique desert place. We need to rest awhile and be kind to ourselves, patient with our weaknesses. In our respite, we will experience the miracle of two becoming one flesh.

"It is no longer I who live, but it is Christ who lives in me!" (Galatians 2:20). We two are one.

What God has joined, let no one and nothing tear apart.

For Reflection and Discussion

- What constitutes rest for you? What could you do to make rest a sacred nourishment? How do you live in the creative tension that Paul describes as being pulled in two directions at once, simultaneously wanting to do God's will and yet not doing it? In what ways are you helping to gather God's scattered people and leading them out of their fear and trembling?

Prayer

O God, Shepherd of my soul, light to my darkness, help in my times of distress, I turn to you. You are the one who can do all things in me and with me and through me. You are my inspirer, the breather whose breath I inhale for vitality and exhale to give life to others. Give me the patience and mercy that will keep me from scattering your people instead of gathering them, punishing them instead of impelling them into your magnificent presence. For this, I pray, believing that my desires are also your wishes for me. Amen.

Gathering fragments so that nothing is lost

Every time I read the Johannine account of the feeding of the five thousand, I think of the many times I have been miracled by stretching my resources. I can tell numerous personal stories of "stone soup," the tale that speaks more about the nourishment derived from sharing than it does about finding extra food for unexpected guests. Especially for a first-generation Italian woman, it is always so comforting to know that people will eat well and have some left over.

However, this time different words from the story struck me. This time I was captivated by the possibility that the miracle to be discovered is in the gathering of the leftovers, the fragments that are too often tossed away, discarded and forgotten. While I had concentrated on the multiplication of the loaves and fishes, I missed the importance of preserving the bits and pieces remaining from the feast. How that eluded me is a wonder because—to the dismay of many, especially a husband who discards anything I inadvertently leave behind—I am a notorious gatherer. My refrigerator is a testament to conservation. Not a speck is thrown away if it can be saved, reused, or recycled. I have but one impulse, constant and clear. Always, I "gather up the fragments left over, so that nothing may be lost" (John 6:12).

Though there are cookbooks galore containing recipes to enhance the presentation of second or third go-rounds of food, I usually choose a plain and simple repeat of the original. My husband's response is identifiably positive, "Tastes better the next day." For him, for me, and perhaps for uncountable other folks, there is a misunderstood miracle in the simple, straightforward gathering of fragments. We had looked for and found excellence in the original meal. A surprising delight now lies in the even more fragrant feast rendered in remnants.

In addition to the lesson offered in miraculous multiplication, I suspect that Jesus was attempting to leave another message. While stressing the importance of satisfying the needs of God's people, it seems to me that he was urging his disciples, then and now, to pay attention to what remains after the meal is completed. Pay heed. Tend to the residue, not because we have received insufficient nourishment but because there is much left over for us to gather lest it be lost. Having eaten our fill, we may grow lax and lazy, sleepy with satiation. We may forget the sparseness of our starting point, remembering only the miracle of multiplication.

When we stop to gather the fragments, we face the fact that God uses the fragments of our faithfulness, the leftovers of our life, as the genesis for future increase. Quite often, faith is built on those fragments, a misunderstood miracle!

Bundling up the bits and pieces of our life is a marvelous method of remembering and re-membering them. Because it is what I term a "mindless task," we involuntarily begin to muse over the meal. I know I often smile with the memory of all the pleasantries evoked with sharing the food of my day. At other times, I frown at its imperfection and mentally take measures to improve the presentation, preparation, and even the accompanying conversation. Always, I am stashing everything away for another day.

There is such a sense of satisfaction and relief in the process. I feel good about the fact that I have given with generous hospitality. I feel even better that I now have sufficiency for yet another meal that needs only to be reheated. I can relax because I have been a gracious gatherer whose work has helped to prepare a future meal. I can only surmise and ponder the possibility that God must feel similarly satisfied with the gift and results of divine generosity.

God takes who and what we are, gives thanks that we have received the gift, and assists us in distributing it to all who are hungry. We are the meager five loaves and two fishes. Apparently insufficient to feed the multitudinous hungers of the world, we are, in fact, more than enough to satisfy human needs. Blessed by God, our gifts and talents, energies and empathy, are multiplied until there is satiation. Blessed by God, our vocation to lead lives of humility and gentleness, to bear patiently with one another in love, to make every effort to maintain the unity of the Spirit in the bond of peace gains depth and breadth.

Who we are proclaims but one message: "Take and eat, take and drink. Blessed by God, this is my body and blood, my life, given up for you." No one is left wanting in our presence. Not only is it obvious that we have lost nothing in the process, but it is equally clear we have much left over to gather lest it be lost.

No matter how wonderful and uplifting those words are, they still scare me. I have a holy fear of the call for me to be miracled into multiplication. I believe with all my heart that I'll not be consumed into nothingness. I am convinced that there will, indeed, be fragments remaining that can be gathered and saved lest they be lost. Yet, I am afraid.

My lifeboat of belief rocks in the rough seas of life. I tremble in the darkness of faith that cannot see and shake with the strong winds that buffet me. Rowing furiously toward the safety of land, I am distraught with the possibility of drowning. Intellectually, I know that Jesus is present with me, but I lack a "gut" belief. I need to see him walking on the seas. I need to take him into my boat. I need to hear him saying, "Here I am; do not be afraid."

What I need and want is not a miracle of multiplication. What I need and want is the "other miracle." I want Jesus, my God, to gather up the fragments of my faith. I want to be gathered up so that nothing of me will be lost. All of me will be found and saved, to be reheated, warmed for use another day.

For Reflection and Discussion

- What do you think are the dreams of Christ that only you can fulfill? In what ways are you bread for others? What are you doing to gather the fragments of people who do not know Christ? How are you bringing them into the loaf that is the Church, the people of God?

Prayer

R. The hand of the Lord feeds us; he answers all our needs.

V. All your works shall give thanks to you, O Lord, and all your faithful shall bless you. They shall speak of the glory of your kingdom, and tell of your power, to make known to all people your mighty deeds, and the glorious splendor of your kingdom.

R. The hand of the Lord feeds us; he answers all our needs.

V. The eyes of all look to you and you give them their food in due season. You open your hand, satisfying the desire of every living thing.

R. The hand of the Lord feeds us; he answers all our needs.

V. The Lord is just in all his ways, and kind in all his doings. The Lord is near to all who call on him, to all who call on him in truth.

R. The hand of the Lord feeds us; he answers all our needs.

—Psalm 145:10–11, 15–16, 17–18

Eighteenth Sunday in Ordinary Time

2 Kings 4:42–44; Ephesians 4:17, 20–24; John 6:24–35

The bread of life brings breath and breadth

In *A Midsummer Night's Dream*, Shakespeare's Puck proclaimed, "Lord, what fools these mortals be." The statement was correct. It continues to be an accurate observation of humanity to this very day. We humans seem driven to see and seek the right things for quite errant reasons. Even our songs proclaim that we look for love in all the wrong places. We ignore the good staring us in the face while we chase illusory benefits, only to discover disappointment plaguing our steps. Impelled, perhaps compelled, by quaking self-images, we alternately provide disclaimers for our actions and assert protestations of our own grandeur. We work for food that does not last, never noticing the imperishable store of love and life prepared, ready, and perpetually available for our intake.

Fear forces us to complain about our lot in life. It also causes us to look for wondrous events or people that will be and do for us what we refuse to be and do for ourselves. Essentially, we simply keep stumbling over the substantial and permanent nourishment contained in the Bread of Life as we persist in searching for instant sustenance in the morsels of existence. We are stuck in our humanity. We are always asking "What is it?" and never noting the miracle of life daily presented for our consumption and delight.

Oh, what fools we mortals be!

I wonder how often I have responded and reacted in exactly the same fashion as those wandering Israelites in the wilderness or the crowds looking for Jesus on their side of the sea. How many times have I grumbled about life's inadequacy and stumbled past its nourishment? How many times have I been like a spoiled child who will not taste and see how good "strange" food can be? I can hear myself in those young ones who wrinkle their noses, determinedly fold their arms, and ask their parents "What is it?" They have already set their minds against any possibility of liking that which is foreign to them. They'd rather do without necessities than succumb to surprise and lose their prideful stance.

The words catch in my throat as I read what I have written, so closely do they capture my own reality. I have my personal sense of what I need and want.

I have my own perception of who Jesus is and what he does, my individual idea of community, adventure, and spirituality. With those views firmly entrenched, I seek only the bread of my desires and understanding. Unaware of all else, recognizing nothing more, I stumble over the bread of life. Vitality becomes a matter of like seeking like. It is my watery self finding its own level, and I am less than I started, though I think I am more.

I search, not for signs of God's presence so much as indications that there will be a perpetual replenishment of food, an ongoing satiation of my human hungers.

This could be a sad tale of lingering hopelessness. But it isn't. The distress dissipates with my growing consciousness that even my complaining has not deterred God from being God. My grumbling has not dismayed the One who cares for me more than I will ever know. In fact, my miserable malcontentedness has had an unbelievable effect. It has drawn me ever nearer to the God who listens more relentlessly than I can complain! When I look toward the desert of my discontent, I see the glory of God appearing in the cloud of my own contrariness. God is there, in the midst of my misery, to give me nourishment beyond my wildest dreams. God gives me all that I need in order to know that God is God, Lord of my life, Savior of my spirit.

In the twilight of my terribleness, God gives me meat, recognizable food, to sustain me. God meets me where I am so that I will know the divinity I am!

This reality is so simple that each and all of us try to complicate it. If it is all that simple, why then do we seem to stumble over the bread of life? I suspect the simplicity itself is the problem. If something is made complex and complicated, we would have reason to cease trying. We could say, with impunity, this is too hard for me to do. It is too difficult for me to be. Life's hungers would continue to gnaw at us. Our spirits would grumble with emptiness. Our throats would become dry with thirst. Our hearts would grow weak and faint. Lacking vitality, life itself would begin to ebb away.

Despite the dire prospects, we choose that negativity. We manage to spend most of our time stumbling over the bread of life. We ask questions to deflect truth-telling. We want to know what we need to do to earn our bread. We question what is needed for us to perform God's works. As a result, the concentration is on us and our participation. All the while, the simple truth lies elsewhere, not in earning God's presence, but in believing in the one whom God has sent. It is discovered while learning God's potency.

Simplicity is both the problem and the reality.

Believing does not end with intellectual assent. Nor does it reach completion in an accurately recited creedal statement. It may not even begin there! Believing is the ongoing process of a lifetime. It both takes from us and gives to us the time of our lives! Believing brings us into union with Christ, our brother and savior, companion and friend. Believing unites us with the one who gives life to the world.

Believing in the bread of life brings breath and breadth to our life!

Jesus says, "I am the bread of life. Whoever comes to me will never be hungry, and whoever believes in me will never be thirsty" (John 6:35). That's as simple as can be—and as good as it gets. Come to God. Believe in Jesus. Live in God's spirit and let God's spirit live in us. Complain if we must. Grumble if necessary. That is not an issue with God. Just come to God through all the moaning and groaning. Don't stop when we stumble over the bread of life. Let God pick us up and help us to keep on going.

Always remember, never forget, believing in the bread of life brings breath and breadth to our life!

For Reflection and Discussion

• What steps have you taken to lessen the times you have grumbled about life's inadequacy and stumbled past its nourishment? When have you been offered "strange food" in your spiritual journey? How have you responded to that unique growth opportunity? How have you met God in the process?

Prayer

Bread of Life, you are the God who nourishes and sustains me. You fill my hunger and quench my thirst for eternal life. And yet, I am not satisfied. I turn my back on you and seek the food and drink that offers instant gratification without unending peace; short-term success without permanent conversion. Help me to recognize the bread you offer, the food of grace you give me to eat. Help me to partake of the daily nourishment you provide without anxious concern or angry complaint. Help me to see beyond the bread I eat and touch the God who loves me. Amen.

Nineteenth Sunday in Ordinary Time

1 Kings 19:4–8; Ephesians 4:30–5:2; John 6:41–51

Mangia, Bella Mia, mangia!

"Mangia, Bella Mia, mangia!" Those words, spoken by my grandmother, repeated by my mother, proclaimed by Italians over the ages and across nations, still make my lips turn upward in a smile of memories. They warm my heart, nourish my spirit, and comfort me in myriad ways. Eat! was the encouragement, if not the command.

Initially, my grandmother was referring to meals she had prepared for us. But, I think she had more in mind than that. Nonna's heritage was one of denial. Life in the mountains outside of Naples was sparse and rigidly monitored. Everything was scarce, not just food. Often, "going without" was the only option. Here in America, the land of plenty, even in her poverty, she had more than ever anticipated. So, her word for me was a powerful urging to partake of life's banquet. Try, taste, enjoy, even gorge myself on all that life has to offer. *Abundanza* was both the cry and the reality!

Nonna was a believer. She gave credence to the fact that bitterness, anger, harsh words, slander, malice of every kind did more harm to the participant than to the recipient. These are the things that erode life's abundance, rendering it meager and malevolent. How can anyone eat to their heart's content if they have a diminished capacity for enjoyment?

Life within the expansiveness of *abundanza* has its price. Nonna knew that as well as anyone else. She loved her fresh vegetables from her garden. She loved them too much. Annually, Nonna suffered the consequences of that abundance. Eating tomatoes until her system could bear no more, she knew that hives would plague her. But, eat she would to her heart's content. The painful price paid was definitely worth the surfeit of pleasure she had.

My Nonna expanded her abilities and capabilities. In the face of mockery, sarcastic remarks, and all sorts of disparagement from family as well as "friends," she taught herself to read and write English using her beloved movie magazines as teaching tools! Standing firm in a ghetto environment that sought to downgrade her existence, she maintained a "can do" attitude. Misunderstood and feared, even by those she loved, she never gave up, never gave in.

Her anguish stemmed mainly from a debilitating heart condition that imprisoned her in a third-floor apartment. Nonna viewed life from a sunny porch. She watched the antics of children in the street; heard neighbors' conversations, and felt the pain of being unable to participate.

Nonna died when I was just ten years old. My mother, her only daughter, was silent in her devastation while I was scarcely aware of what had happened. The enormity of loss came later, much later, as did my realization of how much I had gained in those ten short years.

Whether or not it is an accurate medical diagnosis, my mother and I have always believed that Nonna died of a broken heart. Unable to understand how people could be so cruel to each other, her heart ached. Having been cheated by family members she trusted, a little bit of her died. Being intelligent and able in a time and place where those qualities were neither honored nor accepted, her pain increased. Even her own husband, a man of simple tastes and simpler desires, seemed incapable of the compassion and empathy she so needed. He could rest easy with an "X" for a signature. She never could!

With all of this, however, in her own way Nonna tried never to sadden the Holy Spirit. She followed the way of love and gave herself as an offering to God and to us. Nonna was a gift of pleasing fragrance. My grandmother gave me the most precious gift I would ever receive, total, absolute, unconditional love. Her cry, "Mangia, Bella Mia," rings in my being as the voice of an angel of the Lord. (Perhaps it was not coincidence but providence that her name was Angelina!) Was she trying to tell me to "get up and eat, otherwise the journey will be too much for you?" (1 Kings 19:7).

Was my grandmother more in tune with the Real Presence than I ever appreciated? Although her education and experience were scant, she was wise in the ways of divinity. Nonna was also practical. One has to eat to live. Eating well empowers abundant life.

Nonna's earthly journey was brief. Lasting fifty-six years, it was just long enough to help her overburdened son by bringing his son, her eldest grandson, into her home and raising him. It was long enough for her to enjoy seeing eight other grandchildren come into the world. We were the living bread come down from heaven that gave her eternal life. She believed, ate, was nourished and sustained by this "flesh of Christ" and her world had life despite its imprisonment.

What Nonna received she gave, freely and unstintingly. She followed her own advice, ate her fill, was strengthened, and walked her half-century pilgrimage to the mountain of God. Her heart may have been broken but her spirit gloried in the taste and sight of God's goodness. It is there, nestled in the warmth of *Abundanza*, that I believe she has found complete refuge. From her new porch, high above our earthly street, I can hear her calling to all of us: 'Mangia, Bella Mia, Mangia!" "Get up and eat, otherwise the journey will be too much for you!"

We hear you, Nonna! We hear you!

For Reflection and Discussion

- What names come to mind as you think about people who have been heavenly bread in your life? Relate ways in which you have been this bread for others, ways in which you have enfleshed life for those who were in a spiritual cardiac arrest. How have you empowered your family and friends to get up and eat? In what ways have you encouraged them so that their journey is not too much for them?

Prayer

Dear God, too often I have sat down under the broom tree of my life and called a halt to conversion. I have declared that my journey and your call were too much for me. Each time, someone came to my assistance and urged me onward. Each time, I gained the spirit and strength to continue. Each time, I have seen your divine hand drawing me nearer to you. I praise you and give you thanks for being my God, for bringing me closer, for surrounding me with your friends who are my friends. You have given me your flesh, for my life and the life of the world. I promise to take and eat of this gift. I promise to share your life with all whose paths cross mine. In Jesus' name, I pray. Amen.

Twentieth Sunday in Ordinary Time

Proverbs 9:1–6; Ephesians 5:15–20; John 6:51–58

Walking in the way of insight

While writing this reflection, I am a mere month away from the celebration of my sixty-fifth year of life. Medicare's entry date stares me in the face as do the wrinkles and furrows of aging. Gravity continues to have its way with me. Inches drop from my height but not from my frame. What was once solid flesh now jiggles like jello. Agility has been replaced by careful steps. Vitality is found and used sparingly, before and after nap time. Despite the two-pound weights I use to build muscle that I pray will scam the scales and save my pride, I still seem to be slowly sinking into the earth from whence my humanity came. If I listen to some who trod my path with me, I would be despondent or depressed with the sight of vanishing vigor.

They have chosen to walk in the way of sight. I, instead, have opted to walk in the way of insight.

There lies all the difference.

Certainly, I need to face the mirror of my life and look intently at its reflection. But, I need also to see beyond the surface image into the reality underlying the facade of middle age. Unless the years have simply passed by in a chronological parade of clowns, cars, marching bands, and beauty queens, much wisdom has been gained and gleaned with the passage of time. In all of us entering or part of the community of elders, all who have the eyes to see and the ears to hear, "Wisdom has built her house, hewn her seven pillars. She has slaughtered her animals, mixed her wine, she has also set her table" (Proverbs 9:1–6). Wisdom resides in our house, in the abode of wrinkles and falling flesh. It is there that she takes her meals and provides her nourishment.

Wisdom walks with us in the way of insight.

Sadly, it seems there continues to be societal pressure, media madness, that both promotes and projects an image of sight rather than insight. Body beautiful is attainable even into twilight years, if only we would expend time, energy, and lots of money in its pursuit. Willowy wisps and "biceped beauties" dominate the scene, seductively smiling success and beckoning entrance into their illusory world. Wisdom never enters the picture. There is no allusion to its value, virtue, or vitality. Visual fallacy, disguised as healthy living, is far more important than the wise life of balance and moderation where simplicity is sought and nonsense is negated.

It would be just as sad for us to ignore the wonders and wonderfulness of youth. Those who are wise, like the scriptural Lady Wisdom, send out the young serving women to invite the maturely simple ones to the feast. Recognizing our own abilities and limitations, we match them with those who possess other, but equally limited, talents and treasures. Together, we partake of sage thinking and drink the cup of discernment.

When sight intensifies to insight, maturity makes its way into our lives. We all walk together with wisdom, and no one stumbles.

As I look back on the years gone by, I can note the changes I have embraced. I smile, remembering how I mocked the old Italian grandmothers who walked along the path to the beach ahead of me and my young companions. Those elders were probably younger than I am now, but seemed wizened with age then. I recall their heavily oiled faces and broad brimmed hats, protection against the sun in the days before sunblock and tanning beds. Ample bodies crammed into ubiquitous black swimsuits, they chattered away, seemingly oblivious of their mocking attendants. How we snickered as we marched behind them, aping their slow-stepped trek to the healing waters of the sea. The more their bodies jiggled on the downward slope, the greater we giggled with glee. Drunk on the wine of our tender age, we vowed never to look as silly as they! Filled with the spices of our salad days, we refused to believe that passing years would or could take their toll on the freshness of our youth! Filled with the spirit of immature innocence, we found music in the madness of mimicry. And we walked by sight rather than insight.

It has taken six decades for me to realize how wise those women were. Surely, they knew what we were doing behind their backs. Our giggles were scarcely stifled. They chose to let us enjoy our days of wine and roses. They opted to allow us the freedom to believe we would grow into maturity without aging. Though their experiences could have taught us much about living simply but deeply, they permitted us to discover that reality in our own way and time. Perhaps their conversation included reminiscences of times when they, too, had considered themselves to be invulnerable and invincible.

Somehow wisdom was absorbed during those summers in the silent camaraderie between sage Italian women and sassy Italian girls. It was a sagacity that has sustained me through many trials and tribulations, and has evoked laughter from my deepest spirit of joy. Their jiggling black swimsuits are now mine. The giggles hidden behind my hands so long ago echo today in the "Oh, Mom's" of my children and the mirth of my grandchildren.

Over the years, I have eaten Wisdom's bread and drunk the wine she has mixed. I have become the serving woman who calls others from the highest places in the town of life. While welcoming the simple, I have learned how to lay aside immaturity and live freely with intention, promise, and love. Foolishness has fled. Understanding has entered. I know with trusting faith that I have life in me that will not be taken away.

It no longer matters that firm flesh has vanished into flabbiness. Nor do I worry that wrinkles crease my face. Those are matters of sight, and fright. The wisdom of age impels me, and you, to relinquish the path of sight, to walk in the way of insight.

Walk in the way of insight. Sing and make melody to the Lord in our hearts. Jiggle, giggle—and be filled with God's spirit of life eternal.

For Reflection and Discussion

- Describe situations or occasions when you traveled from simple sight to deepening insight. What happened at those times when you took a second look at life and saw everything differently? What did you see? How did you respond? Perhaps God is asking us, "Do you see what I see?"

Prayer

God of Wisdom, my Sophia, you enfleshed your word into humanity and incarnated us with your divinity. Give me the grace to listen to you in the playfulness of the young as well as the maturity of the elderly. Let me wiggle and jiggle and giggle with delight that you are my God and I am your child. Give me the grace to empower others and call them to go higher and deeper, to grow more profoundly in love with you and be recreated each day of our lives. Amen.

TWENTY-FIRST SUNDAY IN ORDINARY TIME

JOSHUA 24:1–2, 15–17, 18; EPHESIANS 5:21–32; JOHN 6:60–69

Choices, choices, choices

I can remember the early Howard Johnson days when ice cream flavors expanded from the basic trio, vanilla, chocolate, or strawberry, to a mind-boggling twenty-eight flavors from which to choose. What a quandary for tiny tykes, and their elders! We'd stand and listen to the rapid fire rattling off of the entire list, think for a moment, and invariably decide on vanilla, the first listed and easiest to recall. Then came the blue light specials of the original K-Mart, once known as Korvette's. The choices arrived with the sight and sound of flashing cerulean bulbs accompanied by a piercing, "Welcome Shoppers! For the next ten minutes, for just five dollars you can buy…." It was too much for me. I left the store, determined not ever to spend one shopping moment in any place that was that confusing.

Today the dilemma is even more daunting. Supermarkets display brand upon brand of cereals, breadstuffs, dairy products, cleaning aids, and more. Sizes and prices vary, not necessarily in the manner expected. Sometimes, the largest amount costs more per unit than its tinier counterpart. Other times it is far less. When I shop, I truly do drop, with the fatigue of picking and choosing, selecting and rejecting. The temptation is to discontinue snipping coupons, not look at prices or contents, and opt for vanilla—the first listed and easiest to recall.

Then I hear the echo bouncing off the walls of my mind. Not to choose is already a choice! Never will I be free from making and taking an option. My life and yours, human existence itself, is defined by our choices and their consequences.

When Joshua gathered the tribes of Israel and summoned the elders, heads, judges, and officers of God's people, they presented themselves before God. But, presentation alone was not sufficient. Their statements of presence had to be commitments that both pronounced conviction and were demonstrated in action. To turn to God demanded their turning away from all other gods. They had to say what they meant and mean what they said. The assertion is no less absolute for us today.

Perhaps the gods have different faces, less overt, more subtle. They may not be golden statues as much as they are stated goals. If my god is money, then my decisions will be based on the premise of gaining lucre. If it is prestige or prominence, I'll opt for whatever leads me in that direction. If it is service, my selections will follow accordingly. The fact is that Joshua's mandate remains accurate. "If you are unwilling to serve the Lord, choose this day whom you will serve" (Joshua 24:15).

I am crushed by the concreteness of his command. It seems so much easier to float through life riding on the waves made by the choices of others. Some days, I can only do that. Those are the times when I sit like a vegetable, a veritable couch potato. Exhausted and dispirited, I let the noise of the television drown out the sounds of life. At first blush, that kind of retirement appears appetizing. But, the consequences quickly loom large. Neither the exhaustion nor the lack of spirit disappear. Instead, they exacerbate. The god I have chosen does not give me life. It sucks life from me.

As did the Israelites of old, so do we begin to look anew at our choices from the perspective of life or death. Why would any of us forsake the God who continues to bring us up from the varying lands of our individual "Egypts"—our personal places of bondage? Why would we want to leave the God who has freed us, once and for all, and yet is always ready to free us again from the houses of slavery we have entered and now want to leave.

Unreasonable as it seems in the face of those truths, we are still reluctant to do more than give lip service to our options. It is not the choices that cause our angst but the consequences that inevitably follow them. To choose God is to opt for servanthood. It means that henceforth we are to be subject to one another out of reverence for Christ, the Christ who dwells in each of us and wishes to live his life in us. Even the disciples who lived and walked with Jesus on his earthly journey complained, "This teaching is difficult; who can accept it?" (John 6:60).

This teaching is surely difficult, especially for disciples. It is made more tedious when we focus solely on the required, possibly odious, task of service. Too often we hear erroneously. Though it is not what is said, we hear that we are asked to be slaves. Untrue! Christ has freed us into the renewed relationship of friendship. We are no longer slaves. We are sisters and brothers, family members of the Body of Christ. The service in question is simply and solely to reverence the Christ who is in all. That's it. And, it is ours to choose or reject. What remains to discern is the manner and method of serving, the ways through which we enact our mission and achieve our goal.

Will there be tough moments, laborious chores, dreaded drudgery? Of course. Will those events and experiences kill us? No! At least they won't if our perspective matches God's. While we work by the light of love, we'll live in that illumination. To allow the light to dim is to live less and die more.

We have the facts. All the information we need is wrapped up in Jesus whose unity with God explodes into the Spirit of Love. There is but one thing missing: our choice. We can fixate on the consequences of our decision, the difficulties that will arise, and turn back because we fear hardship. Or we can choose to stay, trusting that ardor will supersede any arduousness.

There is but one question remaining for God to ask and for us to answer. It is both poignant and plaintive, "Do you also wish to go away?"

How will we respond? If not God, who? To whom can we go? Choices, choices, choices. So few choices. So little time!

For Reflection and Discussion

- Where are your choices leading you? How are you spending your time, talent, treasure? In what ways are you a floater instead of a chooser, a procrastinator instead of a serving spiritual friend? Can you describe your choices as life-giving or life-sapping, enlivening or stifling?

Prayer

The time has come for me to choose the way of God
To win—despite apparently insurmountable odds!
I pray, this day, for courage and strength
That I might sustain the journey's length
Whether mountain high or valley low
I want to continue this way to go
And live each moment as if it were my last
Gracing the present with the hopes of the past
Entering future's surprising arms
With trust in goodness, not in harm.
With praise and joy I make my plea,
God, my God, remember me.
Amen.

Twenty-second Sunday in Ordinary Time

Deuteronomy 4:1–2, 6–8; James 1:17–18, 21–22, 27;
Mark 7:1–8, 14–15, 21–23

Jesus was an angry man

Most people would not classify Jesus of Nazareth as an angry man. He walked the roads and pathways of Palestine peacefully forgiving, doing justice, welcoming the children, teaching the crowds, healing the sick, and explaining the Scriptures. His was a journey of love, a pilgrimage into truth. Jesus' mission was one of revelation and redemption. He revealed the presence of God through his spirit of love and gave his life to this mission. In the process his life became ours to share and give. It was our turn to live as gift and givers.

Jesus of Nazareth would not be called an angry man.

Yet, Jesus displayed anger at times. Jesus evoked angry reactions. He disturbed people with his undaunted truthfulness. He challenged people to see who they really were, and to rejoice in the vision by becoming ever more human, holy, godlike. Jesus demanded honesty and despised hypocrisy. It was not the sinners who felt his wrath, but those who would not admit their sinfulness. Busily judging others, they scarce had time to evaluate themselves!

Those who broke the law did not hear Jesus' reproach as much as those who used the law to burden people to the breaking point. He did not mince words when it came to exposing surface servitude that contorted the divine image. "This people honors me with their lips but their hearts are far from me. In vain do they worship me, teaching human precepts as doctrines" (Mark 7:7).

Jesus was angry!

It was not that Jesus was angry with what was being done as much as with was not being done. Justice was not being done. This angered Jesus! "The one who does justice will live in the presence of God," recalls the refrain for Psalm 15. This is God's promise to all. Micah reminds us of God's desire, the simplest of dogmas. "He has told you, O mortal, what is good; and what does the Lord require of you but to do justice, and to love kindness, and to walk humbly with your God" (Micah 6:8).

That's it! All the laws, precepts, commands, demands, find their totality in just action, tender love, humble walking with God. The Pharisees and Scribes heard but they did not listen. They could find no "law" in words that were commanding a heart response. They lived the letter of the law, knowing that its spirit would demand genuine commitment and constant growth. The Pharisees and scribes made their choice. It was to remain in a stage of lawfulness that would allow them to avoid any questioning of human tradition. They did something even more frightening. They chose to make the law their god. They opted to revere the law as divine.

With such disproportionate reverence for the law, they asked Jesus a loaded question, one for which they obviously wished no answer. "Why do your disciples not live according to the tradition of the elders, but eat with defiled hands?" (Mark. 7:5).

The law, created and intended by God to be life-giving, was being diminished and misused. It now brought defilement, destruction, and death.

Jesus' anger needs to be ours as well. We need to be angry with ourselves for giving lip service to God. We need to recognize that our hearts are far from God's heart. We need to be angry enough to "let it all out" in order to let God touch our hearts and allow God's word to take root in us with its power to save.

Does that sound like a strange request? Perhaps it is. But I am not speaking about the kind of anger that underscores depression. I intend the fiery blaze we feel when we've made a terribly stupid mistake and know it. When that happens to me, I become enraged at my own stupidity, clumsiness, laziness, forgetfulness, whatever it might be. That anger is neither destructive nor long lasting. It is a holy anger. It is a healing power that allows us to take a second look at ourselves, take note of our limitedness, and start again.

In this "angry" time we are empowered with vision. We begin to see ourselves not so much as lawful people, but as "awe-ful" ones who listen to the words of God before acting. Our prayer becomes a plea for God to "place in our hearts a desire to please you and fill our minds with insight into love, so that every thought may grow in wisdom and our efforts may be filled with your peace."

Now we can embrace the law, not as a stop-gap measure to keep within safe lines but as a guideline to deeper loving. We can "welcome with meekness the implanted word that has the power to save our souls" (James 1:21). Our welcome is affirmed and confirmed when we act on this word knowing that if we are "hearers of the word and not doers (we) are like those who look at themselves in a mirror, for they look at themselves and, on going away, immediately forget what they were like" (James 1:22–23).

The people of God clothe justice with mercy. They suffer with the downtrodden who are beaten into mindless submission. They join hands with those who are spurned and shunned by those who pay God lip service and teach human precepts as dogmas. Their hearts break as they walk with the outcasts.

Refusing to trod the path of injustice, remaining outside the lines of merciless traditions, God's people journey in faith alone.

Are we among them? Or is ours a hypocritical Christianity? Do we dare to be the kind of people Jesus summoned the crowds to be? Can we hear the beckoning, the begging, of the just Jesus as he cries, "Do you not see that whatever goes into a person from outside cannot defile...It is what goes out of a person that defiles. For it is from within, from the human heart, that evil intentions come, and they defile a person" (Mark 7:21–23).

Listen. Act. Do justice. Live, love, and serve within the presence of God. Then, and only then, will the law be truly observed. Only then will our reverence for God be full, glorious, and gracious. Only then will the deep recesses of our hearts be filled with the goodness of God and the peace of God's spirit. Only then will we be able to understand the great depth of kindness which God shows to those who live, love, and serve beyond the limits of law.

The time has come for us to become angry people—angry enough to do something, for God's sake!

For Reflection and Discussion

• What word, insight, conviction, call, with the power to save souls, do you believe God has implanted in you? How have you integrated it and responded to it? In what ways are you preparing and opening yourself to receive and respond to the daily word God is giving uniquely to you?

Prayer

Dear God, my arms are open to receive your presence; my ears to hear your word. Let me not sit in somber silence, or stay in slothful serenity without giving heed to the cries of the poor, oppressed, and violated ones who live in my house, my neighborhood, my workplace, and my church. Make me angry as Jesus was angry. Increase my awareness of injustice and make me a doer of good, one who empowers life. I ask this in the name of the Christ who is my companion and savior, lover and friend. Amen.

Twenty-third Sunday in Ordinary Time

Isaiah 35:4–7; James 2:1–5; Mark 7:31–37

Doing everything well by being hearing aids

In the religious education programs of the seventies and eighties, it was common practice to participate in group meetings where feelings were shared. Various devices were used to ease folks into that deeper mode of communication. One that I recall was for each of us to compose our epitaph, our gravestone engraving. I remember well what I wrote: "She tried and failed and tried again." It seemed to be a grand summation of my life at the time.

I had tried hard to be a good wife, mother, and religious educator—sometimes even simultaneously—only to discover my imperfections within each role. Missing the mark was disappointing. Often I avoided believing it, or became angry with my own "dis-abled," frail, and fallen humanity. With each occurrence, I dusted myself off and tried once again. It seemed then, and continues, to be an ongoing process marked both with angst and anticipation, ecstasy and agony.

However, now there are other words that catch my eye and tug hard at my heart. They are the simple ones the Marcan community used to describe Jesus. With the gracious faith that trusts we are all called to be other Christs, I can boldly profess my banner existence in like manner. "S/he has done everything well; s/he even makes the deaf to hear and the mute to speak" (Mark 7:37).

This gospel phrase strikes me as one I might strive to approximate. It is certainly a grand measure of godly life. I'll leave the epitaph writing to those who outlive me and can attest to my progress or lack thereof!

It is not that the trying, failing, and retrying have ended. More to the point, I have been able to isolate the particulars of the process. As a result, the concentration shifts from a focus on me, painstaking though it might be, to others. In the final analysis, when all is said and done, has transformation occurred in my presence? There is the question. Are the deaf empowered to hear and the mute to speak because I am in their lives? Or is there continued silence and speechlessness because I refuse to share my own empowerment?

Often I am myself a person who is spiritually hard-of-hearing. God's words come to me in distorted fashion. When the pitch is out of my range, I cannot accurately discern the message. So, I take whatever I can hear and repeat it, loudly and vociferously. I decide that increased volume equals intensified hearing. But, all I do is create noise, both for myself and others. With imperfect hearing, speech becomes more and more garbled. The message is mistaken, credibility is flawed, the accompanying ignorance is far from bliss. Finally, only muteness remains to replace the shouting. What I need is a hearing aid or two. It's what we all need, all of us whose hearing is impaired.

Perhaps that is the essence of our call to Christianity: to be hearing aids. The message has already been announced and pronounced. It simply has not been heard clearly. The words hang in the air, awaiting an aid to assist our hearing them in the depths of our hearts. "Be strong, do not fear! Here is your God…God will come and save you" (Isaiah 35:4, 5).

Be strong. Do not fear. Take a chance on God. Dare to confront God as did the Syrophoenician woman, the Gentile who had the temerity to beg a Jewish rabbi for assistance. Her hearing was keen. She had heard about Jesus and desired to be an aid for her little daughter afflicted with an unclean spirit. It did not matter to her that she and Jesus had differing religious affiliations. Nor did her gender deter her boldness. Might I suggest that it was more likely an asset? She had nothing to lose and everything to gain.

This unnamed woman had but one goal in mind: cure for her child, a girl so afflicted with a demon that her speech and hearing could be nothing less than impaired. She was a fortunate youngster, though. What she could neither speak nor seek for herself was spoken and sought by her mother, her hearing aid. As the story goes, Jesus begins with a delaying tactic, if not a refusal. "Let the children be fed first, for it is not fair to take the children's food and throw it to the dogs" (Mark 7:27).

What a strangely harsh response! This certainly does not sound like the good and gentle Jesus. Was Jesus testing the woman's intent and sincerity? Was he repeating what he had been so carefully taught in the synagogue? Was this a test for the incipient Marcan church, and ours, to measure our authenticity in light of our universality?

Whatever the reason, it was not going to dismay this mother from her stated mission. She boldly challenged Jesus with his own words. "Sir, even the dogs under the table eat the children's crumbs" (Mark 7:28). This Gentile woman became a hearing aid for Jesus. She helped the Rabbi, whose integration of the Torah was so profound that he was himself the Word of God, to hear God's call to cure her daughter.

Healing happened with her hearing aid.

The incident left its mark on Jesus. Soon after he returned to the Sea of Galilee in the region of the Decapolis, a deaf man with a speech impediment was brought to him. As unnamed as the woman, so was there an anonymous "they" who brought the man to Jesus and begged for his healing. Jesus responded with the courage of the Syrophoenician woman. His touch, sigh of compassion, and command "Be opened" became hearing aids for one who had been deaf. And everyone was astounded beyond measure.

Healing happened because Jesus was the deaf man's hearing aid.

In like manner, so are we called to be hearing aids for all who are deaf to the Word of God and mutely refuse response. In our healing presence, they can be touched. With our continued compassion, they will receive more than crumbs from God's table. At life's end, it will be clear that we had not lived in vain. In fact, our epitaphs will be identical, both as individuals and in community. Our mark on the world will bear these words,

"They have done everything well. The deaf hear, and the mute speak."

For Reflection and Discussion

- What words would you want on your epitaph? In what ways have you done everything well? Have the lives of others been transformed because of your presence?

Prayer

Dear God, so often, my hearing is impaired. Your words are garbled, your message mistaken, your credibility becomes flawed, and I remain incredibly ignorant. I ignore your call and refuse your invitation to grow. I need a hearing aid. God of my deafness, come to me. Bring into your light, life, and love by way of people who hear your words clearly and can both translate and interpret them for me. Let healing happen in my life because of them. Remember, O God, I am your child and it is not fair to throw the children's food to the dogs. Amen.

TWENTY-FOURTH SUNDAY IN ORDINARY TIME

ISAIAH 50:5–9; JAMES 2:14–18; MARK 8:27–35

The worst of times can be the best of times

Days and nights were marked by the passage of thermometer-bearing, blood pressure cuff-carrying, intravenous-poking hospital personnel. Persistent pain made time seem to stand still. Fear of the unknown crept subtly into my heart and head. It invaded my waking moments. I became anxious, worried, concerned. Every idea and concept I had thought, taught, preached, and believed about living in the "now" was being challenged. The precious grace of the present moment faded in the face of my fright. Possibilities, probabilities, questions filled all the spaces where faith had once reigned secure. It was, for me, the worst of times. It was also the best of times.

There I was, awaiting and then enduring unexpected surgery. Beyond that, I was informed that further hospitalization and surgery was in the offing. I was rendered weak when I had been so proudly strong. I was became unable to "do for myself" when I had always been able to manage. Dependent on others for my most basic needs, I felt totally out of control. Minute after minute, hour after hour, I was recipient rather than donor, being served, not serving. Even my "thank you's" were minuscule and whispered in pain.

I lay in my bed unable even to pray, a scary thought. I could not even seem to "offer up" the experience in solidarity with and empathy for all those whose sufferings far surpassed my own. Even the knowledge that others might need my pain to help them pull through their crises was insufficient to rouse me. All that held my attention was my own terrible vulnerability. All I could summon was the piercing hurt I found so difficult to bear.

Probing questions soon followed. Would I be accepted in my weakness by those who only knew me as the strong one? Would I be loved for who I am, even if I could not do as much as I had done previously? Did I love myself in my incapacity? Did I really love the "me I am" without having that love depend on what I did and could do? Would I have the patience to be, just to be, and know that "being" is good?

So often, so long, so reflectively, had I spoken and written of faith. It was the faith that I witnessed in people whose lives touched my own in myriad ways.

Now my turn had come. The words written in the letter of James became hauntingly vibrant. "What good is it, my brothers and sisters, if you say you have faith but do not have works? Can faith save you? If a brother or sister is naked and lacks daily food, and one of you says to them, 'Go in peace; keep warm and eat your fill,' and yet you do not supply their bodily needs, what is the good of that? So faith by itself, if it has no works, is dead" (James 2:14–17).

Now, it was I who was naked. I was the one robed with fragility, covered only by a hospital gown, vulnerable to the view of all. I was the one denied food and drink, dependent on the nutrients provided by tube and needle. Now I was being asked to practice the faith of receiving, trusting that dependency and vulnerability were open pathways to God, the God whose power is found in painfully passionate response.

I saw faith in action. As nurses, doctors, aides, loyal friends, loving parishioners cared for me, I was nourished. Laughter fed me, even when it hurt to laugh. Cards, letters, flowers, visits quenched my thirst for inclusion in the life I thought I had lost. I was sustained and encouraged by the loving admonitions to "take each day as it comes." I witnessed profound love offered to me in a land I could never again claim to be alien and strange.

It was, indeed, the best of times in the worst of times.

Although this experience happened years ago, it continues to rise to the surface of my consciousness. Because it was a turning point in my life, I clearly recall even names and dates despite the fact that I find it difficult to remember other occasions. Major surgery, followed by complications that brought me to death's door, also provided me with a wake up call. No longer could I consider life a "given." Instead, I began to appreciate each day as a treasured gift containing surprises I needed to unwrap with reverence.

There was more. Always, there will be more for me to learn of pain and powerlessness. I began to taste a small portion of God's banquet feast, a table set for all. My own experience made me see more concretely the frequency with which I had judged by human standards and not God's.

I never "thought" I had, but, there it was. I evaluated my life, and thus the life of others, by the human standard of productivity. There were tasks to be performed perfectly, goals to be set and met with success, work to be done on schedule, no matter what! Strength and control were admired, respected, and accepted as appropriate and virtuous. They are all very good objectives, no question. Yet, I had forgotten that the table of God is set in giving, not rebelling. It provides places for those who do not shield themselves from the buffets and spittings of real living.

Only now have I begun to understand the profundity of God's command to each of us, "If any want to become my followers, let them deny themselves and take up their cross and follow me" (Mark 8:34). The truth is I had been extremely selective regarding personal denial. I had denied myself only those things, situations, pleasures that I determined to be bearable pain. I had not denied my very self, the strong, proud, healthy self. Too fearful of failure, too scared to be trusting, I skirted that kind of sacrifice.

God knew I possessed, but had not fully used, a different sort of health. God's view is salubrious!

God's plea is simple. Love yourself. The request is that I love enough to cry out in supplication, to plead and pray to the God who loves me into life. It is a divine communication sent to all peoples everywhere.

God asks me, God asks you, God asks us, to deny our very selves. Self denial is the cross I must accept. Give up the false "me" I present to the world and be real. Be authentic and know that inauthenticity is sin. Masks are madness. Hang up the effigy I offer the world and let it burn in the Sonshine. Follow in the steps of Jesus. Suffer, stumble, fall, cry out in pain, and know, as never before, that God keeps the little ones safe. Know what it means to be brought low and be saved from myself. Know that we "walk before the Lord in the land of the living" (Psalm 116:9).

Ah, yes, it is indeed the best of times in the worst of times!

For Reflection and Discussion

- When has vulnerability brought you closer to God and what did you learn in the process? How have you allowed others to serve you when you would much rather have been serving them? In what personal ways have you experienced illness as a grace? How do you understand the words, "denying my very self"?

Prayer

Courteous God, be the foundation of my being. May I sit in you in true rest, stand in you in sure strength, and be rooted in you in endless love. Reveal yourself more to me so that I may know my true nature better and act as I truly am.

— "Night Prayer," from *All Will Be Well*

Twenty-fifth Sunday in Ordinary Time

Wisdom 2:12, 17–20; James 3:16–4:3; Mark 9:30–37

Made in the image of God who remains, lasts, and serves us all

The heart of Christian justice can be summarized in one sentence: "Whoever wants to be first must be last of all and servant of all" (Mark. 9:35). Before we can speak about or try to live justly we must experience what it means to be last, to be servant of all. For too long we have been carefully taught that those words indicated passivity and self-deprecation. They were transmitted as demands for us to be Casper Milquetoasts whose service begins and ends with our being no more or less than doormats. Certainly that is a service of some sort. Doormats are both helpful and welcoming. However, the service they render is not one that empowers either giver or receiver to be transformed.

The Scriptures do not portray Jesus as a passive man or one who constantly puts himself down as less than a good, worthy person. On the contrary, Jesus was in the "resurrection business." Life lived abundantly, experienced to the full, was his stated goal, for himself and those who followed him. To serve with authenticity is to accept with action the paradoxical and crucial reality that last is first.

Jesus lived, died, and rose from death believing the truth of that reality.

Parents and caregivers of all sorts learn this lesson early in life or suffer the pain of denying it. I hear my children complaining about the times that they cannot do what they wish to do because their children need tending or occupational duties call for their presence. They harbor regret regarding their decision to marry at what appears in retrospect to have been a young age. "Too early" marriages prevented the living of life, in their estimation. Children hampered carefree fun and frolic.

Frequently, I am in the same place. I also want to be first. The argument, whether spoken or kept hidden, revolves about who is more important. Sometimes, decisions are made erroneously because they emanate from the argument of importance. Children may be given too much liberty or too little opportunity because somebody has to be first in line of importance. Jobs may override life or get short shrift for the same reason.

At the opposite end of the spectrum, retirees announce that they are spending their children's inheritance. They have earned the right to do as they please; speak what they wish; be where they want and when they want. In other words, the belief is that later years end the cost of discipleship. Retirement is seen as relaxation from responsibility. Ending years bring with them the right to be the most important and to choose me, first. There is no indication of retirement or "me first-ness" in Scripture. In contradistinction, there is clear statement of lifelong commitment in the Gospel message: "Whoever wants to be first must be last of all and servant of all."

What, then, comprises the just life? Answers are not easily found, except through the process of trial and error, faith and trust. There are powerful clues, though. Mother Teresa certainly unearthed those signposts in her life. She accepted her call to be a physical presence with the poorest of the poor and remain servant of them all. She was constantly one of the least. Interestingly, her life among the unwashed and unwanted continued for at least ten years before it came to anyone's notice. Mother Teresa heard her own individual, personal call to remain last, to be servant. She followed it where she found herself, on India's crowded streets. Unlike the disciples who heard the words of Jesus, failed to understand them, and were afraid to question, Mother Teresa heard, possibly questioned, listened, learned, and lived the answer.

We can do the same. We can look closely at the way we spend our time, energy, talents, and money. We can prayerfully ask questions of God. We can attend to God's questions posed for us. "Those conflicts and disputes among you, where do they come from? Do they not come from your cravings that are at war within you?" (James 4:1).

We need to sit in silence with the questions, difficult though that may be. We need to be acutely honest with ourselves; be just with our assessment. Each of us alone and all of us together need to give ourselves time to listen to the responding voice of God. Perhaps it will come by way of a friend's request to have lunch. It might be the pastor's call to assist at a parish event. Maybe God will speak to us through the media where stories of injustice seem to be the main fare of each day. In grand fashion or tiny bits, the call to serve justly is everywhere, even in the church itself! Justice demands an active response to the statement, "It's just not right."

No one can tell us how, where, or when to respond. No one can evaluate the success or failure of our service. At the same time, a praying community certainly has enlightenment to offer, suggestions to make, challenges to place before us. Justice, for example, demands that children be welcomed. A praying community will notice whether or not children of all ages are welcome in its midst. Are the childish infirm brought to the center of our lives? Do we find joy in being children who laugh, play, and delight in life? Are we people who celebrate each moment and each person? Justice demands such a welcoming presence on this planet.

There is one other way to assess our life of justice. It is by way of those who seek always to be first, to be the most important, to be served rather than to serve. They will set a trap to ensnare the just ones whose pilgrimage is service. When we who choose the way of justice and service as our lifestyle are beset because of our determined pointing to and speaking out against injustices, we know that we are on the right track. When our gentleness and patience are tested, when our words are scrutinized for accuracy, we will know that we are, in deed and truth, among those who remain the last of all and the servant of all.

Obviously, this is not the life of the fainthearted or frivolous. It is a journey into the depths of peace where our sole consolation rests in blind faith. It is entry into a faith that opens our eyes and hearts to the core conviction that God will take care of us, for it is God who remains, lasts, and serves us all.

For Reflection and Discussion

- How do you serve others so that you will not be seen as "the star" or as a fulfillment of your drive for power and prestige? What ways can you find to listen, learn, and live the Gospel imperative to be last, to be the servant of all? When have you empowered others to be servers?

Prayer

Servant God, I come to you in humble acknowledgment that I have not always sought to serve others. I have also failed to accept the willing service offered to me. Instead, I seek to control situations and people. I look for that which "serves" me best, provides me with feelings of worth and power while denying others that same privilege. My pride is my downfall. For this I am sorry. I beg forgiveness of you, my Servant God, and of my brothers and sisters whom I have failed to serve as well as denied their gift of serving me. Amen.

TWENTY-SIXTH SUNDAY IN ORDINARY TIME

NUMBERS 11:25–29; JAMES 5:1–6; MARK 9:38–43, 45, 47–48

The sharing of seasoned saints

One of the first and most difficult lessons taught to each of us is the painful task of sharing. I do not put that in the past tense because the tutelage continues to the day we die. I hear my mother's voice mimicked in my own and repeated in that of my children as they command their own offspring to "Remember to share." I even find myself looking enviously at a perfect Manhattan or a luscious piece of cake that my mate has carefully husbanded and commanding, "Sharesies!"

I watch my little grandson share delightedly anything he has in abundance or does not appreciate but tightly grasp his last, favorite morsels for fear that sharing means losing. Pressed to charity, he measures carefully, gauging his own degree of "half" and pinches off a smidgen more for himself and less for his sister. I smile at the humanness of his actions. How many times have I "halved" more than my share of life's goodness? Whether it is a piece of cake or a parcel of ministerial service, it seems that we all find it difficult at worst and challenging at best to participate in the sharing commanded by those who would be seasoned saints.

Our church communities are no less watchful, frugal, or miserly. There seems to be a concretized sense of who is called and inspirited by God. We refrain from considering change unless it is ordained from on high. For years we have lived this way with no apparent ill effects. But, roiling beneath the pacific surface is an oceanic wave waiting to erupt. One might question its origin, but we need not look beyond the very words we proclaim in the Scriptures, the word of God, to discover the source of our angst and the secret of our animation.

We read in the Hebrew scriptures of Numbers "the Lord came down in the cloud and spoke to him (Moses), and took some of the spirit that was on him and put it on the seventy elders; and when the spirit rested upon them, they prophesied" (Numbers 11:25). When God spoke to Moses there may well have been a divine request that he share. Moses must have given his permission, else God would have had to override him and the story doesn't bear that evidence.

But, there is more to this apportioning than permission or division. The tale continues to speak of another separation. Eldad and Medad allowed the spirit to rest on them outside the tent. God's spirit and prophecy was shared in the unexpected, surprising site where they remained. Sacred space expanded to include the place where seasoned saints shared the mystery of divinity! And everyone ran to stop it. Even Joshua, son of Nun, assistant to Moses, and his chosen one, demanded the arrest of such audacity. Moses must have given his permission and enthusiastic approval with delight that God's generosity could be seen, given, and freely received.

Jesus perfected Moses' range of approbation. When Jesus heard that his disciples were trying to stop a man from casting out demons in his name simply because the man was not a follower, he responded with a different cease and desist order. "Do not stop him; for no one who does a deed of power in my name will be able soon afterward to speak evil of me" (Mark 9:39).

Let him go and see what happens! Share your gift and there will be a seasoning of saints!

When I reflect on the daily operations of any given church community, I see more people who resemble Joshua than Moses, myself included. The cry goes out for volunteers but the "best jobs" are already taken and held secure by those who are "chosen ones," self-appointed or otherwise. Spiritual direction is sought but authorized only if it occurs "inside the tent." Any prophecy that happens "in the camp of life" is suspect or ridiculed. Imprimaturs and nihil obstats hold prime importance. Truth is enclosed and encapsulated within the camp of orthodoxy. God's spirit is only allowed breath, and breadth, in certain places and under specific circumstances. There are very limited "sharesies" permitted! In the midst of such stinginess, Jesus issues a constant reminder, "Whoever is not against us is for us" (Mark 9:40).

I wonder what would happen if we really decided to make those words our personal and communal mission statement. Would we begin to realize that the largest of all stumbling blocks to the belief of the little ones, God's precious anawim, is our frugality? It is the hoarding of God's spirit and our own. When we limit God's generosity by confining personal sharing to those who are tented with us, we hang a millstone around our neck. We drag ourselves around, burdened by gifts we choose neither to impart nor accept. We forget that God's word is replete with wishes and warnings regarding the search, seizure, and sharing of treasure.

We are the five loaves and two fishes that will feed thousands, if only we bring ourselves to God and accept God's blessing. We are enough for God. Amply blessed, we can generously give, and be amazed at the abundant leftovers. We cannot bury our treasure in the field for fear of reprisal or imperfection without paying the price of jealous acquisition. To our wonderment, God would rather we risk giving the whole of our giftedness than to dig a hole for its safekeeping.

If we lay up treasure for the last days by denying treasure to those who are in need of it today, we lose the saltiness of life itself. Without seasoning, we are neither saints nor prophets.

Salt is good. Differences do not minimize faith. They do not undermine belief. Differences give voice and vigor to life with God. Minus the flavor found in encampments outside the tent, the insiders become staid and stagnant. They become obstacles to those whose vision does not match their own. It would be better for all of us who are "in-tent" on separation, division, and ecclesiastical measurement to excise our boundaries and enter life maimed by possibilities than to keep those borders intact and find ourselves in the unquenchable fire of self-imposed limitation.

God's command is simple and direct. "Have salt in yourselves and be at peace with one another" (Mark 9:49). Share magnanimously in the camps and tents of God's people. Welcome all who are not against Christ with the radical belief that they are for Christ.

Remember, each sharing empowers and enhances the seasoning of saints.

For Reflection and Discussion

- How does your stance on ecumenism help you to assess your views and the behavior of the Spirit's presence in unlikely places and people? What examples can you give to demonstrate the primary mission of evangelization as one that brings people to Christ rather than simply getting them into a church? In what ways did this reflection cause discomfort and questioning?

Prayer

God of all creation, Maker of the universe who is present everywhere, open my eyes and heart and mind to see you in unlikely places and people. Help me to understand that universality is not uniformity. Give me the grace to listen to those who live outside the tent of my life, my family, my culture, my educational background, my church. Let me have the wisdom to honor and revere their thoughts, to learn from their opinions, to communicate my own with charity, and to grow in the process. Amen.

Twenty-seventh Sunday in Ordinary Time

Genesis 2:18–24; Hebrews 2:9–11; Mark 10:2–16

Hardheartedness and the law

I am always amazed at the human capacity and instinct for separation. We categorize our budget items and alphabetize our filing systems. Our driver's licenses indicate gender, height, eye color, and race, putting each of us into identification boxes. Little children know instinctively they are being compartmentalized according to ability when they are put into groups euphemistically called Butterflies, Grasshoppers, and Tadpoles. Church people excise one Scripture passage from another in order to prove biases and cement opinions. And so it goes, on and on!

Our focus, if not emphasis, is on fracture rather than union. We seem to fear the vulnerability and perceived weakness of compassionate unity. Fear intensifies our focal point and diminishes understanding. The questions we ask become inquiries that seek to separate the licit from the illicit, no matter the circumstances, situations, or changes that might be mitigating factors. Without interest in the persons, only in the product, righteousness becomes rigidity and charity calcifies. Resulting laws, not resilient love, emerge from hardness rather than softness of heart.

This attitude is frequently attributed to the Scribes and Pharisees of Jesus' day. However, even the disciples seemed unable to stop themselves from putting people into categories. When parents brought their little children to Jesus in order that he might touch them, Jesus' followers spoke sternly to them. They were deciding who was to be admitted into Jesus' presence and who was to be kept at a distance, who was considered to be worth the time and effort and who was simply a pest!

How often have we, like those men of old, fallen into the trap of using questions to test one another, rather than to search sincerely for truth! With queries that contain hooks and underpinnings, we manipulate responses to suit our desires and substantiate the status quo. Our hardheartedness becomes both impermeable and impervious to change or reformation.

In this midst of this stultifying stubbornness, God's word determinedly pushes and probes its way into human life. It provides a radical reminder that we are no longer divided into male and female, young and old, learned and ignorant. Gone are any sorts of division. We humans are wedded to each other in the most primeval ways. Partners in a marriage of life, we are "no longer two, but one flesh. Therefore what God has joined together, let no one separate" (Mark 10:8–9).

When we remember that reality, all of life's experiences change dramatically. I experienced a vivid example of this "wedded life" when a major incident of inadequate communication caused a ruckus at the local firehouse. The chief, upon the advice of a financial officer but without informing the board of directors, placed an ad in the paper to hire a second full-time firefighter. Technically and legally, there was no problem with his action. Both chief and financial officer had responded lawfully. The difficulty lay with the fact that each person involved in the process had a different understanding and interpretation of the implications of that decision.

Feelings ran high and hot. Old, unresolved issues surfaced and unhealed wounds opened. A special board meeting was called to give everyone an opportunity to speak their truth. Individuals arrived separately with personal opinions, biases, and tightly held agenda. A certain distance was retained as each took a seat and the gavel sounded. However, this "church" community also began, as it always did, with prayer to God for wisdom and guidance. And that made all the difference.

In lieu of an ordinary business meeting, there was heartfelt liturgy. Each man and woman pronounced their belief and gave voice to their sense of exclusion. In the process, the total truth was slowly unearthed amidst apologies for misspoken words and unspoken questions. All was resolved, and celebrated in the eucharist of ice cold watermelon shared at a picnic table as stories were told of the old days.

Separation is not a viable option when God is a member of the wedding party! No one will be permitted to split our union, not even one of our own rank and file. The potency of that union is such that we leave past prejudices with comparative ease, just as husband and wife leave their mothers and fathers to join each other in the stability of a new life. We begin to realize the value of being like little children in the family of God, children whose awareness of dependency and interdependency is both powerful and empowering. We are recognizing that imitation of Jesus needs to incorporate a Christlike indignation when we are confronted with situations or people whose intent and purpose is to separate us one from the other. Our childlike approach to divinity commands the comfort and challenge of a close-knit union with God and each other. We cannot allow either dismissal or denial of our very selves. We must not permit the dysfunction of disjunctive dismemberment!

This is not to say that differences disappear. Nor does it mean we are to become robots marching in lock step with unthinking motion. More to the point, it is to say we are incorporating into our being, both corporate and individual, the reality that "the one who sanctifies and those who are sanctified all have one Father" (Hebrews 2:11).

We are the family of God, whole and holy in God's sight.

With hearts softened by this familial relationship, our shalom is true discipleship. Peace emanates from the discipleship which encourages unity and dispels dissension. True discipleship also empowers the communication and sharing of dissenting voices, not for the sake of dissent but for the revelation of truth. True discipleship opens minds and hearts to hear God's voice speaking to us and about us in these words, "This at last is bone of my bones and flesh of my flesh. These ones shall be called Godlike, for out of my divinity have they been created."

In God, and in the people of God, there is no room for the hardheartedness that evokes law.

For Reflection and Discussion

- Give examples of times when you have "hard-heartedly" used legalism to resolve a challenging difficulty. When have you, instead, evoked compassionate love? What does it mean to you to be described as a person who is called Godlike?

Prayer

God has joined us, each to each,
In a union that cannot be breached.
Within this partnership, tried and true,
I find who I am in companionship with you.
I learn to respect, honor, and revere
All that you are, whether hidden or clear.
I come to find a treasure trove of goodness and light
Where once had been but shadowy night.
And so, I pray, with God at our side,
Nevermore from each other shall we hide;
But, always be open and honest and true
Children of God, that's me and you! Amen.

Sadly rich; richly sad

It was a hot, dusty, dry day. The air was still, so still that the sounds of locusts seemed to pierce the atmosphere with a shrill cacophony. Palpable, the heat was almost visible. Certainly its odor could be detected in the sweaty stickiness endured by both humans and beasts. It was the kind of day when one would prefer to find and enjoy the comparative coolness of a pond or fountain than to endure the suffocating embrace of sunshine. Even the questionable shade of a palm tree would be an appreciated respite.

Despite the enervating drain of the day's radiance, plans were still in progress. They were to set out on a journey. Heat, fatigue, thirst, and hunger were not going to deter them. The journey was too important. This was not travel for the sake of travel. It was a movement of the total person. It was a voyage of mind, heart, and body meant to clarify priorities, force choices, command decisions, and elicit responses. This was a trek into becoming.

Soul and spirit, joints and marrow would be penetrated and divided. Reflections and thoughts of the heart would be judged. Not the activity of a day but the action of a lifetime, this journey was an invitation to continuing growth. All those who were readying themselves were instinctively aware of its challenge. This was to be a pilgrimage that would reveal the truth and beauty of life. Ambivalence was tangible. Everyone was both eager and fearful, excited and questioning. Most of all, they were willing to risk the comfort and security of the life they knew in order to walk the way of the "yet-to-be-known." Letting go of what they possessed in order to travel lightly, freely, unencumbered was a gamble they dared.

Among the travelers was one who unnerved the others. They watched him with grave intensity. His call to be a journeyer seemed to come from depths they could only imagine. He possessed an uncanny awareness of himself and the heat and his surroundings. With acute self-consciousness, he knew precisely what he needed to relinquish in order to travel freely. A sensitive person, he felt the pain of those losses quite deeply. Yet he exuded a certain peace and love. People paid attention, drawn to him as if by a powerful magnet. Without any effort or overture on his part, he was the center of every group, the star attraction of every community, the awe-inspiring leader of every gathering. Because of his charisma people often came to ask questions and seek answers. They also came to mock and deride him. His was not an easy life but it was a dynamic one.

No one was surprised when, on the very day he was setting out on a journey, a man came running up, knelt down before him and asked, "Good Teacher, what must I do to share in everlasting life?" (Mark 10:17). Obviously attracted to the uniqueness of this pilgrim, the questioner was eager to share the man's secret for deeper living. He wanted to discover the formula for the peace-filled love he saw emanating from this Rabbi. Excited, he could not constrain himself. Walking would not suffice. He ran to the pilgrim, to kneel before him in homage, a gesture that momentarily called a halt to the journey.

Neither dismayed nor annoyed with the interruption, the pilgrim was immediately gracious to his questioner. However, he did not respond with a series of commands, formulae for successful living. He only reminded the seeker that the journey into life begins in one's own heart. It starts with the wisdom and authenticity found in our truest self. "You know the commandments," he said, and then listed them to make certain there was clear communication.

"The commandments," the man eagerly replied, "I have kept since my childhood." At this, the journeyer smiled. His statement to the questioner was not one regarding his keeping of the commandments. It was one involving his knowing them. Deliberately or not, the point was missed. Still, he did not chastise the young man. Instead, he accepted him with love, a love that saw deeply into the man's desires to do more. He also knew that those desires could be burdensome. Perhaps they would be too difficult to carry on the journey he was about to ask the man to walk. The pilgrim fervently hoped his love alone would be enough to encourage the man to be more, not just to do more. He wanted to grab him, keep him close, and convince him to join in the journeying. But he knew he could not. He could not intrude on freedom and call it discipleship.

The pilgrim waited, for just a brief moment, before responding to the initial question posed. The interlude was deliberate. He had to give his questioner a chance to look directly at him and feel deep, deep love. To be loved, to feel love and be embraced by it, was absolutely essential. The journey ahead was too important to be hampered by lack of love. It was too deeply compassionate and filled with the painful joy of suffering to be traveled by a minimalist.

So, looking at him with love, the journeyer went on to say, "You lack one thing; go and sell what you own, and give the money to the poor; you will have treasure in heaven; then come, follow me.' When he heard this, he was shocked and went away grieving, for he had many possessions" (Mark 10:21–22).

Incarnate love offered this rich man the one thing he did not yet possess. But he could not own it, no matter how great his desire, because it would involve dispossessing himself of all he held dear.

The commandment was too consuming for him to hear. He wanted so much. Proffered love could not override his attachments, the things with which he had filled his life, the things that owned him. He was willing to give up so little. Immeasurably saddened, possessed by his dejection and suddenly conscious of his own enslavement, he could not risk the freedom of letting go.

The journeyer, in turn, was also sorrowful. To see the man's sadness hurt him. He ached with the pain of knowing his love was not enough to impel free choice. He wanted so much to stay there, to try again, to offer more powerful persuasion. But he knew he could not. The journey was vitally important. He had done all he could do. He had invited the man with all the force of love and hope. Now he must be on his way, knowing that the man would live in sadness and he in sorrow. He felt the agony of his disappointment as well as his compassion and gave them both as gift to God saying, "For God all things are possible" (Mark 10:27).

Belief flooded his being. His sorrow was edged with joy. Holding in his heart the memory of the sadly rich man, the richly sad journeyer began his long trek home.

The story has just begun.

For Reflection and Discussion

- What feelings are generated in you when you read this demanding passage from the Markan gospel? What "wealth" or "riches" own, control or possess you? When have you dared to ask Jesus, "Good Teacher, what must I do to inherit eternal life?"

Prayer

Repeat these lines from the Prayer of St. Ignatius four or five times as a mantric prayer. Then sit in silence to absorb their meaning.

Take, Lord, receive all I have and possess
Give me only your love; that's enough for me.

Do the crime and pay the time

My son-in-law Rob is a corrections officer in a maximum security facility. The work has both taken a toll on him and been a gift for him. Because he has seen the value in demands for discipline, and the harsh lesson discovered in its absence, he teaches his children the concept of taking responsibility for their action or inaction as he smilingly states his favorite expression: "Do the crime and pay the time." Obviously, Rob is not speaking of profoundly criminal activity in his declaration, just the typically human tendency to avoid duty and opt for delight, to look for acclamation while ignoring accountability. Although his children—my grandchildren—are yet young, they understand their father's sense of commitment and its cost.

Audrey must adjust her schedule to accommodate a paper route. When she is unable to do her job, her Dad asks her what she wants. If her desire is to go on vacation, to dance in her recital, to spend an overnight with family, she must find and secure her substitutes, as well as pay them for their time. If not, her reputation and "job security" are at stake. Before he can watch the television program he loves, Justin knows that toys are to be picked up and put away. If not, they will be packed away to be given to a child who has less and would appreciate the gift. Little by little, each one learns that "wants" have prices attached to them. Admittedly, these are hard lessons but necessary steps toward the children's development into mature adults.

I can hear God speaking to us with Rob's loving logic. Certainly, Jesus of Nazareth clearly informed his disciples of a similar truth. When the thunderingly overt sons of Zebedee, James and John, asserted their wishes, "Teacher, we want you to do for us whatever we ask of you. Grant us to sit, one at your right hand and one at your left in your glory" (Mark 10:35, 37), Jesus responded, "You do not know what you are asking. Are you able to drink the cup that I drink, or be baptized with the baptism that I am baptized with?" (Mark 10:38).

If one chooses to "do the crime" of seeking the glory of discipleship, then one must also "do the time" of a lifestyle that suffers with love.

It is as simple, and as radically profound, as that!

There is no easy path to glory. It is the way of the cross, the way of Christ. The road is paved with the crushing blows of unwarranted oppression and damaged by the perversion of justice and the powerful presence of injustice. Like our ancestral prophets, we will face being cut off from the land of the living, led like lambs to slaughter, stricken for the transgressions of others. Despite the fact that we have done no violence, violence will be meted out to us. Through it all, though we might well have shouted our anguish and proclaimed the unfairness of it all, we will be silent. Our silence becomes a disturbing quiet that offers no explanations, absorbs the noise of deceit, and proclaims the potency of God's will.

Do the crime of discipleship; live a lifetime of crucifying and redemptive love!

Some may be upset with labeling discipleship as crime. It is a startling concept and a scary one. Yet, discipleship, in the minds of many who would choose facile fidelity, is both criminal and insane. After all, disciples are asked to surrender themselves, in entirety. Followers of Christ are led along a paradoxical route where death is life, afflictions are salvific, and service is a potent potion. This would appear to be a crime against human nature's desire for pleasure, power, and prestige. In a world where the lifestyles of the rich and famous make headlines and television programs, those who choose poverty and powerlessness in the name of Christ are oddities at best and idiots at worst.

Do the crime of discipleship and pay the price of a lifetime!

While I ponder that thought, yet another comes to me. Granted the outrageousness of James' and John's statement, it was also amazingly authentic. They knew what they wanted, expressed it overtly, and expected a positive response. However naive or, perhaps, ignorant their request, they were honest men with honest desires. Jesus responded positively to that authenticity. He made clear the extent to which their intent would lead them and asked if they were ready for the consequences of their command. Interestingly, the men were not reprimanded for their desire. Nor were they judged to be greedy, audacious, or proud. Only a simple remark, "You do not know what you are asking," preceded Jesus' explanatory and responsive question. "Are you able to drink the cup that I drink, or be baptized with the baptism that I am baptized with?" (Mark 10:38).

Honest men with honest desires faced an equally honest assessment of the price tag for glory, answered directly and without hesitation. They got more than they asked for and less than they thought. Jesus gifted them with the opportunity to drink from his cup of passion and be baptized into the sacrament of his sacrifice. Positions of glory were not his to give. And yet, they did not turn their backs on him. They were willing to pay the price of a lifetime because they had chosen the crime of discipleship. Understood or not, they opted to have the potential to serve rather than to possess the power of being served.

It would be nice to have the story end here with a neat conclusion and a discernibly tidy moral. However, like most tales of humanity, there were and are complications. Anger reared its ugly head among the other ten followers. Like most of us who timidly hang back, not daring to chance being reprimanded and waiting to see what will happen to those who do speak up, the remaining apostles did not like the fact that Jesus said nothing to reprove the brothers for their audacity. Nor did they appreciate the implication that James and John might be well rewarded for their outspokenness. I suspect they were even more upset with their own cowardly silence, and surprised that it was not praised as noteworthy!

James and John wanted to be great and said so. The others were equally desirous but kept a pretense of humble silence. Jesus saw through the subterfuge and labeled it. "Whoever wishes to become great among you (and they all did!) must be your servant, and whoever wishes to be first among you (and we all do!) must be the slave of all. For the Son of Man came not to be served but to serve, and to give his life as a ransom for many" (Mark 10:43–45).

There it is in a nutshell. The cost of discipleship is crucial. It is a lifetime and lifestyle of crucifixion, of pouring oneself out for others, of being numbered among the transgressors, bearing their sins, carrying their infirmities, and making intercession for them.

It is a crime if we do not accept the call. We'll have the time of our lives, when we do!

For Reflection and Discussion

- What kind of "time" have you done for the "crime" of discipleship? When have you opted for delight and neglected duty, refusing to postpone pleasure in order to serve? What advice would you give to someone who is seeking to be at the right hand of the Lord?

Prayer

Dear God, in your endless friendship thank you for being patient with me. Help me to be patient with myself. Let me see my contrariness as leading me closer to your love and peace. Thank you for your presence in the midst of my disquiet which I know will be turned into true beauty and endless love.

—From *All Will Be Well*, Ave Maria Press

THIRTIETH SUNDAY IN ORDINARY TIME

JEREMIAH 31:7–9; HEBREWS 5:1–6; MARK 10:46–52

The continuing adventure of taking a second look

Lately, when I read the story of Bartimaeus, I picture my grandchildren hiding their faces behind outstretched hands so that they will avoid seeing scary sights on television, videos, or in the world of nature that surrounds them. Once in a while they will spread their fingers slightly and temporarily, just long enough to glimpse what they fear. Immediately, the fingers are compressed again to form a solid barrier between their fright and their faith. While they are making the sight go away, they try hard to believe the scare will disappear along with it.

Adults act similarly. Usually we use words and phrases, not fingers, to dispel what we refuse to see. "Don't go down that road!" we say. Or, "Do I really need to know about this?" What we mean is that we prefer being blind to seeing what may cause us sorrow. We would rather opt to avoid and deny reality than to affirm and deal with it. Fearing the responsibility involved with sight, we choose the paralysis of blindness and the pleasure of blissful ignorance.

Strangely enough, the choice propels us into yet another phenomenon. Apparently content with our own lack of vision and light, we are determined to deny sight to those who seek it. Like the Markan disciples, we sternly order the blind who eagerly cry for sight to silence their desires. Perhaps subconsciously, we have a sense that their sightedness will encumber our blindness and cause us pain. So our stern message is, "Stay as you are, where you are! Do not become a bother to us."

Thank goodness, Jesus doesn't view life as imperfectly as we do. His command calls us to approach him with our needs, our very selves. His desire is to give us sight, but only if that is our wish as well.

Jesus knows the power and price of vision. In his human journey, he learned to see clearly and precisely what was, what is, what could be. His experience with family, friends, disciples, outcasts, enemies, and the curious crowds that followed him taught him to see deeply into human hearts and view their most private attitudes. Jesus' life, spent traveling the roads of Palestine, provided him with an expansive point of view.

No one was considered to be out of his range of vision. No matter their status or lack thereof, their gender, educational background, or life experience, people were worthy of his attention. However, he did seem to pay special heed to those who sought redemption. Anyone who requested assistance in achieving profound change immediately commanded his concentration. And it often seemed that the louder and more persistent the cry for help, the more quickly Jesus responded. It never mattered to him that others thought differently with far more narrow a perspective than he. Nor did it matter that his response would be a contradictory one. In fact, he countermanded his disciples' dismissal of Bartimaeus by calling the blind man forth. The invitation gave both disciples and beggar a new opportunity to see and, pointedly, to see again.

Life with Jesus is the continuing adventure of seeing again.

To live a godly existence is to take a second look at everyone and everything, beginning with my very own self. When I do that, I have discovered, two things happen. My first reaction is to recoil at the sight. Applying what is revealed to me, either by my own admission or the observation of others, causes me to cringe because my first sight is critical and frequently negative. My husband suggests that it would have been better for me to have presented a Scripture lesson without mentioning a specific denominational stance. I hear "You failed!" My feelings are bruised, my ego is shattered, and I become defensive.

However, with a second look, a second response takes shape. I become much more calm. I hear, "Your audience would be more responsive if the presentation did not always include limited examples." Taking the information to heart, I become more aware of my own biases and shortcomings. I change.

All of this happens when I am adventuring into the surprises to be found in taking a second look and regaining true sight.

With regained sight, life is renewed and I am both reinvigorated and empowered to revitalize my companion pilgrims on faith's journey. Together we ask God to save the people, the faithful remnant which gives us hope. As we make our plea, the scales continue to fall from our eyes. The cataracts that had prevented each and all of us from seeing God's people have been extracted. Clearer vision now allows us to see what had always been but had not been recognized. God "gathers them (and us) from the farthest parts of the earth, among them the blind and the lame, those with child and those in labor, together; a great company. With weeping they shall come, and with consolations I (God) will lead them back" (Jeremiah 31:7–9).

Renewed sight is such a relief! I do not have to worry about who is in the motley crowd. That is God's concern. All I need to know is that my vision not only includes this nondescript remnant but gives me the ability to deal gently with them. My renewed sight reveals my allegiance to them and my membership among them. I am among the weak, ignorant, "wayward-yet saved" sinners who comprise God's people. I am one of them and they are part of me. We are inseparably brothers and sisters, sons and daughters, begotten by God and called to be God's priestly people.

Our commonality is a unique unction. It calls us to deeper union, challenges us to profound commitment, and critiques the clarity of our sight. When we journey together as persons in community, both our individuality and the community we share is enlightened. What I fear to do alone, I gain faith to achieve with others. What God's gathered people find impossible, single-minded prophets urge into possibility. Each helps the other to discover what we really want and need. Each of us prays with the other, "My Teacher, let me see again." Individually and collectively, we will hear the words of Jesus, our brother and companion: "Go; your faith has made you well."

Then, like Bartimaeus, we will follow Jesus on the Way, the venture of a lifetime, the continuing adventure of seeing again.

For Reflection and Discussion

- What do you think and feel about this statement: "The most painful act that the human can perform is the act of seeing. It is in that act of seeing that love is born" (Anthony De Mello, SJ). When have you dared to ask God to give you sight? What happened? If you have never asked, what is holding you back?

Prayer

God of my blindness, hear my plea
I want to know; I want to see
The universe as you observe it, with clarity,
And treat all who reside here with infinite charity
The task is more than I can bear or do
Unless it is accomplished hand-in-hand with you.
So, give me sight, but do it gently
And give me patience to see intently
All that you are and all that you wish
For me to be in eternal bliss.
Amen.

THIRTY-FIRST SUNDAY IN ORDINARY TIME

DEUTERONOMY 6:2–6; HEBREWS 7:23–28; MARK 12:28–34

The gainful losses of a divine life

I come from a long line of "*abundanza* apostles." With an Italian heritage, all of us tend to live long, enjoy much, laugh loudly, argue boldly, shriek joyously, weep copiously, but not frequently. Generally, we are larger than life. If we do nothing, we embrace life and gift it with abundant pleasure.

With the passage of each year, I also find that I am frequently participating in the paradoxical services that pronounce death as they celebrate life. These are ultimate moments when friends, acquaintances, and family alike are called to ponder the losses and gains of a divine life. As a result, I often cogitate over what I'd like done at my own funeral liturgy. Though my choices change with circumstances, I return to Isaiah's magnificently consoling declaration. "On this mountain the Lord of hosts will make for all peoples a feast of rich food, a feast of well-aged wines, of rich food filled with marrow, a feast of well-aged wines strained clear" (Isaiah 25:6).

I revel in the promise contained in those words. They provide perspective for my spiritual myopia. They transform deep, dark valleys experienced during my faith journey into temporary weigh stations, incredible rest stops of re-creation, as I travel toward my eternal mountaintop. All that I had considered to be loss in my life can now be seen as gain. Conversely, the "gains" are now perceived as illusory and falsely golden. More than that, all is *Abundanza*!

In fact, I begin to realize with astonishment that the valleys are more than purposeful. They are essential to understanding and attaining the profundity of godly paradox: the upside-down mountain whose peak pierces deeply into our innermost being. It is the grace found in "deep down things," in the words of Gerard Manley Hopkins.

This is the apex upon which God destroys the shrouds we cast on ourselves and others. This is where death is swallowed up and life is resurrected. Here is the place to discover that "the Lord God will wipe away the tears from all faces" (Isaiah 25:8). It is in the valleys of life that revelations occur. These are revelations celebrated on and shouted from mountaintops so that their echoes can be heard across chasms and abysses, and travel up and down the slopes to permeate with hope what would otherwise be valleys of despair. These are the places that fill us with the flowing milk and honey of divine surprises that multiply before we can ever deplete them.

Through them we learn this God is the one for whom we have waited. Here is the God who enters life's losses and turns them into gains, bringing us carefully into divinity's land of milk and honey. This is the God who demands and commands total commitment, who seeks the entirety of our life, love, heart, soul, understanding and strength. This is the God whose emission of love is endless.

God's expectation is our corresponding love, the passion and compassion with which we love ourselves and others with divine endlessness! Wise persons recognize, believe, and live the reality that there is no commandment greater than this! It is more important, by far, than all the burnt offerings and sacrifices we might proffer. It is the way we continue to learn and express the heavenly promise that wipes away all tears from all faces. It is the Way of the Messiah. There is no doubt this way leads inexorably to valleys with inverted heights and crosses with splinters. To think otherwise is to be an obstacle in the path of the grace found deep down things. It is to love self more than God. It is to lead more than follow, to set our mind on human things rather than those of divinity. It is to be far from the dominion of God.

Refusal to hear is already deafness. Avoidance of sight is its own blindness. We are called to be people who deny ourselves so that we might be empowered to take up the cross God has prepared for us and be strengthened for our walk with the God of heights and depths, gains and losses.

For years, I have restricted my caloric intake during the day when I know I am going to enjoy a nice evening meal with friends. My denial was and is a practical one. If I am nothing, I am the quintessential, daily dieter! However, I am now realizing that meal planning also has spiritual connotations and ramifications. If it makes sense on a physical level to prepare myself for the enjoyment of what is to come by initial restriction, how much more essential is it to act similarly on a spiritual plane? The emptying of spiritual wants, like that of bodily desires, is not being done for its own sake, but as a necessary element to allow fulfillment. Lighter fare during the days of one's life gives rise to the marvelous banquet feast awaiting our evening enjoyment.

Anticipation cools desert heat and gives hope to despairing days. Eating lightly makes traveling easier and intensifies expectancy. It allows us to be more aware of feelings and sensations. As we come into contact with our own "lacks" and losses, we become more compassionate toward the inadequacies suffered by others. In turn, looking forward grows into a pleasurable experience that is integrated into the present moment, not separated from it.

What is "lost" in the mountains of disappointment, disillusionment, discouragement, and desolation, is gained in the valleys of courage, conviction, companionship, and creativity. God will attend to those shrouded mountaintops by wiping away our tears and swallowing up the death we find there. God will overpower all the enemies we fight within the boundaries of our own weaknesses and failures. God will make us alive, again and again. God will reveal the hope to be found in hopelessness and the saving graces hidden in great suffering. God will lead us from false heights to true depths. All we need do is to get behind the God who saves.

Follow the Leader God. Revel in the wonders waiting for us. Find joy in the gainful losses of a divine life.

For Reflection and Discussion

- List one or two concrete ways in which you might be more loving this week. In your experience, how has love's vision allowed you to see new beginnings and giant possibilities? When has loving meant great sacrifice to you? How was that kind of giving redemptive for you as well as the recipient?

Prayer

Courteous Lover, thank you for your presence throughout the day. Help me to see that everything leads to you and that you lead me toward the bliss you wish me to enjoy. Let me share your love with my neighbors. May they see how your courtesy lifts me up and may they sense in me your love for all creatures.

— All Will Be Well

THIRTY-SECOND SUNDAY IN ORDINARY TIME

1 KINGS 17:10–16; HEBREWS 9:24–28; MARK 12:38–44

Deadly fear or delightful faith

A tiny child stands, almost steadily, on wobbly legs. Only recently has crawling been relinquished as the sole means of mobility. Tightly, he grasps a chair's edge for support. He "holds on for dear life," we say. Smiling, encouraging parents stand a short, but scary, distance away. "Come on," is the gentle call. "Come on. Come to Daddy and Mommy. Don't be afraid." The teetering almost-toddler thinks a moment and then lets go. He lets go of all he had held onto, for dear life. Stumblingly but purposefully, he walks for the first time.

A little preschooler climbs, step by step, higher and higher, to the top of the playground's longest slide. Looking down from dizzying heights, she sees her mother waiting at the slide's end. "Let go," her mother urges. "I'll be here to catch you. Don't be afraid." The youngster waits for one interminably long moment, sits down at the top of the slide, squeezes shut her eyes just long enough to calm herself. Then, she lets go and zips down the slide with astonished, openmouthed glee!

School-bound youngsters, from kindergarten through college, fearfully anticipate the terrors of the unknown. With great anxiety, they contemplate the impending "dangers" of quizzes, tests, examinations of all sorts. Brains are crammed full of information while stomachs jump with nervousness. Whether the task is as simple as reciting the alphabet or as complicated as understanding higher math, the whole person is on edge with expectation and fear. Will I be asked the questions I am prepared to answer? Will I pass or fail? Will I be accepted or rejected, praised or admonished, rewarded for my efforts or punished for my deficiency? In the midst of it all, the nurturing parent gives a hug and says, "You'll do all right. Don't be afraid!"

Days, months, years go by. We are no longer taking our first baby steps, or sliding down a great, long playground slide, or awaiting a school exam. But, the fears are still part of our life. Sometimes, perhaps too often, they exert an overwhelmingly powerful influence on our thoughts, and subsequently on our actions. Sometimes, fear looms so large that we are paralyzed by it. We render ourselves incapable, unable to be, do, act, think, or even to care.

Afraid to fail and afraid to succeed, we remain stuck in the mire of mediocrity. Cowering, we can neither challenge nor be challenged; give nor receive. Choosing, changing, moving, growing, becoming—all are terrors at night and dreaded by day. We fear rejection, reprisal, alienation, loneliness, suffering, aging, death. We are afraid of hurting a relationship, of losing what little we have, of being ignored, of horrible things happening. We fear ourselves. We fear others. We fear God. Fear. Fear. Fear!

All of us must face the fact that we do have our experiences, whether frequent or seldom, of that painful emotion. In those dark silences the words of Scripture tug, gently but urgently, at our hearts. In the scary stillness, we hear God speaking a parental encouragement, "Do not be afraid!" Do not let this human feeling fill the senses so that paralysis—emotional, physical, spiritual, or psychological—takes place. Do not allow fear to become the lord of life. Pray, instead, into the fearfulness. Enter the very depth of the worst fear. Face it squarely. Admit to the God who loves us as we are, the God whom we love as best we can, that we are afraid!

Ask God to "protect us in (not from) the burdens and challenges of life." Ask God to "shield our minds from the distortion of pride and enfold our desire with the beauty of truth." Ask God. Ask, not so that we will be relieved of fear, but that we will deepen our faith and "become more aware of God's loving design and more willingly give our lives in service to all" (quotes from the Opening Prayer B. Ask and be ready to receive divine encouragement. Do not be afraid!

I find it interesting that God does not say "I will take away your fear." Then I remember the toddler's unsteadiness and tight grasp. I remember the tiny girl on a tall slide. I remember all the "first days" of my life. And I remember my own parents standing by. They knew they could not do it for me. They knew I had to learn on my own, making my own mistakes and learning from them. In turn, I watched with similar, heart-pounding powerlessness as my own children, followed by my grandchildren, went through identical terrors.

Life consists in giving, not taking away. God does not take away. We are left free to give our fears to God or keep them as invisible fences to prevent our escape into vitality. God even leaves us free to give fearfully with scant faith, or generously with greater faith than we believe we have. No matter when or how or why, God simply says, "Do not be afraid!"

And then God waits. God waits with outstretched arms ready to catch, hold, and hug us as we take our first baby steps. God waits at the bottom of that long, tall slide of becoming, ready to scoop us up and rejoice with us in the happiness we find in trying. God waits as we encounter all the tests, challenges, and examinations that are part and parcel of living and learning sanctity. God waits, saying, "You'll do all right. Do not be afraid!"

Our waiting God loves us all the time. Time after time, incident upon incident, we learn that God loves us more than we know and more than we can imagine. Slowly, in the warmth and weight of God's love, we begin to lose our "fear of disturbing a comfortably fixed pattern and a fixed routine."

God waits until the day we are ready to take a giant leap into profound faithfulness. When we are ready, God repeats the divine encouragement and promise. God makes sure that we hear it. "Do not be afraid. The jar of meal will not be emptied, and the jug of oil will not fail until the day the Lord sends rain on the earth" (1 Kings 17:13–14). Having reminded us, God repeats what was asked of the widow of Zarephath and the poor widow of the Markan gospel. God asks us to give, not from our surplus wealth but from our want, from all that we have to live on. God asks for our trust. God requires our belief in the divine promise.

Ultimately, God asks us to give all we have. It won't kill us. It will give us life. Why are we so afraid to respond?

For Reflection and Discussion

- Describe an incident, your own or that of another, where fear was dismissed by faith, where you took a chance on God and deepened your life. In what ways can you be Elijah for someone who has little to give? What feelings are aroused in you when you hear the words about the widow in the Gospel, "She, out of her poverty has put in everything she had, all she had to live on."

Prayer

Dear God, I am scared. It is hard to trust that my poverty is your abundance. It is hard to believe that I will not be left empty, helpless, vulnerable, and impoverished. I do not want to let go and ride the high slide of life in love. My intellect tells me that you are not just waiting at the bottom, you are riding with me. But, my innards quake with fear. So, I give you that poverty, the poorness of my faith, the last smidgeon of fear. Take it, my God, and replace it with courageous trust. Let me know in my heart that the jar of my faith and the jug of my hope will never run dry. Amen.

Thirty-third Sunday in Ordinary Time

Daniel 12:1–3; Hebrews 10:11–14, 18; Mark 13:24–32

Preparing is to be prepared

The day was gray and somewhat forbidding. Some would say "No one in her right mind would be walking the beach." Yet, walk I did. Faster and faster, I pounded the hard sand trying to dispel the painful feelings that were overtaking me. I nearly broke into a run when I heard the sea speaking. Roaring, rolling breakers shouted, "Be prepared. Beware, keep alert; for you do not know when the time will come. You know not the day nor the hour. You know not when the Son of Man is coming." In my terror I looked around and saw doomsday signs surrounding me.

I noticed shells broken by trampling feet. They had already been worn thin by the ceaseless movement of the waters and were eaten through with holes. Marine predators had preceded human ones. I walked past trees whose roots were laid bare to the ravages of nature. Sea, sun, and sand had taken their toil. Flotsam and jetsam clung precariously to one tree's naked rootedness, a tree that refused to give up its existence, no matter how slender it was. I saw the corks, bottles, and beer cans that spoke of careless people. These were the ones who used everything and everyone to satisfy personal needs and pleasures, then threw away the remains. Carelessly, they never gave a second thought or stopped for another glance to see if anyone would come along to pick up the remnants. It was of no consequence to them. Only the sea would roar its anguish and carry away life's forgotten traces.

There were a few hardy, perhaps obstinate, people sitting in beach chairs. They were far enough removed from the scene to be oblivious to the plight I had witnessed. Chattering mindlessly, they traded bits and pieces of everyday trivia, the sound bytes that preoccupied their days. Never did they see what I saw. Shattered shells, bared roots, broken creation remained invisible to eyes blinded by affluence. Never did they hear the angry roar of an outraged sea screaming her warning, spewing her wrath in the crashing foam that coated the shoreline with bubbles of despair. "But about that day or hour no one knows, neither the angels in heaven, nor the Son, but only the Father. Beware, keep alert; for you do not know when the time will come" (Mark 13:32–33).

No one listened. No one heard. No one seemed to care.

Suddenly, a gentler, a more determinedly persistent, sound whispered its way through the crashing surf. At first I could scarcely hear it. The roar of the breakers was so loud. But, the whisper inched its way into my heart-calming my fear of impending doom. The whisper gave me hope. I even had hope that the deafened beach chair folk would somehow open their ears long enough to pay attention to it too. The whisper I heard was the fluttery voice of little waves as they tentatively kissed the shore before the pounding breakers crashed and dashed their way upon the sand. Quietly, they spoke to me. "Be preparing. Keep on trying. Don't give up because the way looks dark or the task seems impossible. Be preparing. The end is not yet here. There is always hope."

Just then I noticed that I was not alone at the water's edge. Sandpipers scampered past. Hearing the message, they continued to poke the sand for their coquina meal. They had heard the roaring waves, but listened more intently to the fluttery sounds, and kept right on doing what they were doing. Little ghost crabs also heard and raced across the sand dunes, stopping along the way to burrow their way home. In the distance, seagulls followed fishing boats, dipping into the sea to make a meal of the discarded catch.

I heard, too. Attentively, I took to heart the psalmist message, "I keep the Lord always before me; because he is at my right hand I shall not be moved. Therefore, my heart is glad, and my soul rejoices; my body, also rests secure" (Psalm 16:8–9).

I listened to hear the God of Hope reminding me, "The plans I have for you, plans for your welfare and not for harm, to give you a future with hope. Then when you call upon me and come and pray to me, I will hear you. When you search for me, you will find me; if you seek me with all your heart. I will let you find me, and I will restore your fortunes…I will bring you back to the place from which I exiled you" (Jeremiah 29:11–12, 14).

God had spoken in the crashing roar of the breakers. Because I am so often deaf to my Creator's call, God had to speak loudly to get my attention. But, I had also heard God in the gentle whispering! Clearly, I needed to attend to the fact that my journey is in the preparing as well as in the end result. I needed to hear again that God waits for me and waits with me while I engage in the ongoing process of being made whole and holy.

There are inklings of divinity in all who walk the beach of life as I do. All of us are eagerly awaited, no matter where we are in the process of accepting the perfection that is already ours, whether we know it or not. "By a single offering he (Jesus) has perfected for all time those who are sanctified. Where there is forgiveness of these, there is no longer any offering for sin" (Hebrews 0:12, 18).

Each day brings new possibilities of death and ever-deepening life. Each day takes us closer to end-time and nearer to "beginning- time." Each day provides us with unlimited opportunities. Daily we can learn that God keeps us safe and offers us hope. Yes, doomsday signs are all around us. Prophets of doom and gloom shout warnings that the end is near. Striking fear into our hearts, they hope the fright will last long enough to cause a radical change in the way we live. They trust it will assist us in preparing for the coming of the Lord. They beg us to believe in that second coming. Warning of trials, their cry is frantic: "Be prepared!"

Fear wanes. Interest dies. Routine returns. We get tired of waiting for God. That is the time when the crashing, thundering prophets of doom are supplanted by the whispering harbingers of trust. Roaring breakers are followed by gentle waves. The message is modified, but not minimized.

Be preparing. Be living. Be continuing. Be growing in the belief that God will not abandon us. God will not suffer faithful ones to undergo corruption. Instead, we will be shown the path to life, fullness of joys in God's presence. We will be and have delights at God's right hand forever.

To be preparing is to be prepared!

For Reflection and Discussion

- What steps can you take to assist you in preparing, being alert, being aware of the signs of God in your life? When have you heard God thundering a message to you? When has God spoken in gentler ways? How have you reacted or responded?

Prayer

Dear God, each ending moment brings me to a new beginning. Yet, I fail to live it deeply. Like the flotsam and jetsam of the sea, I toss my life away on triviality, shattering the shell of my existence and laying bare the roots of my mediocrity. But, I have not lost hope. I know that you are with me in the exactness of every hour and every day. I know that you are preparing me, even when I am not aware of the preparation. I thank you for being my God, my Savior, my Friend, but most of all for being my Preparer. Amen.

Feast of Christ the King

Daniel 7:13–14; Revelation 1:5–8; John 18:33–37

A royal homecoming

The village square was buzzing with excitement. Everyone was hustling and bustling about. Consumed with the anticipation of the special event that was to occur that day, the shopkeepers paid scarce attention to their business. Farmers from the countryside came into town, bringing their wives and children with them. Townspeople flocked to the central meeting place. Street merchants half-heartedly plied their wares. Children raced from one spot to another, absorbing the energy of the atmosphere. The King was coming to their town!

Everyone was overflowing with eagerness. Just to catch a quick glimpse of His Majesty would be a treat. Their King was no ordinary royal. Their kingdom was like no other. Actually, the story began a long time ago. The town crier began to chant it as he walked among the waiting crowd.

Many, many years ago our grandfathers and grandmothers, and their grandfathers and grandmothers before them, were ruled by a king called Chaos. The land was wracked with wars and turbulence. Anger, hatred, and brutality were seen and felt everywhere. Neighbor fought neighbor; friend cheated friend. The law of the land was violence and abusive power. Only the strong, the able, the cunning, the clever survived. Oppression became a way of life. Tyranny was a virtue. Honesty gave way to savage lies. No one seemed immune to it. No one was ever happy. The country was steeped in this tragedy, and no one seemed to care. All were powerless, or so it seemed.

There were only two kinds of people in our kingdom, the oppressor whose rule was dread and the oppressed who were robbed of their dignity. Parents wept when their children were born into this tyrannical terror of Chaos. Yet, they bore their young. Somewhere deep in their hearts was a tiny but unquenchable spark of hope that someday things would be different. Someday, someone would come to confront the reign of Chaos and change his rule.

In each household, hope grew steadily stronger. Slowly and stealthily, children were taught to cling to trust, to live with dignity, to believe in the richness of their abilities. Despite all they lacked in material goods, position in life, social status, families spoke of the wealth invested in dreams and hopes and visions of a better life. In each newborn child, they saw promise and possibility. Perhaps one of them would be king. Despite all that might hamper them, the people of the kingdom of Chaos dared to dream.

One day, the hopes and dreams of the grandfathers and grandmothers, and their grandfathers and grandmothers before them, came true. A babe was born to a humble carpenter and his wife. He was taught, as all the others, of his people's hopes and dreams, and the child listened with all his heart. He was committed to the cause of freedom, justice, and truth. He walked the way of his countrymen. He experienced the pain of their oppression. He felt the pangs of their hunger and thirst for justice. He sought to break the power of evil and strove to make all things and all people new. He spoke of love where hatred had always been the word. He preached of patience rather than power, forgiveness in place of fearfulness, openness as the onslaught to oppression, virtue as replacement for violence, serving instead of savagery.

The poor and oppressed heard his words. They believed in him but they thought he meant to lead them into war against their powerful ruler. Cheering him on, they wished to crown him King and thus challenge Chaos to duel, if not to full-fledged battle. But the young man ran from the title. His way was not the way of violence but of peace. They had not understood.

The crowds were disappointed. Even his closest friends did not understand him. All hopes of conquest had been dashed to the ground. Were they to be bound forever by the ruthlessness of the powerful? Was poverty always to be their lot in life? Would oppression continue to be the food that poisoned them? No one seemed able to answer these questions.

There were some people who heard this man of peace. They also feared him. They paid attention when he was called king and were fearful that he might claim the title and dethrone Chaos forever. They were so fearful that they killed him.

The town crier stopped his story at this point. The villagers gasped. How could this story be true? Here they were, all of them, standing in the village square awaiting the arrival of their king. Had they misunderstood? Was there no king after all? A terse, tense silence fell. Suddenly, sounds of joyous laughter and song filled the air. Heads turned. People craned their necks and stood on tiptoe to see—but no one was there. Slowly, one by one, they realized that the joyful sounds were rising from the depth of their hearts. They were the rulers of peace and justice. The reign had come from inside-out!

This king of theirs was not dead at all. He was alive and living among them. He always will. "His dominion is an everlasting dominion that shall not pass away, and his kingship is one that shall never be destroyed" (Daniel 7:14). The king reigns in their laughter and love. He rules in their freedom and service. His voice is heard in the way they live.

The village square bustled with excitement once again as the villagers danced with joy. Husbands and wives joined hands with their children. Children linked arms with the elders. Friends and neighbors hugged. Harmony reigned in their hearts. Their voices mingled as they sang, "The Lord is King; he is robed in majesty. He has established the world; it shall never be moved; your throne is established from of old; you are from everlasting" (Psalm 93:1–2).

The King had come home to live in their hearts. The party began.

For Reflection and Discussion

- In what ways does Christ reign supreme as companion and ruler in your family, among your friends, and in your church community? If Christ does not reign in your hearts and theirs, what is keeping that from happening?

Prayer

Pray, with song or in the silence of your hearts, the words of this hymn.

Refrain
The King of glory comes, the nation rejoices.
Open the gates before him, lift up your voices.

Who is the King of glory; how shall we call him?
He is Emmanuel, the promised of ages.
Refrain
In all of Galilee, in city or village,
He goes among his people curing their illness.
Refrain
Sing then of David's Son, our Savior and brother;
In all of Galilee was never another.
Refrain
He gave his life for us, the pledge of salvation;
He took upon himself the sins of the nation.
Refrain
He conquered sin and death; he truly has risen,
And he will share with us his heavenly vision.
Refrain

—Willard F. Jabusch

Church
Feasts

193

PRESENTATION OF THE LORD

MALACHI 3:1–4; HEBREWS 2:14–18; LUKE 2:22–40

When the student is ready, the teacher will come

I just re-read an e-mail I received a while ago from a young person who was struggling to become an adult. Chronologically, that age and stage of life had been reached. Psychologically, it was still a terrifying shadowland.

Here was someone who was beginning to face human frailty head on, trying to clean out the closets of life and let go of old habits that were detrimental to growth. Here was someone who clearly wanted to fully engage in life, a person who recognized that ingrained patterns can hold us hostage. But change must be practiced daily, bit by bit, to avoid feeling so overwhelmed that all we do is shut our eyes and step over life—instead of stepping into it. The last line of the e-mail read, "I am willing to walk, so here I go, scared but going."

The student was ready. The teacher was on the way.

It is never easy to be a student. Nor is being a teacher without its hardships. There are mixed emotions surrounding both, the intermingling of blessing and curse, joy and sorrow, progress and setbacks—entanglements that remind me of the double helix of DNA. Life itself is a commingled spiral of surprises. On the one hand, we are delighted with the approach of the teacher called Covenanted Life. On the other, we wonder if we can endure the day of arrival. Will we be able to stand the appearance of one who calls us forward, who asks only that we let go and live? It is written that such a messenger is "like a refiner's fire and like fullers' soap" (Malachi 3:3) This is someone who will work to remove blemishes and dross, burnishing the subject until the reflection of the teacher is clearly seen in the student.

Each of us is called, in turn, to be teacher and student. Perhaps it is more accurate to say that we are student-teachers. Recognizing that we are all members of the human race, we also realize our common finiteness and flawed natures. In order to teach, we need first to be students who are in touch with our humanity. We need to become like our brothers and sisters so that we might empower them to become like us. Then, together, we will be able to image the God who created us.

The labor is one of love—tough love that will cause the rise and fall of many. We are to be signs that will be opposed because our presence is to provoke the revelation of inner thoughts. As a result, we will also experience the piercing of our very souls, an agony of spirit that accompanies the ecstasy of being God's chosen ones. When the time for our purification comes we will know that our only task is prayerfully to present ourselves to God as designated holy ones. We need to believe that the Teacher will be there in the presentation.

This bring to mind a well-worn tale. It may be rather simplistic, sentimental, even sloppy theology but it does contain truth. The story tells of a sleeping man whose bedroom suddenly filled with light as God appeared to him to tell him that there is work to do. God showed him a large rock in front of his cabin and explained that the man was to push against the rock with all his might. So this the man did, day after day. For many years he toiled from sun up to sun down; his shoulders set squarely against the cold, massive surface of the unmoving rock, pushing with all of his might. Each night the man returned to his cabin sore, worn out, and discouraged, feeling that his whole day had been spent in vain.

Satan decided to enter the picture by placing thoughts into the weary mind: "you have been pushing against that rock for a long time, and it hasn't moved." Giving the man the impression the task is impossible and that he is a failure, the thoughts discouraged and disheartened him. "Why kill myself over this?" the man thought. "I'll just put in my time, giving just the minimum effort; and that will be good enough." And that is what he planned to do, until one day he decided to make it a matter of prayer and take his troubled thoughts to God. "God," he said, "I have labored long and hard in your service, putting all my strength to do that which you have asked. Yet, after all this time, I have not even budged that rock by half a millimeter. What is wrong? Why am I failing?"

God responded compassionately. "My friend, when I asked you to serve me and you accepted, I told you that your task was to push against the rock with all of your strength, which you have done. Never once did I mention to you that I expected you to move it. Your task was to push. And now you come to me with your strength spent, thinking that you have failed. But is that really so? Look at yourself. Your arms are strong and muscled, your back sinewy and brown, your hands are callused from constant pressure, your legs have become massive and hard. Through opposition you have grown much, and your abilities now surpass that which you used to have. You haven't moved the rock, but your calling was to be obedient and push and exercise your faith and trust in my wisdom. This you have done. Now I, my friend, will move the rock."

When everything seems to go wrong, just P.U.S.H.! When the job gets you down, just P.U.S.H.! When people don't react the way you think they should, just P.U.S.H.! When your money looks "gone" and the bills are due, just P.U.S.H! When people just don't understand you, just P.U.S.H.!

P.U.S.H.: Pray Until Something Happens.

Joseph and Mary "pushed" their way to the temple to present their son to God as good Jews obeying God's word. Simeon accepted his dismissal from life peacefully after he had "pushed" his way to a vision of salvation meant for all people. Anna "pushed" with praise, worshiping in the temple with prayer and fasting night and day. Jesus grew and became strong. Filled with wisdom, he "pushed" his path from Nazareth to Jerusalem, from carpentry to the cross. My e-mail correspondent is preparing to "push" into wholeness.

When the student is ready to P.U.S.H., the Teacher will come and the favor of God will be upon us all!

For Reflection and Discussion

- When did you last experience the "push" of prayerfulness? What happened? What sorts of things do you need to clean out of the closet of your life? How are old habits tying you to the past and preventing your walk into a renewed present?

Prayer

God of my rock hard determination to succeed
Let me see that you are the power I need
To continue, to stay, in faithfulness true
So that your will be done and I'll be made new.
Let my P.U.S.H. be your pull into life in its grandeur
Will never a thought that my way is grander.
Gift me with goodness I could never attain on my own;
In wisdom and grace let my spirit be honed
Until one day I see you as you really are,
God of goodness, God of bountiful love without mar.
Amen.

ACTS 12:1–11; 2 TIMOTHY 4:6–8, 17–18; MATTHEW 16:13–19

Ordained into the power of paradox

Because it occasioned the ordination of many priests who have had and continue to have a great influence on me, I always link priesthood with June twenty-ninth, whether or not it is the actual moment of ordination. My mind races with memories emblazoned with faces of men who were CYO chaplains, college professors, or coworkers, dear friends all, then and now. This year there is additional happiness as I remember philosophic conversations punctuated by laughter and riddled with mutual teasing, exchanges that I enjoyed with a priest friend who has just been ordained a bishop.

These memories merge and forge new understandings of the Scriptures set aside for this day. They evoke a picture of two priesthoods modeled in the lives of two great men: Peter and Paul. We all are drawn, in one way or another, to Peter and his role as the rock upon which the church is built. Images of popes and power mingle with ideas of authority. Suddenly, the priesthood becomes a fraternity of brothers who hold the keys to the kingdom of heaven. The church emerges as a duality and division of "us and them." For all practical purposes, there were centuries of accreted distance between altar and people; church and kingdom of God.

I see a different concept of priesthood described in the Scriptures, however. I see the priesthood of Peter, "ordained" as one of the Twelve, as one that is coexisting and in collaboration with the equal but different priesthood of Paul, an apostle by virtue of his painful conversion process. Both were leaders. Both knew and showed the Way. Both made, admitted, and were sorry for their mistakes. Both suffered the pain of persecution and imprisonment. Here are two persons, viewed in their unique, historical moments, who cause us to look and see dual priesthoods. These are priesthoods lived side-by-side, each integral to the other. Neither is separate from nor subservient to the other.

This is what I envision in our church today. I see a church led by those who are Paul as well as those who are Peter. It is a church that protects the people of God with necessary boundaries while it affords them limitless horizons. It is a church that lives powerfully in paradox. It is a church in painful process.

Unfortunately, I also see a church that takes people into its custody, arrests their spiritual growth, and holds them bound. Imprisoning them as Peter was detained in prison, this church fastens with double chains. It has guards to keep watch. It would seem that those who would speak disconcerting truth cannot escape. It would seem that freedom is forever lost .

But, escape is not prevented. For there is a third model: the church is also a priesthood of fervently praying people. Their prayers bring angels of the Lord. Light shines in the cells of darkness, sleep, and submission. Leaders, awakened to their own imprisonment, are again called to follow the Lord, even if they have no clear realization of what is taking place! The coupled priesthood of Peter and God's people is marked by prayer and surprising awakenings. There is nothing stagnant, stifling, or static about it!

No less exciting is the priesthood of Paul who is described as "fighting the good fight" and "finishing the race" (2 Timothy 4:7). There is no room for complacency here. There is only one task to be done; one vocation to be pursued: completing the preaching task so that all might hear the gospel.

The call of Christianity is so simple: to complete what Christ has started. Look at the life of Christ and pay attention to the priesthood he began. See a priesthood that includes outrageous people. See a priesthood that embraces outsiders, that forgives the unforgivable, walks the way of the world to sanctify it. See a priesthood that listens intently, hears the unspoken, responds to demands, especially the demands of women and all who are powerless, admonishes only with a look of love and always, always, leaves people free to be who they choose to be.

Life has no limits for those who would be Paul. It is a matter of pushing onward, stretching limits, pondering possibilities, and growing, ever growing into Christ. It is a matter of "already being poured out as a libation" (2 Timothy 4:6). It means seeking the truth in all its forms and places, believing that the Lord will stand by our side and give us the strength we need to do God's work. "The Lord will rescue me from every evil attack and save me for his heavenly kingdom" (2 Timothy 4:18).

Whether we look to Peter, Paul, or the fervently praying community of God's people, there is but one reality that comes to light: no one and nothing can imprison the word of God. Why, then, is it that we are so afraid of being free to speak and hear truth, the truth that is God's word, the truth that holds great promise, escape from imprisonment? Why do we allow guards to keep watch at the doors of our freedom, enslaving us to unthinking responses that substitute for faith?

The answer might be found in the response we give to the single question posed by Jesus to his disciples: "Who do you say that I am?" We may hedge, as did those early followers, and give answers without personal response. But the question is so important that Jesus asks until someone answers. In the Matthean account, Peter speaks for all. Peter proclaims Jesus as Messiah and Son of the Living God. Peter becomes rock, the steadfast bedrock of faith. On this bedrock of faith, the church is built. Against this bedrock of faith, nothing can prevail. Because of this bedrock of faith, the keys of the kingdom can be entrusted to frail, fragile, often fragmented people.

The faith of Simon Peter answered for the others. It continues to answer for us today, just as our parents responded in our name to baptismal promises and requests we were too young to proclaim. Each of us is eventually empowered to face and respond to Christ's question. Throughout our lives of discipleship, we will hear him ask us by name: "And you, who do you say that I am?"

We cannot live only on Peter's response. We must answer alone on our individual quest and pilgrimage to God with the courage of Paul who claimed his unique apostleship with his life. We must also respond as a searching community, journeying together to discover the truth contained in our answer.

For Reflection and Discussion

- How would you describe the ideal priest? What would be the most important characteristics to look for? How do you approximate these ideals in your baptismal priesthood?

Prayer

Dear God, you have called me and I am yours. In my baptism, you named me priest and asked that I serve you and your people. Through my parents, godparents, and faith community, I responded "yes" and grew into the priesthood you claimed for me. I promise to offer you the eucharist of my life, giving you the praise and glory in thanksgiving for all you have already given to me. I promise to hear the confessions of those who need a listening ear, to confirm them in their goodness, and commune with them in our common faith journey. I promise to marry my presence with yours and theirs and lay the hand of hope upon any discouragement I see. I will do all of this until I breathe my last breath and receive the crown of righteousness. Amen.

FEAST OF THE TRANSFIGURATION

DANIEL 7:9–10, 13–14; 2 PETER 1:16–19; MATTHEW 17:1–9

Jesus of Nazareth was a dreamer

As I contemplate the readings for this day, an old Christmas tune, "Do You Hear What I Hear?" keeps running through my mind. Like the little lamb, I am bombarded with one, continuing query: "Do you see what I see?" Did the little lamb see a star dancing in the night, a star with a tale as big as a kite? Do I? Do we?

Do we chance viewing life from new perspectives, daring to look at things and people without preconceived notions or anticipated results? Do I see what you see? Do you see what I see? The question presumes innate ability and prescribes active, personal involvement. It hangs in the air, the night wind, awaiting perpetual response.

At the same time, I clearly remember sharing a conversation about mystical experiences with a friend. She and another woman were part of a large group who had journeyed to Medjugorje, where they became separated from each other in the movement of the crowd. Each, from her own spot, had been gazing at the altar encircled by a number of priests. Everyone else, priests included, were concentrating on a spot overhead, anticipating a vision of the Blessed Mother. These two women, alone but together, saw the air in front of the altar begin to pulsate like a beating heart. Each knew she had had an unexplainable, mystical experience that could be shared and understood only by one who was open to see what she had seen. At the first opportunity, they tentatively broached the subject. It was then that they acknowledged, recognized, and realized a profound truth: each woman, separately, had seen what the other had seen!

Then came the next step: how to communicte a mystical experience? To elucidate what one can scarcely comprehend is both necessary and fraught with difficulty. So, the questions continue. "Do you hear what I hear?" said the lamb to the shepherd boy, "a song, a song, high above the trees/ with a voice as big as the sea!"

Seeing, we share. Sharing, we hear. Hearing deepens sight, and the process continues with cyclic intensity. This is the life story of God's people.

The prophet Daniel had a dream. Though terrified by visions in his head, visions that plagued his mind, Daniel watched, wondered, and pondered the meaning of thrones being set up for the enthronement of an Ancient One. Daniel saw white, snow-bright clothing and hair, fire, and thousands attending the presentation of the Son of Man before God's throne. His was the viewing of dominion and glory—everlasting, unconquerable kingship as it was universally received by all nations and all peoples. The awesome, even frightening, power of God was unfolding before him. Seeing, he understood that his sight was but a fraction of his vision.

Daniel was a dreamer, and dreamers see the real hidden in the unreal. They notice the unreal hidden in the real. For dreamers, this paradox is life's paradigm because they walk with the God who is the really Real. Their mountain top existence nurtures them, feeding desert days and making unavoidable valleys viable.

"Realists" mock the dreamers' life, dishonoring and dismissing it with ridicule. "Dream on!" they say, never once considering that dreams are heart wishes and soul desires. Dreams transform night terrors into daytime triumphs. They unscramble a puzzled unconscious, readying us for transfiguration by surfacing suppressed truth. Dreamers give voice to the basic goal of Christianity: transfiguration. All God's people are called to be dreamers.

Dreaming about all that is and all that can be allows us to continue the process of becoming and being eyewitnesses of God's sovereign glory. It empowers our uniqueness, gives wings to our declarations, and sensitizes our attention. Dreaming fixes our hearing and attunes our listening to divinely prophetic messages. When the day's distractions melt into nighttime reflections we are more able to distinguish prophecy from pomposity.

Jesus of Nazareth was a dreamer. He dared to dream impossible dreams. Jesus steadfastly believed that they could come true and invited others to an identical belief. For him, all things were possible. Jesus took Peter, James, and John with him on his dream journey. He led them up a high mountain, far from the madding crowds of naysayers stuck in their mud of negativity. He led and they followed, leaving the hazy, valley atmosphere to enter the rarefied air of clarity. In that place, in that revealing moment where vision became sight and sight became vision, Jesus was transformed. Transfigured before them, he gave them permission to see what he saw; hear what he heard—and they were overwhelmed with joy, overcome with awe.

The goodness of their experience was so overpowering that Peter wanted to capture it. He wanted to nestle it into a building and keep it safely protected from danger. Lost in the here and now, Peter stopped dreaming and became a pragmatist—until God interrupted his plans. "Then a cloud overshadowed them, and from the cloud there came a voice, 'This is my Son, the Beloved; listen to him'!" (Mark 9:8).

All God's people are called to be dreamers, hearing and listening to God's voice speaking in the clouds. When we answer that call and respond to God's voice, we will no longer see anyone but Jesus. There will be no more fear. Jesus' caroling questions will be answered. "Do you see what I see?" Yes, we see what Jesus sees. "Do you hear what I hear?" Yes, we hear what he hears.

Transfigured, our dreams will be realities.

For Reflection and Discussion

- When have you had an experience of seeing and hearing what others do not envision? When have you shared a vision with someone else? In what ways are you a dreamer like Daniel and Jesus? How have you helped to make your dreams and those of others become realities?

Prayer

Dreammaker God, I call on you
To give me visions, daring and true,
Dreams that will lead me to lands new and bright
Dreams that will bring me to ever-deepening sight.
No tents to enclose you, I promise, my God
Only openness to paths you and I will trod—
Into valleys of hope where others await
The dreams we bear in our message of faith.
Amen.

Feast of the Assumption of the Blessed Mother

Revelation 11:19A; 12:1–6A, 10AB; 1 Corinthians 15:20–27; Luke 1:39–56

Going up?

As each August fifteenth rolls around bearing its special Marian feast, my mind conjures up strange images of Mary being assumed into heaven. I can envision a body in levitation or a casket-rocket zooming through space—even an elevator carrying one passenger who is "going up!" Icons and mosaics depict a woman clothed in glowing garments, ascending from a tomb while surrounded by angels who remain nearby but do not touch her.

Neither a statement affirming resurrection nor one of resuscitation, this dogma is one that defies description or definition. All of us can parrot the credal phrases, but what does Mary's assumption really mean in our lives? How do we relate to a woman riding the skies, "clothed with the sun...the moon under her feet and on her head a crown of twelve stars" (Revelation 12:1)? Worse yet, the story continues to read like the most terrifying of Grimm's fairy tales. "Then another portent appeared in heaven, a great, red dragon, with seven heads and ten horns....His tail swept down a third of the stars of heaven and threw them to the earth. Then the dragon stood before the woman who was about to bear a child, so that he might devour her child as soon as it was born" (Revelation 12:3–4). Before we can even react to the horror, the child is snatched up to God and the woman flees into the desert where a special place had been prepared for her by God.

How strange is that? What has this to do with us? I wonder what would happen to our relationship with God if we put ourselves in the place of this pregnant woman, this woman full of grace? In what ways do we expectantly and enthusiastically labor to give birth to life, even when the pain involved causes us to wail aloud?

It seems to me that our experience of this feast gains relevance when we make the effort to unpack the scriptural descriptions in meaningful ways. Just as the apocalyptic woman of the skies carrying the child of promise was accosted, so all of us are assailed by demonic forces ready to devour the child we are bearing into birth. That child, a child of God, is our truest self.

We spend a lifetime working to free the child within, the God-image we are. Equal to our liberating effort is the tireless toil of those prepared to strangle such existence in its infancy. At times, even God seems not to care. Often, the only course of action open to us is flight into the desert. No sooner have we experienced the result of fertile faithfulness, then we are forced to race into aridity! It scarcely seems fair, yet it is here that God has prepared a special place for us. Life is nothing short of a mixed blessing, a paradoxical paradise.

When we move from a focus on her assumption to fix our thoughts, minds, and hearts on the person of the earthly Mary, it is apparent that she was consumed by godliness long before being assumed into God. Awareness of her unusual pregnancy did not prevent Mary from continuing to image the divinity she bore. She went about her normal routine as if nothing unusual had occurred, continuing to find the extraordinary presence of God in all the ordinary people and situations she encountered. It was that "unique normalcy" that cried out to others, informing them of all the possibilities hidden in the apparently impossible. It was her Mary-ness in their midst, a voice of greeting and compassion, that announced her blessedness among women and called others to proclaim the greatness of God emergent in human lowliness.

Mary's pregnant presence in our lives today continues to cause the child within us to leap for joy. She consistently gives witness to and exemplifies the blessedness of those who trust that God's words to them will be fulfilled. Mary remains with us as she did with Elizabeth, as our companion. She stays to assist each and all in the labor of giving birth to the child who dwells within.

The process begins, in a way that is similiar to the human work of physically birthing a baby. It is both a solitary endeavor and one in which we discover our dependency on others, including the child who cooperates in the movement from a covert relationship to an overt one. To give birth is to admit and avow the graciousness of a mighty God who does great things for us. It is to know the holiness of God's name and the extent of God's mercy. Obviously, this "birthing" is not limited to the physical entry of an infant into the world. Birthing is what each of us does daily as we struggle to free ourselves, leaving our comfortable wombs and expanding our lungs with the oxygen of spirituality.

Giving birth is a commitment that cannot be retracted. Once begun, there is only forward movement. Mother and child are consumed with the process and assumed into it! Babe and mother are unified in their push to new life. Mighty Mom is deposed from her position as encaser of existence. Lowly babe is raised to the height of independence. The child emerges. The umbilical cord that once served as a conduit for nourishment must be cut. Nurture now lies in detachment. Attachment becomes an opportunity for death to snatch the child and devour it with morbidity. Yet, each mother remains hungry for her child, and child for mother. Emptied of limited richness, each individual is now allowed a fulfillment never dreamed possible.

Mary learned from her birthing process and lived it all her life. As she lived, she died—always being emptied and filled, always dying and rising, always giving and receiving. Death was her final birthing, her ultimate detachment and eternal forward movement. Having remained where God wanted her to be for as long as God desired, Mary then returned home.

Consumed with the divinity within her, she assumed the special place prepared for her. Going up? Perhaps. Or maybe, it is going in—to God.

For Reflection and Discussion

- In what ways do you live expectantly and enthusiastically labor to give birth to life, even when the pain involved causes you to wail aloud? What have you learned from your spiritual "birthing process"? How do you understand the statement: "Attachment becomes an opportunity for death to snatch the child and devour it with morbidity."?

Prayer

Beloved Mother Mary, I come to you as a child in need. I want to find joy in giving birth to life and love. I want to set out in haste to assist my brothers and sisters. I want my being to proclaim the greatness of God. I want my spirit to rejoice in God my savior. But I am so weak and afraid of the labor pains involved in the birthing process. Please be with me as my mother. Stay with me as my friend. Pray with me as my sister. I ask this in the belief that God will entrust me with the graces given you. I ask humbly as a lowly one. Please hear and answer me. Amen.

Exaltation of the Holy Cross

Numbers 21:4b–9; Philippians 2:6–11; John 3:13–17

The cross our only sword

Back in the "fabulous fifties" when families were not nuclear and neighborhoods were often ghettos, Roman Catholic teenagers rallied around their unique flag of Christianity. It was an emblem loosely knit as religious education, but strongly maintained as a social club. A place where boys and girls could meet with adult approval, CYO, the Catholic Youth Organization, was the authorized outlet for our youthful vim and vigor. It was our rallying place.

As soon as I conjure up an image of those days, a song hums in my memory bank. "We're an army of youth flying the standard of truth and fighting for Christ our Lord. Arms lifted high, Catholic action's our cry, and the cross our only sword. On earth's battlefield, never a vantage we'll yield. Led dauntlessly on, we sing. Comrade true, dare and do 'neath the queen's white and blue. For our flag, for our faith, for Christ the King." In years to come, that militaristic stance would be questioned and finally disappear. But for that time and place, it was a sign of our strength. We were young people whose professed goal and greatness lay in our proximity to God. In turn, we somehow sensed that God-nearness would be found in bearing a cross. So we sang of its potency and marched to its pace.

In adolescence, we found identity, exaltation, honor, glory, praise, and a certain degree of pride in the presence of the cross. However, we saw ourselves wielding it rather than yielding to it. We understood the need for a sword to do battle in life. The cross was a handy one. It gave us a sense of holiness while simultaneously allowing us the power and punch of warfare. Our might was akin to the Crusaders. We also dreamed of conquest and victory as we concentrated more on the attributes of piercing "sword-ness" than on the wood of crucifixion.

Now, with vintage years, we are more attuned to the pain of that cross. We wince with its splinters. Bearing it is not an easy task, although it does bring a certain ease. Nor is it a peaceful one despite its promise of profound peace.

Yet, the truth remains. The cross is our only sword.

This structure of death is also a sign of defiance. Its ability is paradoxical.

The cross has the potential to exhaust us to the point of expiration while it provides the opportunity for our exaltation as well. Death on a cross is ignominious to the ignorant, but a sanctifying grace to those who have accepted their salvation. Outstretched arms signal receptivity and welcome. Vertically poised bodies link earth with heaven. There is pain in the outreach as well as suffering in the wrenching rise from earth and descent from heaven. Despite the anguish, or perhaps because of it, transformation occurs. Aching muscles intensify our human sensation and increase awareness. Outreach enhances vulnerability and empowers us to approximate the mind of Christ who lay on such a cross, once and for all.

Just as he did not regard equality with God something to be exploited or abused for privilege nor are we to use our likeness to divinity in erroneous ways. Holiness is a grace to be shared, not a gift to be hoarded. With God as Lord, it is virtually impossible to lord it over others.

If the cross is truly our only sword, we cannot use it to strike a fatal blow without splintering consequences. Its beam could easily imbed itself in our flesh. History has proven the truth of these statements. Crusaders, with crosses proudly displayed on the flags of violence, were marauding murderers. Their proclamation of the cross as their sword was a provocation of fear, not a declaration of faith. If they began as protectors of Christianity, they ended as warriors against heathenism. Their efforts were not to include and embrace the enemy with arms of love. Instead, they sought to isolate and destroy the enemy with arms of hate. In reality, the sword was their only cross, to bare and bear against those whose understanding of God differed from their own.

Interestingly, Nazi Germany chose a stylized cross as its banner of crucifixion. Yellow stars of David were gassed into nonexistence by soldiers with armbands crisscrossed with a twisted sense of Christianity.

It is no less true today. The people of God continue to kill each other under the aegis of a cross turned into a weapon of destruction. Fundamentalists of every ilk, from Islam to Judaism, neo-Nazis to fanatical members of the IRA, leftists to rightists, all have forgotten that the cross lifted by Moses in the desert and the one upon which Jesus was lifted are instruments for resurrected life, not tools of remorseless death. "And just as Moses lifted up the serpent in the wilderness, so must the Son of Man be lifted up, that whoever believes in him may have eternal life" (John 3:14).

When the cross is indeed our only sword, we choose to relinquish our gains so that others might attain what they need. We opt for the humility of truth rather than the treachery of high exaltation. Our goal is not solely personal power but equally the empowerment of others. With the cross as our only sword, we will be able to strike mortal blows at the poisonous serpents of greed and pride, lust and envy, covetousness, sloth, and anger in our midst. We will discover an uncanny ability to recognize that we will not die of hunger and thirst in the desert wilderness. Instead, we will find surprising oases of food and water in apparent desolation. True, the food will be different from our usual fare, but it will also be astonishingly nourishing,

When the cross is our only sword, it becomes ever more evident that God loved the world in this way, the way of the cross. "For God so loved the world that he gave his only Son, so that everyone who believes in him may not perish but may have eternal life. Indeed, God did not send the Son into the world to condemn the world, but in order that the world might be saved through him" (John 3:16–17).

So I hum my tune as my fingers race across the computer keyboard. Chronology aside, I am still part of a gathering of youth. You are there with me, all of us flying the standard of truth. Militarism has mellowed with maturity. We now fight a battle of love for Christ, our Lord. Our arms are lifted high in a universal embrace of peace, shalom.

The sole triumph we profess, the solitary exaltation we accept, is the cross of Christ we bear as our only sword.

For Reflection and Discussion

- How do you see the cross as your only sword? What is your understanding of this feast, the exaltation of the cross? In what ways have you experienced transformation in the midst of crucifying anguish?

Prayer

Jesus, my protector, hear my complaints, my pains, my woes. Show yourself to me in my darkness. Increase my hope and trust in you. Help me sense and feel your presence in my confusion and blindness. Give me confidence that through your cross this unpalatable mixture will work to my good.

—Night Prayer from *All Will Be Well*, Ave Maria Press

SOLEMNITY OF ALL SAINTS

REVELATION 7:2–4, 9–14; 1 JOHN 3:1–3; MATTHEW 5:1–12A

Saints are survivors

When the word "saint" is mentioned, it is all too easy to conjure up notions of plastic people whose emotions are held totally intact. Perhaps we see "holy" pictures of haloed serenity. "She's a saint, he's a saint" might describe persons who endure, uncomplainingly, all things that come their way. None of these images is bad, but they tend to lead us into impossible comparisons. We feel that we cannot measure up to that kind of sanctity. If we go that route, we have missed the message of Scripture. We have misunderstood this feast day which proclaims the solemnity of *all* saints!

God's word and wish is universal. No one is excluded. There are no labels, denominations, rigid codes, or lists of entry requirements—only a vision of inclusivity. "I looked, and there was a great multitude that no one could count, from every nation, from all tribes and peoples and languages, standing before the throne and before the Lamb..." (Revelation 7:9). God says that all are saints. This is *our* feast day. Any misunderstanding lies in the way we have defined sanctity. Any problem occurs with our descriptions and list of demands which supersede those of God. "Who are these and where did they come from?" (Revelation 7:13) are the scriptural questions. The answer is clear: saints are survivors.

Saints are not simply people who endure the hardships of life. To be a saint is to run the race and live. Saints are not self-styled martyrs who walk through each day with grim forbearance. Nor do they deny the pain and passion of their humanity. They are not individuals who simply "go with the flow." They run against the tide with all their might. They embrace what life brings. Theirs is a providential view.

Plaster of Paris people cannot be saints. Sanctity demands a flesh and blood engagement with each day. Sanctity is found *now*. Today is the day of surviving. Yesterday is gone. Tomorrow has not yet come. All that each of us knows is that "We are God's children now; what we will be has not yet been revealed. What we do know is this: when he is revealed, we will be like him, for we will see him as he is" (1 John 3:2).

In those words we find the essence of what it means to be a survivor—a saint. All that we are and do is based on the reality that we are children of God. No matter what the trouble might be or the illness or the disaster, saints survive because they have a visceral belief that God is there with them. God is with us as a father who would not leave his child to suffer alone. God is with us as a mother whose heart breaks with every heartache her child endures.

Saints are survivors who see God's light in the dark tunnels of life.

Saints have a "be-attitude." It is more than optimistically viewing a glass as half-full rather than half-empty. It is awakening to an understanding of the meaning of happiness. To be happy is to live always with God. Dependent on God's presence and help, the saint is empowered to live in sorrow and be consoled, to know worldly powerlessness and inherit the power of authenticity.

The vocation of all humanity is to be saints. It is a solemn call that brings with it both passion and pain, agony and ecstasy. Its rewards are profound, potent, and permanent. At the same time, they are often not immediately palpable. To be a saint is to trust and survive; to survive in trust.

The holy life is not for the fainthearted. It will bring the incomprehensible blessings found only as we journey into the depths of Christianity. Saints will be insulted, persecuted, and bear the hurt of slander simply because they are who they are: holy people.

I have often heard complaints about the removal of saints' statues from our churches. There is a point to be made regarding their symbolic value as reminders of our heritage. I think, however, that a greater value has been served in their removal. All the pedestal people are gone. Plaster people are no longer in our midst. We now have real people living as saints.

Pregnant women are saints—not because they have accepted life but because they are experiencing and celebrating it. The poor and homeless are saints—not because they have no money or property but because they are living from their poverty. The elderly are saints—not because they are aged or infirm but because they are vibrant with wisdom. Saints are not stoic statues; they pulse with divine dynamism.

Room has been made for the enfleshed saints—real, flesh and blood persons who see well, say well, and pray well. Look in the mirror. Look all about you. Take a long look. They are there. We are among them. It is true. Be glad and rejoice. We, the saints, survivors are marching on!

For Reflection and Discussion

- In what ways have you been a faithful survivor? How have you survived the slings and arrows hurled at those who follow in the way of Christ? Give examples of times when you have experienced and celebrated life.

Prayer

God, my God, you are the light I find
Within the darkness of my life tunnel;
The glow that defies any neon aura
That pierces blackness into sparkling dawn.
I offer you my thanks and praise, today,
And all the days that you have numbered
For me to give you glory and know my worth
As a surviving saint dancing the march of goodness—
Prancing my delight that I am yours and you are mine.
Amen.

Feast of the Dedication of the Lateran Basilica

1 Kings 8:22–23, 27–30; Ephesians 2:19–22; Matthew 5:23–24

What does it mean to be "church"?

As a hospital chaplain, I am often asked what church I belong to. The expected answer is that I mention a particular denomination. I respond "St. Brendan Roman Catholic Church." Invariably, the ensuing conversation suggests that this is only a partial answer. It opens the door to a statement I hear repeated time and again by patients, despite their own affiliation or lack of one, and that is: "It doesn't matter what church you go to. It only matters that God counts in your life." I know each person is trying to affirm my belief, even if it is not theirs. At the same time, they are testifying to the fact that we are all in the same boat, even if we are not in the same buildings. We are all searching to discover what it means to be "church."

Marvelous though our cathedrals, basilicas, and sanctuaries, they do not define or provide meaning to the word "church." The people of Assisi came face-to-face with that reality as an earthquake destroyed the frescoes and paintings that had drawn tourists and locals alike to come to their church. The temples we build cannot contain God. Perhaps that is not news to us who already know that church is more than any building. We know what church is not: church is more than a place. But we have yet to plumb the depths of what church *is*!

Today's readings give us direction. Church is all about the awesome truth that God dwells among us on earth. We cannot fully comprehend that fact; it is too big for our minds to grasp. To be church is to celebrate what we cannot understand, but are trying to live. To be church is to put God first, always. It is to come to grips with the reality that God is in charge. To be church is to be people of prayer. It is to be people who ask God to "regard your servant's prayer and his plea…heeding the cry…heed and forgive" (1 Kings 8:28–30). The prayer may be offered from a building but it is important that the place be one which is filled with persons who are strangers and aliens no longer.

The heart of any church building is not in its statues, mosaics, crucifix, or even in its liturgies and homilies. The heart of the reality is in the exact middle of the word church: you are, I am, we are.

The heart of the church beats with the presence of God among us. Now we are getting close to understanding the answer to the question, "What does it mean to be church?" It means that we first engage the reality that we are fellow citizens of the saints. We are members of the household of God. To be church is to live as saintly members of God's household, God's family. Set apart as holy people who serve as beacon lights of grace to a world blinded by greed, we are "built upon the foundation of the apostles and prophets, with Christ Jesus himself as the cornerstone" (Ephesians 2:19–20).

The church building finds its beauty and definition, its very form, in each and every one of us. Where we are, in Christ Jesus, there is the church. Church is a movable feast. Church is a viable, vital, breathing temple of people who are constantly being built. To be church is to be in process, always being constructed into a dwelling place for the Spirit of God.

To be church is to take time to be with each other. It is to plan and then change plans. To be church is to give and forgive. It is to call and be called. To be church is working and praying. Most of all church is "other-centered." It is more about recalling wrongs that others have against us and reconciling with them than it is about unearthing the hurts we have endured.

When we live in the awareness that we are living stones being fitted together and taking shape as a holy people, we also begin to understand what it means to be church.

For Reflection and Discussion

- In what ways can you "live in the awareness that we are living stones being fitted together and taking shape as a holy people?" How do you understand that we are all in the same boat, if not in the same building?

Prayer

Dear God, when I think of church, let me not narrow my understanding to a building, a place—no matter how wonderful it might be. When I think of church, let me not consider only the hurts I have received at the hands of others. Let me not remember only rejection or alienation or misunderstanding or reprimand. When I think of church, let me recall the body of Christ, hurt and holy; fallen and faithful; sainted and sinning. Let me experience the wonder and beauty of the reality that you are in the midst of Church—and so am I. Amen.

Feast of the Immaculate Conception

Genesis 3:9–15, 20; Ephesians 1:3–6, 11–12; Luke 1:26–38

Opening Eden's Gate

The feast of the Immaculate Conception is one of those mysterious events that is difficult to adequately explain. To add to the enigma, the readings chosen for this day—identical in each liturgical cycle—are ones that emphasize the coexistence of evil in the world and the blessedness of all who are chosen by God and dwelling in Christ. So, what does this feast tell us about God, Mary, the Blessed Virgin, and us?

Richard McBrien explains the concept of being immaculately conceived in these words: "She [Mary] was given a greater degree of grace (i.e., God was more intensely present to her than to others) in view of her role as the 'God-bearer.' So profound is her union with God in grace, anticipation of her maternal function and in virtue of the redemptive grace of Christ, that she alone remains faithful to God's will throughout her entire life" (*Catholicism*, vol. II, pg. 886)

Mary responded so completely to God's gracious call, to God's generously graceful presence, that we can only express her pure response by saying that she was immaculate from the very beginning of her life. Mary is the paradigm of true discipleship, the model for all humanity, of total, free acceptance of God's goodness. She understood the meaning of mercy and rejoiced in being merciful. She comprehended the call of justice and lived it. She integrated her poverty with God's richness, her lack with divine fulfillment, and realized God's love in a way and manner that had neither precedent nor total imitation.

Both the books of Genesis and Revelation present Mary as the antithesis of Eve. The first woman surrendered her innocence, rejecting God's purpose for her desires. Mary surrounded her innocence with response, accepting God's purpose and making it her desire. Eve, with Adam, closed Eden's gate to all humanity. Mary, with Jesus, opened it, for us, again. Mary introduced us to death; Eve presented us with new Life. But both remain models for us. We are sons and daughters of both women, brothers and sisters of Christ.

It is we, the saints, whom Paul addresses when he praises God and says: "Blessed be the God and Father of our Lord Jesus Christ, who has blessed us in Christ with every spiritual blessing in the heavenly places..." (Ephesians 1:3). We, too, are blessed ones, chosen ones, "destined according to the purpose of him who accomplishes all things according to his counsel and will, so that we...might live for the praise of his glory." We, too, "were marked with the seal of the promised Holy Spirit" (Ephesians 1:11, 12). The difference is that Mary gave her fiat, even if it came tremblingly from her lips. She said her "yes" even if "no" was an easier response.

This feast serves as a reminder to us that we are to model Mary's kind of faithfulness, trusting in the destiny God promises as ones chosen before the foundation of the world to be holy and blameless and living solely for the praise of God's glory. On this day, we come face-to-face with the profound truth that a Marian lifestyle is preeminently vital. The passion of its loving does not exclude pain but embraces it. There will be sadness, sorrow, and suffering, but those experiences are keys that empower us to open the gates of paradise once again.

Our lives may not appear to be earthshaking. There may be no measurable heroism to note, at least in the short term. But, we will be counted among those who are in for the long haul. We will be servants of the Lord, waiting upon God's action, allowing God's will to be done in us, with us, through us. We will walk, hand-in-hand with our beloved Mother, watching as she opens Eden's gate and invites us to enter the paradise divinely prepared for all of us.

For Reflection and Discussion

- How do you perceive God's specific choice of you? For what unique purpose do you think you have been chosen? In what ways have you expressed your particular "fiat"?

Prayer

Mother Mary, beloved of my heart,
Keep me close, never to part
From you who lead me without fail
To the Christ whose love does not pale;
To the Father of all, inSpirited in us,
The God in whom we place our trust.
Let me know, and help me to say
Ever so softly, each passing day
My "fiat", my "Yes" in whispery love—
With faith that comes only from above. Amen.